The Dazzling Dark

New Irish Plays

Danti-Dan
GINA MOXLEY

A Picture of Paradise
JIMMY MURPHY

Good Evening, Mr Collins
TOM MAC INTYRE

Portia Coughlan
MARINA CARR

Selected and introduced
by Frank McGuinness

faber and faber
LONDON · BOSTON

First published in 1996
by Faber and Faber Limited
3 Queen Square London WC1N 3AU

Photoset by Parker Typesetting Service, Leicester
Printed in England by Clays Ltd, St Ives plc

A CIP record for this book
is available from the British Library

ISBN 0–571–17770–0

2 4 6 8 10 9 7 5 3 1

The Dazzling Dark
New Irish Plays

GINA MOXLEY

Gina Moxley was writer/performer on *The Basement* (RTE), *Hidden Agenda* (RTE Radio), *Sunday Miscellany* (RTE Radio), *Ten Minute Tales* (RTE), *Crack 90s*, and on *Stitch That* (Irish Arts Centre, New York). Her theatre appearances include *The Playboy of the Western World* (Almeida Theatre), *Way of the World* (Rough Magic), *New Morning* and *Digging for Fire* (Rough Magic and Bush Theatre), *Boss Grady's Boys* and *Prayers of Sherkin* (Peacock Theatre), and *Fear of Feathers* (Andrew's Lane Theatre). Her television credits include *Family*, *The Lilac Bus*, *Act of Betrayal*, *A Song for Europe*, *Nighthawks*, *The Basement Comedy Show* and *The Late Late Show*. Her film credits include *Hear My Song*, *Joyriders*, *Lapsed Catholics*, *Clash of the Ash*, *Snakes and Ladders* and *The Sun, the Moon and the Stars*. She received a commission from Rough Magic in 1992. *Danti-Dan* is her first play.

JIMMY MURPHY

Jimmy Murphy lives in Inchicore, Dublin. He left school at sixteen and started an apprenticeship in house painting. In 1986 he started writing plays and in 1990 took part in the National Writer's workshop in University College Galway given by Garry Hynes. *Brothers of the Brush*, his first play, was originally staged as part of the Peacock New Play, Series '93 at the Abbey Theatre, Dublin. It won the Best New Play Award and was revived in 1994 before transferring to the Olympia, Dublin. It has since been performed in Boston, New York, Glasgow and Edinburgh and has been translated into Welsh. He was also awarded the Stewart Parker Memorial Prize for new writing in 1994. For Radio 4 he has written *Peel's Brimstone,* and co-wrote *The Mandarin Lime* with Gary Mitchell.

TOM MAC INTYRE

Tom Mac Intyre is a Cavan-born poet and playwright. He has had many plays performed by The Abbey Company, most notably *The Great Hunger* (1983–86), which toured internationally. He has published four volumes of poetry (including a collection of translations from the Irish) and several collections of short stories. He has been a member of Aosdana since 1982.

MARINA CARR

Marina Carr was born in 1964 and grew up in Co. Offaly. She graduated from University College Dublin in 1987. Her plays include *Low in the Dark, The Deer's Surrender, This Love Thing, Ullaloo* and *The Mai.*
Portia Coughlan was commissioned by the National Maternity Hospital in Dublin to celebrate its centenary. *On Raftery's Hill* is forthcoming from Druid Theatre, as is a new play for the Project Arts Centre, Dublin.
Marina Carr lives in Dublin. She is currently Ansbacher Writer-in-Association at the Abbey.

Contents

And we have come,
Despite ourselves, to no
True notion of our proper work,
But wander in the dazzling dark
Amid the drifting snow
Dreaming of some

Lost evening when
Our grandmothers, if grand
Mothers we had, stood at the edge
Of womanhood on a country bridge
And gazed at a still pond
And knew no pain.

'Girls on the Bridge'
by Derek Mahon

Introduction

MASKS

I'm writing this introduction as October comes to an end and we're nearing Hallowe'en. Since Celtic times we've celebrated this festival and recently, in a mad fit of sanity, the Irish government declared it a public holiday. All Souls' Night, Hallowe'en, is our Mardi Gras, a time for wearing masks and remembering the dead, as if by remembering them we resurrect them. And the mask is the outward sign that we are engaging in this ritual communication between the living and the dead. These four plays all wear that mask, each at their unique angle.

Marina Carr is a writer haunted by memories she could not possibly possess, but they seem determined to possess her. This haunting is a violent one, intensified by the physical attack on the conventions of syntax, spelling and sounds of Standard English in the language of *Portia Coughlan*. It is a violence that avoids resolution to its conflict. Through the disruption of its narrative, Portia herself, like the ghosts of Japanese theatre, lives, dies, comes back to relive her suffering. By the play's end she stands by a river, a river that does not carry her to peace. The war goes on, the war of words where the weapons are the fighting talk of mother, father, son and daughter, sister, brother, wife and husband. The landscapes where they conduct their campaigns begin by seeming to be familiar. Yet they, by the perverse logic of love and hatred, grow foreign through their very familiarity. The unhappy, unholy family is the only constant in this universe, and it is in the process of tearing itself to pieces. Tragedy is so often the consequence of a fatal lack of self-knowledge. Marina Carr rewrites that rule. Her characters die from a fatal excess of self-knowledge. Their truth kills them. And they have always known it would.

That sense of predestination does not control Gina Moxley's *Danti-Dan*. Her's are dangerous children hellbent on discovery. Cactus is wise in her wickedness. She guesses that hell itself would be better than this middle-of-nowhere where she has been landed. Her intelligence turns her into an alien here. She befriends to manipulate, invents rules to defy them, and all that she must learn is patience, for with patience she can achieve anything that comes within the focus of her ambition. If time is the enemy in *Portia Coughlan*, in *Danti-Dan* it is a golden opportunity. Time is the means of escape into adulthood and freedom. Time is the method of learning how to cope with, even celebrate, loneliness. But Cactus is, above all else, a wise woman. She has already felt that time is a hard master. It does not allow any to forget, let alone forgive. These children are shaped by what happens to them in the play, and what happens to them is what they do to themselves. No outside influence affects them. Snatches of pop songs punctuate the action, a banal music of the spheres, barely impinging upon their consciences. *Danti-Dan* is a wonderful indictment of childish innocence. Its comedy is laughter in the face of lies.

Laughter is bitter in Jimmy Murphy's *A Picture of Paradise*. It cures nothing. It does not lighten the load nor dispel the fears of this family whose native city, Dublin, is turning before their eyes into a wasteland, a nightmare. They have lost the fixed bearings of a home in this place. Rootless, luckless, they are even violently evicted from the kip of a flat they attempt to squat in and make their own. They do not have the bare comfort of a tribal allegiance, for their working-class neighbours display as much determination to be rid of them as did the council that put them first on the streets. Imagination has dwindled into the excitement of buying a lottery ticket or backing a horse. They make a gamble with their destiny and lose. And propelling all this sense of loss, undermining it excellently, is Murphy's own sense of rage; justified, articulate rage. That rage is ultimately centred on his characters themselves. He tempers pity for their plight with a refusal to brand them as victims. Each of them shares a complex responsibility for their disintegration. Like Moxley's dangerous children, here are dangerous adults, aiding and abetting in the game of their individual destructions. They themselves have thrown the dice to decide their fate. And there are no gods to save them.

Michael Collins, a God of Irish history, is at the heart of Tom Mac Intyre's *Good Evening, Mister Collins*. For the past twenty years Tom Mac Intyre has confounded and intrigued Irish theatre, giving to it some of the most inventive and challenging fictions it has had to encounter. Behind all the diversity of Mac Intyre's writing lie a terrific sense of play, an imaginative disturbance, and a darkly creative obsession with Ireland's past, particularly in his major works *The Great Hunger* and *Rise Up, Lovely Sweney*. *Good Evening, Mister Collins* continues that obsession. Through the fluency of his dialogue, the earthiness of his politics, and the accuracies of his psychology, Mac Intyre reveals Collins not as action man nor martyr, but as a deeply confused, highly imaginative and wilful man, all the more attractive for the unpredictability of his temperament and questioning of his role. The subterfuges of DeValera allowed him to outlive the historical Collins, but the histrionic Collins outwits his opponent. And if Mac Intyre's theatre is to be treasured for one quality alone it is for his insistence on wit in dramatic language. His is an idiom as recognisable as Wilde's or Beckett's, as careful and generous in its bestowal of gems as Sheridan's or Farquhar's. His originality is beyond question, but he belongs to that dazzling tradition of Irish theatre that began in the dying years of the seventeenth century. Now in the dying years of this century it is heartening, for me at least, to see it still dazzling in the dark. We continue to make masks.

Frank McGuinness
October 1995

DANTI-DAN

Gina Moxley

Characters

Dan (Danti-Dan), aged 14 with a functioning age of 8
Ber, aged 16
Cactus, aged 13
Dolores, aged 14, Ber's sister
Noel, aged 18, Ber's boyfriend

The action takes place in summer 1970, ten miles from Cork city.

Danti-Dan was first performed in a Rough Magic production at the Project Arts Centre, Dublin, on 21 March 1995 and transferred to Hampstead Theatre, London, on 8 June 1995, with the following cast:

Dan Alan King
Ber Dawn Bradfield
Cactus Sophie Flannery
Dolores Eileen Walsh
Noel Donal Beecher

Directed by Lynne Parker
Set and Costume Design by Barbara Bradshaw
Lighting by Paul Keogan
Produced by Siobhan Bourke
Note re. music: All of these fab songs were used in the original production and worked wonderfully. Those specified without brackets are integral; however, those within brackets are only suggestions.

Act One

SCENE ONE

Afternoon. Early summer 1970. *Ten miles from Cork City.
Bridge, low parapet, with a five-bar gate alongside leading
to the riverside and cornfields. Nearby is a phone box and
a monument to those who died locally in the civil war.
Music: 'In the Summertime' by Mungo Jerry.
Lights up.*

Dan *enters. He is fourteen, and has a functioning age of
eight. He has a downy moustache. He's wearing shorts and
a tee shirt, a gun and holster, a length of rope over one
shoulder and slung across his chest, and a battered cowboy
hat. He's riding an imaginary horse.*

Dan Danti-dan, ti dan dan dan, danti-dan, ti dan dan dan,
danti-dan, ti dan dan, daaan, daaaaanti-dan dan dan.

> *He rides the length of the bridge, slapping his backside
> as he goes, the other hand holding the reins in front of
> him. He anxiously looks behind him. He whips off the
> rope from around his shoulder, makes a slip knot in it
> and skirls it above his head. He gallops towards the
> monument and lassos it, lifts himself off the horse and
> swings round behind the monument. He shoos the
> horse away, coils the rope and peeps out. Gun at the
> ready.*
>
> **Ber**, *aged sixteen, wearing a nylon shop coat, zipped
> up the front, sits at the far end of the bridge. She takes a
> ten-pack of 'Major' cigarettes from her pocket, takes one
> and puts it in her mouth. She takes a Ronson lighter out
> of her bra, lights the fag, kisses the lighter and puts it
> back in her bra. She inhales down to her toes.*

5

Dan Stick 'em up.

Ber I come in peace, didn't you see the smoke signals. Stop it now boy, I'm in fierce form, so don't be bugging me.

Dan puts his gun away and goes towards Ber, arsing his way along the bridge.

Dan Sorry Ber.

Ber S'alright. Jesus, a power cut. Whoever heard of a power cut in the summer? And I would have to be on, oh yeah, of course.

Dan Give us a drag, will you?

Ber Here, have a full one, you'll only be horsing it.

Dan I'd never go a whole one.

Ber passes him her cigarette.

Ber More fool me. They'll ruin your chest. (*Laughs.*)

Dan Is it out all morning?

Ber (*nods*) The register and everything. And you know me, I'm useless at sums. My head's shagging hopping. The shop is boiling. (*She unzips her shop coat to cleavage level.*) And nylon is useless in this weather. Mum, me arse, I'm saturated. And I wouldn't mind like, but I've nothing on under it even. Stop gawking you. You're miles too young for me. I better get back. What time is it?

Dan Fifty-six minutes apast one.

Ber What's that? Oh yeah. Listen, if you see Dolores tell her to call up. Tell her get money off Mammy, we'll have to get rid of the meats by this evening. That ham'll be humming if it's there any longer.

Dan She went swimming with Cactus.

Ber I thought that snobby little bitch wasn't talking to her. I wish she'd make up her mind. She had Dolores bawling last night.

Dan Over what?

Ber God knows boy. God knows. (*She goes to leave.*)

Dan Will you be around after?

Ber I might, then again I mightn't.

Dan is embarrassed.

Ber See you so. Oh and Dan, the moustache is coming on lovely.

He twirls his gun on his index finger.

(Music: 'In the Summertime' by Mungo Jerry.)

SCENE TWO

Dan is sitting on top of the gate. Sound effects of cars passing. Good gap between each car. Dan notes the registration numbers in a notebook. He has a bundle of similar books on his lap. His head goes from right, looking at the oncoming car, to left, clocking its number, to centre, writing it down. Occasionally he waves at a passing motorist. His concentration is supreme.

SCENE THREE

Cactus, *aged thirteen, tomboyishly dressed, sticky out hair, climbs through the gate from the riverside and very carefully arranges slices of ham in a line along the parapet of the bridge. Dan is still taking down numbers. The angelus bells ring six o'clock. Dan checks his watch and* *tidies away his notebooks. He goes to Cactus. She stares at him, then gives him a mad smile. He retreats to the monument.* **Dolores** (*Ber's sister*), *aged fourteen, an innocent, slightly gawky, climbs through the gate.*

Dolores Flip's sake, Cactus, what are you doing?

Cactus What?

Dolores The ham. The good cooked ham. I'm going to be murdered all over you. Oh flip. What did you do that for?

Cactus I thought it looked nice, that's all.

Dolores Ah God. You're lousy, you are. That's just pure stupid. (*She tries to peel the slices off the bridge and pile them neatly.*)

Cactus Eh Dolores. . .

Dolores What?

Cactus Don't say what, say pardon.

Dolores Shut up you. Pardon, what?

Cactus Your frock is caught up in your knickers.

Dolores Oh God. Am I puce? Thanks. Did any cars pass? Was he looking?

Cactus Don't mind that langer. He hasn't a clue, him.

Dolores I know, yeah. Ah God love him.

Cactus You sound like your Granny, 'sure gawney love him'.

Dolores Don't forget your togs.

Cactus Who said I'm going anywhere?

Dolores Well . . . your tea.

Cactus I'm not hungry.

Dolores You need it. We're not finished growing you know.

Cactus Jesus, I hope not. I must, I must, increase my bust.

Dolores Ber's a 34C already.

Cactus I know.

Dolores Your man's ears are out on stalks. How do you know?

Cactus (*Shouts at Dan*) Danti-dan, ti dan dan dan.

Dan slopes off.

I know because I can read dummy. I saw the label when you were taking in her bra for yourself.

Dolores Remember, I had more under my arms than I had on my chest. Where's Ber? Mammy'll lacerate us for being late. She's like a bear.

Cactus Over what?

Dolores She heard Ber calling her a cunt behind her back. Ber swore on the bible that she said 'can't'. Daddy gave her an awful clatter. I wouldn't mind like, but I'm sure Mammy doesn't even know what it means.

Cactus Not half, I'd say. She's not that thick is she?

Dolores I never said she was thick, Cactus, I just said she didn't know what cunt means, that's all.

Cactus Oooooh touchy.

Dolores I only said. . .

Cactus Here's her nibs. Look at the walk of her. Septic. She thinks she's it.

Dolores She's breaking in her new shoes.

Ber sits by them.

Cactus Hiya.

Ber Hello.

Dolores We'd better be going.

Ber I'm sitting down for a fag for a minute. I'm crippled. 'Twasn't a power cut at all in the end. Yer man made a balls of the wiring trying to do it himself. Langer. Serves him right. We could've all been blown up though.

Cactus And you with your good shoes on. That would've been desperate.

Ber I don't know what you hang around with her for.

Dolores I don't. She hangs around with me!

Ber When she has no one better.

Cactus Ah no seriously though, are they leather?

Ber Look.

Cactus What?

Ber Look.

Cactus Look?

Ber Leather look, you fecking thick. Leather look, okay.

Cactus They look it.

Ber Watch it you.

Dolores Come on.

Cactus Give me a pull before you go.

Ber yanks Cactus's tee shirt.

You're hilarious. Ah go on.

Ber No Cactus, you're the one who's hilarious. You're the one who's loaded the whole time. I'm up there sweating bricks in the mini-market all day to make enough money for my keep, not yours.

Cactus Ah Ber, go on. It's just I have none on me. Go on, go on, go on. I'll get you back, ten for one. Ah go on.

Ber You have my heart scalded. I pity that poor man putting up with you. Now this is the last time. Honest to God, I'm worse. Here.

Cactus Match.

Ber Your face and my ass. (*She takes the lighter from her bra and flicks it expertly.*)

Cactus You can be so common sometimes.

Ber Shift. Look at the time it is.

Dolores I'm waiting for you. God's sake.

Ber links Dolores and marches her off. Cactus gives her the two fingers, Dolores catches it out of the corner of her eye.

Cactus And hey, you shouldn't call your mother a cunt.

(*Music: 'All Kinds of Everything' by Dana.*)

SCENE FOUR

*Night. Cactus is in the phone box, on the phone but not speaking. She hangs up and taps another number. Again she doesn't speak. Sound effects of a bus stopping and pulling off again. It fades into the distance. Ber and her boyfriend **Noel** (eighteen, wiry, sharp dresser) come into view. Cactus ducks down in the phone box.*

Noel (*off stage*) G'luck John Jo, and thanks.

Ber So?

Noel So what?

Ber I mean like . . . are we saving or what? Jesus.

Noel Yeah, we're saving . . . then I can flah you cross-eyed whenever I like.

Ber You will in your hole. Ah get off me, you animal. Listen will you Noel, Noelie.

Noel Fuck's sake. Ease up will you girl. We'll get engaged, alright. We'll get fucking well engaged. We'll get fucking well engaged for your birth-fucking-day, alright? Loosen your top.

Ber Noel.

Noel Just for a minute. Go on, will you. (*Cupping her breasts.*) Oh dear ol' Flo, I love you so, 'specially in your nightie, when the moonlight flits across your tits, oh Jesus Christ almighty.

Ber Langer. Who taught you that?

Noel The Brothers.

Ber Your hand'll stick up out of the grave for lying.

Noel (*opening her bra*) You're on the last hook.

Ber June is bursting out all over.

Noel Come on down to the cornfield, will you.

Ber They're after cutting it I'm sure. It'd be all stubbly.

Noel That's not all'd be stubbly.

Ber Naw. I'm sure I saw Mammy at the curtain. She'd have heard the bus Noelie. I better go in.

Noel Don't be lousy Ber. Come on, two fucking minutes, that's all. I have an awful horn on me.

Ber I don't know what you think you'll be doing for two whole minutes. It usually only takes you thirty seconds.

He sticks his tongue in her ear.

Stop it will you boy, you have me weak.

Noel Come on, you're gasping for it, admit it.

Ber I told you Noel, I'm due my Auntie Jane. My friend, do you get me?

Noel Again?

They separate. Ber ties her bra. They light fags.

Ber I was thinking, a solitaire, with a white gold band. Or just the shank white and the rest ordinary yellow gold. I can't make up my mind. What do you think?

Noel shrugs, and blows rings of smoke.

I don't want it too high though. It snags your tights when it's too high, apparently. And not too wide either. Then the wedding ring'd look like a washer next to it. Am I going to have to get you one?

Noel Put your hand in me pocket there a minute.

She puts her arm around his waist and her hand in his arse pocket.

The front one, you fucking eejit.

Ber I should've known. Would you say the Topaz suite at the airport would charge a bomb for the reception?

Noel Arm and a leg. Oh, that's the fucking business.

Ber It'd be dead handy though, to be in the airport already. Like, if we were going somewhere.

Ber steps on a bundle lying by her foot. It's difficult to make out what it is.

Oh sweet Jesus Christ almighty.

Noel What? In the name of fuck. . .

Ber Oh, Jesus no. It's a baby. I just know it's a baby. Is it dead? Oh Jesus, that's desperate. Oh God love us.

Noel pokes at the bundle.

Noel It's alright. Fuck's sake. It's nothing Ber. Only someone's togs and towel.

Ber It's after putting the heart crossways on me. (*She unrolls the towel and examines the togs.*) Cactus's. I should've guessed. Christ. I'm not the better of that. I don't know why I thought it was a baby. Feel my heart, it's pumping.

He does readily.

Ah Noel. Cop yourself on, will you. I'm in no humour now. What's she doing leaving her togs here, stupid bitch. I wouldn't be surprised if she did it on purpose to scare the lard out of me.

Noel You're the one who should cop on.

Ber She's a queer hawk that one. Jesus.

Noel There's your old lady at the window. I never knew she had teeth like stars.

Ber Whah?

Noel They come out at night. Get it?

Ber Jesus, you're pathetic. Call up tomorrow?

Noel (*nods*) Hobble a few fags for us.

Ber nods. Noel wiggles his tongue at her, she wiggles hers back at him and runs off. Cactus emerges from the phone box.

14

Cactus (*throws a ten-pack of Major*) Hey, give them to Ber from me, will you?

Noel No bother, thanks very much. What has you out at this hour?

Cactus Not a lot. I have as much right to be out as you have.

Noel Is that a fact?

Cactus Yeah, that's a fact.

Noel Little fucking smartie pants, huh.

Cactus You're entitled to your opinion, even if it is wrong.

Noel I don't need you to tell me what I'm entitled to.

Cactus I'll try and remember that.

Noel Think you're great huh? All fucking grown up. And look at you, two fucking blackberries up your jumper.

Cactus Couldn't be. It's too early for them yet.

Noel Sure what matter, any more than a handful is a waste. Am I right or am I fucking right?

Cactus Again it's a matter of opinion. Hey, would you say the weather would hold up?

Noel I wish someone would hold something else up.

Cactus Whatever that's supposed to mean. Would you say it would be a good summer or not?

Noel What the fuck are you talking about? Every summer is good, that's what summers are for.

Cactus Oh! I remember my mother saying that every summer when she was small was raining. Day in, day out. Lashing the whole time. Imagine.

Noel You should go on away in home girl and take them togs with you.

Cactus Those togs. Not them togs, those togs.

Noel Watch your fucking lip you, I'm warning you.

Cactus You and whose army.

Noel Just watch it.

He backs away from her, pointing at her. She stares at him smirking.

(Music: 'Down the Dustpipe' by Status Quo.)

SCENE FIVE

Cactus is sitting on the gate next to Dan. He's taking down car numbers. She tries to distract him. Dolores appears, walking briskly. Cactus jumps off the gate and danti-dans her way to Dolores.

Cactus Get it?

Dolores Got it.

Cactus Good. Show.

Dolores Hang on, yer man's gawking down here the whole time.

Cactus Hey (*whistles*) Danti-dan. Dan. Hey, your mother is looking for you. She said to send you home if we saw you.

Dan obediently puts his books away and heads home.

Come on, give us a sconce.

Dolores The page where they're shifting, kissing like, is bent down.

Cactus Is it the first time?

Dolores Ehm. Yeah. I think so. I only read as far as the page after that. I think anyway. She's Janet and he's Richard.

Cactus Thanks. I can read. Right, so who do you want to be?

Dolores I don't mind.

Cactus We better get away from the monument, your ma can see us.

Dolores Down there for dancing.

They walk to the far end of the bridge.

Cactus Okay, which one?

Dolores You know me, I'm easy.

Cactus But Dolores you've read it already. You know what happens.

Dolores Yeah, but . . . well, you pick and then we can swop. Then the two of us are the two of them.

Cactus Do it twice?

Dolores It's only fair really, I suppose. D'you know what I mean like?

Cactus Yeah. I suppose. From here . . . 'Janet's chest was rising and falling, she had no control over it . . .'

Dolores Flip's sake, here's Ber. Shove it up your jumper.

Cactus Sugar.

They look very suspicious as Ber comes level with them.

Ber What are ye up to?

Cactus Us?

17

Dolores Us?

Ber Well, there's no one else shagging well here, is there? Take that brazen puss off you, you. What have you up your jumper?

Cactus Two blackberries. Ask Noel, he knows all about it. Sorry, it's two fucking blackberries?

Ber Sounds like him alright. Are you sure it's not two fucking black-fucking-berries?

Cactus Maybe that's it.

Ber What are you wearing a jumper for anyway? It's boiling.

Cactus I hate my arms.

Ber Jesus.

Dolores Were you on time this morning?

Ber Just.

Dolores Mammy said you're not going out during the week anymore. You're too hard to get up.

Ber Fuck her.

Dolores Ber.

Ber I won't have to put up with her much longer.

Dolores How do you mean like?

Ber kisses her ring finger.

Serious?

Cactus To Noel?

Ber We're going into Kings on Saturday.

Dolores Kings? I thought there was a better selection in O'Reillys.

Ber Mmmm, there's the back room in Kings though where you can pick your ring in private.

Cactus Sounds sore.

Ber A solitaire.

Dolores Not too high though.

Ber No.

Dolores Snags your tights.

Ber Apparently.

Dolores When did he ask you?

Ber What? Oh, ehm . . . last night.

Dolores At the pictures?

Cactus What did you see?

Ber Haven't a clue what was on.

Cactus How come, didn't you go?

Ber Listen love, you don't go to the flicks with a fella if you want to watch the film.

Dolores Did ye get the twin seats?

Ber Yeah. I got me ration of passion alright. I was hardly finished my golly bar and he was at me. Look at the state of my stomach after him.

She unzips her shop coat to her waist. She's covered in love bites.

Cactus Oh God. It looks like shingles. Does it hurt?

Ber It sort of hurts for a bit, but then you get all, I don't know, jiggly or something. Hot anyway. You couldn't give a fuck about anything.

Dolores Ber.

Cactus He doesn't use his teeth though, sure he doesn't.

Ber No. Just a good suck.

Dolores Yeuch.

Ber No, you'd get used to it. It's not disgusting, I swear. I mean like, I've a weak enough stomach. No, it's nice . . . ish.

Cactus How hard does he have to suck?

Ber Do it there on your arm and you'll find out.

Cactus Ah, I was only wondering.

Dolores Curiosity killed the cat.

Cactus Who asked you?

Dolores God. I only said. . .

Cactus I only said.

Ber Jesus H Christ, give us a break would you. My lunch time is short enough without having to listen to ye.

Cactus You're right, shut up Dolores will you.

Dolores Flip's sake.

Cactus Joke. Jesus. Fag Ber?

Ber No, you can feck off. Anyway you owe me.

Cactus I do not.

Ber You do so. You said ten for one the other day, when was it? I'm not as green as I'm cabbage looking, you know.

Cactus Oh, I gave them to Noel for you.

Ber When did you meet him? This morning?

Dolores He never saw morning.

Ber Shut up you.

Cactus Last night actually.

Ber When? Where were you?

Cactus Hanging round just.

Dolores Liar. That late?

Cactus I was. Proof? Okay . . . you gave him a hand shandy. You looked bored rigid.

Dolores Is that true? Bored? Naw, Ber's mad for it, aren't you?

Ber Where were you, you spying little bitch?

Cactus I'm like God, I see everything. Watch out.

Ber You give me the willies sometimes, you do.

Cactus I thought it was Noel was giving you the willies.

Dolores That's a good one. Never thought of it like that.

Ber It's none of your business what I do with my fiancé. So watch your face or I'll burst you.

Cactus I'm quaking. Hold me up.

Dan arrives.

Dan My mother didn't want me.

Cactus So what? Mine didn't want me either.

Ber That's an awful thing to say. God rest her. Don't mind her love. You walk me back to work, will you?

Dan She's not even there. She's gone to town.

Cactus We must've been hearing things. Or seeing things, is it Dolores?

Ber What's he on about?

Dolores Yeah, sorry about that. A mistake.

Ber lights a fag, lighter from her bra, as usual. She links Dan.

Ber Dolores, say nothing to Mammy about you know what. I might just keep the, ahem, ahem, on a chain around my neck for a bit. She's like a dog these days, isn't she? God. Can't wait to move out, to give up work.

Cactus For ever?

Ber I might try for a secretarial course in the School of Comm. There's loads of sums though, I don't know if I'd be able for it. Sure, Noel might get something. You'd never know, maybe one of the dogs will get lucky.

Dan It's nearly one fifty eight, Ber.

Ber What? See. Sums again.

Dan I . . . have to get back to my post.

Ber gives him a peck on the cheek. He rides off.

Ber Be good. And if you can't be good be careful.

Dolores And if you can't be careful buy a pram.

Ber Where did you hear that?

Dolores Off of you. Where else.

Ber Are ye going swimming?

Dolores Naw.

Cactus She has her friend.

Ber I'm usually around the same time as you, aren't I? I thought I was getting it yesterday but naw. My chest is killing me. Shag it anyway. I'll probably get it Friday and I wanted to wear my white pants going out.

Dolores Why can't you?

Ber You can see the shape of the S.T.

Dolores Use tampoons.

Cactus Tampons, isn't it?

Ber Mmm. Mammy'd kill me if she caught me with Tampax.

Cactus Why?

Dolores 'Cause you're not a virgin anymore after them or something like that.

Cactus Sure you're not anyway, are you? Have you gone all the way?

Ber Listen girl, this is the kind of place that if you lost your virginity somebody would find it and bring it home to your mother. C'mon, walk up along. I'm dead late already. I'll be slaughtered.

Cactus Have you gone all the way or not?

Ber Jesus, keep your hair on. Well, I sort of have. Not lying down like, only standing.

Dolores What'd you do if you get preggers?

Ber Shut up would you. I'm far too young for that. Anyway, it was only standing.

Cactus Go on anyway.

Ber About what?

Cactus What it's like. What does he do?

Ber Jesus, I don't know. I wasn't looking.

Cactus Had you your eyes closed?

Ber Yeah. When you're weak for someone you sort of go... (*She closes her eyes, head to one side, breathing heavily.*)

Cactus Do you have to close your eyes though?

Ber No, you don't have to, but ... this is like a what do you call it, a court case. Fuck's sake.

Cactus Does he have his eyes closed?

Dolores Couldn't have. Or else how would he know where you were? Flip's sake, you could get your nose broken that way.

Cactus tries out what Ber was doing.

Ber You look more like Saint Bernadette.

Cactus Fuck off you.

Ber Jesus, the time. I'm gone (*She goes off in a hurry.*)

Dolores Me too. See you.

Cactus Where are you going?

Dolores In home. I promised Mammy I'd do the ironing for her. I don't mind it too much really, do you? I love the smell of it.

Cactus Mrs Breen does ours. I think it's even her iron. I don't know.

Dolores See you after.

Cactus Hey, the book.

Dolores Hang on to it. Or plank it somewhere till after.

Cactus Yeah. See you after so. Definitely.

Dolores goes and Cactus starts to give herself a love bite on the arm.

(*Music: 'Sugar' by the Archies.*)

SCENE SIX

Dan is car watching. Noel is hanging around kicking at stones. A car passes.

Noel Renault. CZT 520. Wouldn't take one of them fucking yokes if you gave it to me on a plate.

Dan That's her third time passing today.

Noel Who?

Dan Miss McInerney.

Noel Miss fucking Mc-a-fucking-nerney. A tiger in her tank, that's what she needs, and I know who'd give it to her too.

Dan Esso.

Noel Oh yesso. Esso blue.

Noel ferrets around for five white stones of a similar weight and shape. He starts playing gobs (jacks).

Yeah, I fancy the notion of America too. Maybe the two of us should fuck off out west together Dan, what do you think, huh? Riding the fucking range boy, huh? Saloons bursting with young ones called Lulu, their tits falling out of their frocks. Bottles of whiskey all over the gaff. Shoot the shit out of anyone who looked at you crossways. You could flah the ol' doll without even leaving the place. In the back room like, not in front of the whole town. Yeah. Now that's what I call a pub. And poker with a massive pot.

Dan I can't play cards.

Noel Oh man. You have to be able to play fucking cards if you want to be a cowboy. You have to be able to play fucking cards. They won't let you in otherwise like.

Dan That true?

Noel Gospel boy. The honest to God truth. Cross my heart and hope to die. Rawhide Dan, raw fucking hide. What are you up to boy? Coming down to watch the young ones swimming? Wouldn't mind being an eel in that water, huh? Would not.

Dan Naw. I'll stick here till six o'clock.

A car passes.

Noel Wolsey. Don't see many of them now. Great fucking car. Say what you like about the shagging Brits, and I'd agree with you, but they can put a decent car together. I'll give them that. Do you take down every number or what?

Dan Just the ones coming from town, that's all.

Noel Why like?

Dan 'Cause the gate is on this side and I can tie Trigger up at the monument. I could stand on the other side alright, I suppose. Naw, I like the gate side the best. If there's no cars I can do bucking bronco for a bit. The gang sits this side. As well, there's more people coming out from town than going in. The going in is in the morning and I'm mostly here in the afternoon time.

Noel I mean like, what are you taking them down for, at all?

Dan For my books. I have to keep my books up to date. If I miss one the whole thing is ruined on me. I have a place at home, in a hide, and I put them in there at nighttime. During the daytime I have them with me, mostly. You'd have to shoot the shit out of me to get them.

Noel You're fucking mad, young fella. Fucking mental you are.

Cactus comes along, sits to one side of Dan.

Dan Hello.

Noel Well, look what the cat dragged up.

Cactus just stares at him.

What are you gawking at?

Cactus Not a lot, obviously.

Noel Right fucking smart arse here, Dan.

Cactus I wasn't being smart at all, actually. I wouldn't give you the soot of being smart. You probably wouldn't understand it anyway. You can't even think of a name for your dog, I heard. If that's not thick, I don't know what is. Why don't you call him Blackie? That's nice and easy.

Noel Because, fuck face, it's a bitch and it's a brindle.

Cactus Oooh, excuse me.

Noel And, fuck face, she has a name, she's called Naked Lady. Yes and she's running in the Bitch Classic next Friday night and that lady is going to fucking well win. Then we'll see who's shagging well thick, alright.

Cactus Phew. Who ate your cake?

Noel No one ate my cake, you little prick teaser. No one ate my cake. I just don't like being fucking called thick. Alright? Don't call me thick, alright.

Cactus Yes Noel, no Noel.

Noel I'm warning you.

Cactus Is that a threat? Dan, you heard him.

Noel You're bugging me, I tell you. Really getting on my wick.

Cactus You could always go away. It's a free country you know. Right Danti-dan?

Dan Dan.

Cactus See. No one's making you stay. You're a big boy now. Go if you want.

Noel (*winks at Dan*) Bigger than you're able for.

Cactus Ah just fuck off, will you. A langer, that's all you are. A langer.

He exits, making lewd and threatening gestures at Cactus.

Thinks I'm weak for him. The langer.

Dan And are you?

Cactus No way. God.

Dan Can you play poker?

Cactus Eh no, can you?

Dan No. Just beg of my neighbour and snap. Oh and memory. I have to learn poker though.

Cactus God, would you look at them. Doing that out on the road. Common. And I wouldn't mind but they're nearly engaged, there's no call for that.

Dan Who?

Cactus Ber and that Langer. Don't know what she sees in him.

Dan Ber? Getting engaged?

He gathers his stuff up and goes and sits alone by the

*monument. He's on the verge of tears. Cactus watches
Ber and Noel as they approach.*

Cactus Oh God. He has her bra open. That's . . . oh
God . . . look . . . Dan, Dan?

*She continues to watch them. It's clear that Noel is doing
this for Cactus's benefit. They come close, Ber is
laughing, aroused.*

Ber Tell her Noel. Ah go on, it's a good one.

Noel Cactus doesn't know how to laugh, sure you don't
Cactus? Come on, smile and give your face a fucking
holiday.

Ber Just tell the bloody joke, would you.

Noel Okay. O-fucking-kay. Right, Why don't big trains
have little trains?

Cactus I don't know Noel. Why?

Noel Because they pull out on time.

Ber Good isn't it? D'ya get it?

Cactus Of course I get it.

Noel Why aren't you laughing so?

Cactus Didn't find it funny, that's all.

Noel You couldn't have fucking got it so.

Ber You tarry bastard, take your hand out of there.

Noel I thought you said you had the curse.

Ber Thought made a fool of you. Got my dates mixed up.

Noel Oh good. This is my lucky day. Yabba dabba
fucking do Freddy.

Ber Noelie. Stop will you, she's only a young one.

Noel That one was here before.

Ber Where's Dan?

Cactus Up by the monument. Don't know what's eating him, went off in huff. Anyone any fags?

Ber Noel.

Noel They're in my pocket there. Take one if you want one.

Ber You're desperate. Ah give her a cigarette. (*Shouts to Dan.*) How's my boy?

Noel She knows where they are. Come and get it. Don't try and tell me you're shy.

Cactus Stuff them. I'll get my own thanks.

Noel Please yourself. Don't say I didn't offer.

Ber Dan. Come on down here love. Dan. He's deaf, is he?

Cactus leaves. Ber and Noel kiss.

SCENE SEVEN

There's a transistor radio balanced on the bridge, the top twenty programme is on and 'I'm Going to Make You Love Me' by The Temptations & Supremes is playing. Dan is teaching Dolores to twirl a gun and shoot. They have competitions to draw the fastest. Dan wins by a long shot, Dolores is only humouring him. She takes Dan's hand and checks the time. They hear somebody coming and duck behind the gate, guns at the ready. Cactus appears and sits on the gate. They shoot at her from either side. She falls to the ground. Dan clears the wall and checks the body. The game goes on too long and Dolores begins to try to revive Cactus. Dan is getting worried. He checks the guns. They

*check her breathing. Suddenly Cactus leaps up on Dan
when he's not looking. She twists his arm behind his back
and whispers into his ear.*

Cactus Don't ever shoot anyone in the back again. Do you
hear me? I'm warning you.

> *She pushes his arm until he's almost on his knees. She's
> getting a sexual charge from this, without really
> knowing what it's about. Giddy and confused, she lets
> him go. All three are aware that something has
> happened. They sit on the bridge. The record on the
> radio changes to 'My Cherie Amour' by Stevie
> Wonder.*

Dolores Anyone any fags?

Cactus I thought you gave them up.

Dolores I know yeah. I think I'll take them up again for
the summer. There's nothing else to do like.

Cactus I know yeah. Dan, run up to the shop for us, like a
good boy.

Dan Ah no. They won't sell them to me.

Cactus Danti-dan. Danti-dan. You wouldn't be a minute.
We'd let you hang around with us all evening. Wouldn't we
Dol? Here, I'll give you money to get something for
yourself even.

Dolores Where did you get a fiver?

Cactus Found it. Here Dan. Say they're for your Da. Get
whatever he smokes.

Dolores You're always finding money. It's not fair.

Dan Aftons.

Cactus Flow gently sweet Afton.

Dolores Players please. Thank you so much.

Cactus What are you talking about? Here Dan. You can buy whatever you want. Whatever you want. Imagine.

Dan puts his guns in the holsters, saddles up and takes off. Dolores and Cactus look at each other and shrug.

Did you have your tea already?

Dolores Mammy is in bed sick. Cramps or something. There was blood all over the toilet. She was in there with the holy water bottle, firing it down the jacks as if it was Harpic. Then Ber started going on about someone taking her rollers and not putting them back and how was she supposed to get ready to go out if Mammy wouldn't get out of the bathroom. Then Daddy said she wasn't going out. Ber started roaring. Daddy gave her a clatter. Then Mammy started bawling crying and went into the bedroom and shoved the wardrobe against the door. Flip's sake, it's like Our Lady's loony bin over there.

Cactus I planked the book. Will I get it before Danti-dan comes back?

Dolores Ehm. I don't know like.

Cactus Fuck you. Make up your mind.

Dolores Alright. I'm easy.

Cactus retrieves the book from behind the bridge wall. The radio plays 'Make it With You' by Bread.

Cactus I'll read, okay. Sit next to me. Nearer. Right. 'Janet's chest . . . blah blah blah'.

Dolores Who's who?

Cactus You be her . . . right . . . eh . . . 'no control over it.' Right. 'Richard was silhouetted against the window, his Adam's apple bobbed in a sea of emotion' . . .

Dolores Langer.

Cactus Yeah, ah no . . . 'His brow furrowed, trying to read her thoughts, her mind.'

Cactus furrows her brow and looks into Dolores's eyes.

'Like magnets they drew closer. Janet raised her hand to touch the outline of his square jaw. He caught her and pulled her to him.'

They do likewise.

'It felt good.'

Dolores It!!!

Cactus Shut up . . . 'She surrendered to him, (*Dolores puts her hands up, Cactus withers her with a look.*) sinking into his chest. He brushed her chestnut curls back to reveal her neck, like alabaster, bare but for the velvet choker at her throat. They were breathing as one. Their eyes locked, their lips parted, their bodies trembled.'

Cactus is really getting aroused, Dolores is trying but has trouble not laughing.

'Janet had often wondered whether Richard's moustache would prove an irritant, if and when they ever kissed. The only irritant right now was James. "Take me, oh God, Richard," moaned Janet'. . .

Dolores Take me, oh God, Richard.

They are so close to kissing that it's difficult for Cactus to read the book.

Cactus . . . 'moaned Janet, "take me to the hospital." The hospital was a sprawling gray affair, built in 1879 . . .' Jesus, is that it? What's wrong with him?

Dolores Who?

Cactus James.

Dolores He's after falling off his horse.

Cactus That's all? They don't even shift. That's no shagging use. You said they shifted in it.

Dolores More or less though.

Cactus Where exactly? Show.

Dolores Well, ehm. . .

Cactus fires the book into the river.

Cactus.

Cactus Kiss.

They stare at each other, move closer, close their eyes and kiss very quickly.

Dolores God.

Cactus The mirror is better than that. It's useless if you keep your mouth closed so much. There should be that pwawppy sound.

She practises on her hand. Dolores is feeling awkward.

Come here.

She pulls Dolores to her a bit too quickly. They bash teeth. Both hold their mouths.

Dolores Ouch. God. I don't think that's right anyway.

Cactus You've seen Ber and Noel millions of times, how come you don't know how?

Dolores That's different. He nearly chokes her with his tongue. He's like a camel.

Cactus Try, just a small bit.

Cactus kisses Dolores, softer and longer. Dolores wipes her mouth and makes a face. Radio plays 'Something' by Shirley Bassey.

Dolores Crisps.

Cactus Cheese and onion. That was better wasn't it?

Dolores Ehm, yeah. I don't know. Suppose so. Sort of.

Cactus kisses her again. They separate, both hot around the collar. They listen to the radio. Dolores avoids Cactus's eye.

Cactus Love that song. Clinger.

Dolores I know, yeah. It's ancient though.

Cactus Oh God.

Dolores Phew. Roasting are you? Boiling.

Cactus is tracing her lips with her fingers.

Cactus Was that how, do you think?

Dolores shrugs, embarrassed.

What did it feel like to you?

Dolores Tickly, inside my lips. Quakey kinda. Funny. You?

Cactus Did it make you want to go to the jacks?

Dolores Eh . . . no. For a pee like? No.

Cactus And what about your chest? Did you feel anything there?

Dolores In my chest? A while ago, you mean. Eh . . . no.

Cactus Wasn't your heart thumping?

Dolores My heart? Yeah, I think I could feel my heart alright.

Cactus And that's just with you. God.

Dolores Here's Dan. He took his time. Hiya.

Dan rides up, dismounts and ties his horse up.

Dan I'm going to get caught. I think he knows they're not for my Dad. You'll have to say you made me, Cactus. I'd be murdered. I got a Tiffin for myself, okay. Here's the change.

Cactus takes the cigarettes and change. She kisses Dan, full on the mouth. He pulls away and wipes his mouth.

Cactus Take me. Oh God Richard, take me to the hospital.

Dan is gobsmacked. Dolores is nearly crying with mortification. Cactus lights a cigarette. The two are transfixed by her. She walks off moving with the music. Dan looks at Dolores.

Dolores What are you gawking at? Langer.

She switches off the music and runs off, opposite direction to Cactus, with the transistor under her arm.

SCENE EIGHT

Dan is sitting on the monument, fastidiously covering a new notebook with wallpaper. He has a geometry set, pencil case, rubber and ruler. When he's finished covering the book, he starts to rule columns, slowly and methodically. A car is heard in the distance, Dan's hand slips as he grabs the relevant notebook, leaving a squiggle across the new book. The car approaches and Dan checks his watch, it's too early for him to be taking numbers. He hits himself quite hard with his knuckles on the temples, stops and waits for his breathing to return to normal. He gingerly picks up the new book and the rubber and starts to erase the unwanted mark.

  Blackout.

SCENE NINE

Cactus and Dolores are walking along the parapet of the bridge. Dolores is smartly dressed in her Sunday best. Cactus is in her usual duds, and wearing sunglasses.

(*Music: 'Je t'Aime' by Serge Gainsbourg and Jane Birkin.*)

Cactus There's a pike, look.

Dolores Where?

Cactus There. Look would you.

Dolorcs Naw, can't see it. Give me a go.

Cactus gives her the glasses.

Groovy baby.

Cactus Gravy booby.

A car approaches, Cactus snatches back her glasses. They peer at the car and wave frantically.

Dolores Hiya handsome.

Cactus Hiya handsome.

The car passes.

Dolores The look on his face.

Cactus Yeah. I thought he was going to stop there for a minute.

Dolores God. What would you say?

Cactus Nothing. What would you have to say anything for? Langer. Who does he think he is?

Dolores Who?

Cactus Your man.

Dolores Oh yeah.

Cactus Shhhh. Listen. Car coming.

The car approaches, they stand, one hand on hip, waving with the other.

Dolores Hiya sexy.

Cactus Hiya s . . . oh sugar, it's a woman. Go on Dol, you lezzer.

Dolores Come off it girl, you thought it was a fella too.

Cactus Lesbe friends and go homo.

Dolores Haha very funny. You think you're it don't you.

They sit on the bridge, Cactus firing stones into the river.

Cactus Pike. Filthy ugly looking things. What's the use of them?

Dolores They eat shite.

They sit a while, bored.

Here's Ber. (*Shouts.*) Hiya.

Cactus Brilliant. I don't think.

Ber joins them.

Ber How are ye lads?

Dolores Where's Noel?

Cactus Give us a look at the famous ring.

Ber takes it off the chain around her neck and gives it to her.

Ber Twiddle it three times and make three wishes. He's at home. He can stay there for all I care. Christ almighty he's like a dog himself over Naked Lady.

Cactus She lose? (*Hands back the ring.*) Bit gaudy, isn't it.

Ber It's only for now, till he gets money, then I'll get a good one. Yeah, Naked Lady, she got her leg caught in the trap.

Dolores (*mimicking Noel*) Stupid fucking bitch.

Ber thumps her on the back.

Ber Shut up you, you pup you.

Dolores He said it, not me. God.

Cactus You pup you!

*The girls snigger. Dolores rubs her back. Fags all round.
Ber gives one to Dolores reluctantly, sorry to have hit her.*

Ber I'm up the fecking walls girls. I swear I'll give every bob I have to Concern if I get my friend.

Cactus You're mental.

Ber I'm crooked from praying for it. I even had Dol digging me in the stomach last night, didn't I Dol? No word of a lie.

Dolores She did. I didn't want to like but she made me. Didn't you Ber?

Ber God forgive me. I couldn't be, sure I couldn't?

Cactus shrugs and goes to sit on the gate post, the capping stone of which is loose.

Dolores I wouldn't say so, no. Not really. Naw, you're just late. God, you'd be killed.

Cactus Well, how far did you . . . you know, was he on top of you or what? Like had ye clothes on?

Ber I told you before we were standing up. Jesus. Watch yourself up there you. That stone thing is awful wobbly.

Cactus Only once you did it.

Ber Would you ever shag off. Loads of times, but I always got my auntie Jane before, didn't I?

Cactus Well, it couldn't have been the whole way so. I thought you said you did it.

Dolores She did. Didn't you Ber?

Cactus Did you have to touch his thing? His knob!

Dolores Ol' King Cole (*Cactus joins in.*) stuck a penny up his hole but he never got his ha'penny change, he pulled his knob and got five bob but he never got his ha'penny change.

Ber Jesus, ye can't remember Hickory Dickory Dock and ye have that off by heart.

Cactus Well, did you touch it or not?

Dolores Ah stop, the thought of it.

Ber One of the charms on my bracelet sort of got caught in his zip. I felt it then alright.

   Dolores puts her hands over her ears.

Dolores La la la la la. . .

Cactus And. . .

Ber He was real randy and pushing up against me like that and sticking his tongue in my ear and you know me, that always makes me weak. I don't know where my skirt was, around my oxters I suppose. Ah lads, I'm not, sure I'm not. My savings even I'll give them, the Biafrans is it?

Cactus Ah no, what did 'it' feel like?

Dolores Flip's sake Cactus.

Ber Wait till I think . . . ehm . . . sorta like white pudding. Yeah.

Dolores God Ber, that's disgusting. I'm going to puke.

Cactus What? I like white pudding. And black pudding.

Ber Cooked, yeah. This was raw.

Laughter. Danti-dan comes along, stops short of them. He's wearing trousers.

Cactus Look at him in the long pants, he's like an old man cut down.

Dolores Ah God love him.

Ber Here's my boy. Come over here and give us a kiss.

Dan Howdy. (*He doesn't budge.*)

Ber Who ate your cake?

Dan No one. No one ate my cake. Alright. No one.

Ber Moods now you see. That's more of it. Jesus, you couldn't be up to them. They're all the shagging same if you ask me. Come on, come on in home with me Dol, will you? I don't want to be in there on my own with Mammy.

Dolores Oh yeah, right. See you later, bye.

Cactus and Dan are left alone. Ber links Dolores as they walk off.

Cactus (*shouts*) Hey Dolores. . .

Dolores What?

Cactus Come here, quick.

Ber stops, Dolores returns.

Dolores What?

Cactus Bye.

Dolores Flip's sake. Cop yourself on would you.

Pissed off with being caught out, she runs back to Ber and they leave.

Cactus How's Danti-dan, the little man?

Dan Dan. The horses go danti-dan. Danti-dan, danti-dan, danti dan dan dan.

Cactus Ah shut up would you, cranky pants. Hey, come here. Guess what?

Dan What?

Cactus Come here. I have something to tell you.

Warily he goes to her.

I found out how to play poker. Want me to show you?

Dan Yeah. Sure.

Cactus Don't believe me? (*She takes a deck of cards from her pocket.*) See. Doubting Thomas. I know, come on down under the bridge and I'll teach you.

Dan I'm not allowed down there, Mammy says it's too skeety, I might fall in.

Cactus Sure who'd tell her? (*She flicks the cards.*) Come on Dan. Come on. Dan. Come on.

She walks ahead of him. Dan ties up his horse, pats its nose etc.

Dan Rawhide Trigger. Raw fucking hide boy.

The song 'Rawhide' by Frankie Lane begins gently as he follows Cactus. She looks around to check that nobody is watching, then they both climb over the gate and disappear towards the riverside.

Blackout.

Act Two

SCENE ONE

Music: 'Gimme Dat Ding' by the Pipkins.
  Dan climbs over the gate from the riverside. He looks around to see if anyone is watching, the coast is clear, he whistles and Cactus comes into view. She sits on the gatepost. She's wearing different clothes, a little sexier, nothing too obvious. She's holding Dan's books. Dan is subdued, while Cactus, full of adrenaline, rocks on the loose capping stone.

Dan Give me them. You said you'd give them back now. Give them to me.

  She holds the books out and snatches them back before Dan can grab them. This happens a couple of times. She stands on the post and holds them out again. It's far too high for Dan to reach. He's getting frantic.

Give them back or I'm telling on you. You swore.

Cactus Oh, tell tale tattler, buy a penny rattler. Don't be such a bloody baba. Here they are. Look, I'm giving them to you. Come on, Danti-dan, jump. Woops nearly got them there. Jump. Ah not high enough Dan. Here, jump. You little squirt, you can't reach.

  Dan starts to cry.

Dan I'm straight telling on you.

  Cactus holds the books out over the river.

Cactus Oh no you're not. You're not telling anyone anything, sure you're not Danti-dan?

Dan is fixed to the spot, his eyes glued to his books.

Dan (*whispers*) No.

Cactus Can't hear you.

Dan No.

Cactus What? Still can't hear you.

Dan (*shouts*) No.

Cactus No, what?

Dan No, I'm not going to tell anyone anything.

Cactus hands him his books. He hugs them to himself.

Cactus That's more like it. Good boy Dan.

He heads for home.

Where do you think you're going?

Dan I have to get Trigger and go home. I have to go in for my tea.

Cactus You don't have to do anything Danti-dan, except die.

Dan I'll be killed if I'm late. Mammy'll get worried.

Cactus Mammy Mammy Mammy. Jesus.

She jumps down and grabs him by the arm.

Come under the bridge after.

He doesn't answer and won't look at her.

Tell you what, I'll ring the man in the County Council now, alright. Hang on, alright. And I'll ask him.

She runs to the phone box. She doesn't put in any money and talks very animatedly. She gives Dan a thumbs up sign during the call. He walks to the box, half crying but

44

full of expectation. Cactus comes out.

Well . . .

Dan What? What did he say? Tell me.

Cactus He said . . . eh . . . he said, yeah he said he'd buy them. A pound for each book. Imagine. A whole pound. They need all sorts of statistics he said, that's figures, numbers like, for how many cars are passing. As well they want to know other stuff like, ehm, like how many white cars, say, there are, and red and grey ones too. What else? And ehm, like how many drivers are wearing glasses or are baldy and loads of other stuff. I'll remember it, don't worry. I better mind them for you. (*She takes the notebooks from him.*)

Dan A pound. Phew. For one book. I could do a one of hubcaps and one of . . . loads of things. I'll get enough to go to the Wild West soon so, will I?

Cactus Oh yeah. Real soon, I'd say. And you know how to play poker and all now. See Danti-dan. Don't be stupid now and go telling anyone anything or else I'll have to ring the man. Then he'll change his mind and get someone else. Swear?

Dan Swear.

Cactus Cross your heart?

Dan Cross my heart and hope to die.

Cactus See you after tea so.

Dan Okay.

She kisses him full on the mouth and puts one of his hands on her breast. He pulls away.

Does it have to be in pencil or biro?

Cactus Biro. Yeah, he said biro definitely.

Dan goes off full of excitement. Cactus laughs at him.

Stupid langer.

She throws stones in the river.

(Music: 'You Can Get it if You Really Want' by Desmond Dekker.)

SCENE TWO

Noel is in the phone box. Ber and Dolores are sitting on the monument. Ber is putting nail varnish on Dolores's toenails.

Ber And Sinead's salon is gone unisex, if you don't mind.

Dolores Go away. Who said?

Ber Miss McInerney. She was in this morning. She's as mean as get out that one. One slice of corned beef. Jesus, gumming up the slicer for that. Still, it took my mind off . . . you know. She was giving out about the word sex being plastered up all over the gaff, and the last thing she wanted to be faced with under the drier was sex.

Dolores That's the closest she'll get to it.

Ber Did you ever notice how thick her glasses are?

Dolores You're desperate. There's not an ounce of truth in that, sure there isn't?

Ber If there was, Noel would be led around by a bloody dog by now. Jesus, what's keeping him?

Cactus passes the phone box en route to the monument. Noel leans out.

Noel Where did you get legs all of a sudden?

Cactus Lucky bag . . .

*She wiggles her backside, Noel returns to his call,
watching Cactus all the while.*

Dolores Long time no see. Were you in town or what?

Cactus shrugs.

Ber Well?

Cactus Just around.

Ber Don't mind her.

*Cactus starts messing with the laurel wreaths on the
monument, undoing the tri-colour ribbon and twirling
the wreaths on her fingers till they fly off.*

So which do you think?

Dolores What?

Ber Shoes. Jesus.

Dolores I don't know really like. I'd prefer egg-cup heels
to Cubans, I think.

Ber The ones I liked were fairly pointy. Slingbacks.

Dolores You could always get them for your going away
outfit. In patent. And get Sinead to cover the others in the
same stuff as your frock.

Ber Yeah. Jesus knows where I'll be going away to.
Bessborough. Yeah, scrubbing shagging floors for the nuns
till I'm out to here.

Dolores Ah Ber, stop. They'd never do that to you. Don't
worry. He'll get something and you'll be grand.

Ber We'll see. Here's his lordship. Say nothing. Well

dreamboat, how did you get on?

Noel Not bad, not bad at all. He said to call some day during the week and he'd try to fix me up. No bother.

Ber That's fabulous now. Thanks be to God.

Cactus Do you have to see a man about a dog?

Noel tickles her.

Noel She's very fucking funny this one, isn't she?

Dolores He's going for a job in the chewing gum factory, actually, if you must know.

Cactus For the summer just?

Ber Full time, what do you think? Do you hear her?

Cactus 'I'm forever blowing bubbles.' Jesus, I'd be bored rigid.

Ber Who's asking you? Put them things down, you'll break them.

Cactus Those things.

Dolores Mammy'll have a stroke if you do. She doesn't even like us sitting on the monument, sure she doesn't Ber?

Ber Put them down, I'm warning you.

Cactus I'm quaking. (*She puts them on the ground but continues to fiddle with them.*) So I heard Naked Lady was useless.

Noel Stupid fucking cunt, got her leg caught in the trap.

Ber/Dolores We know.

Noel Jesus, I'm only telling the girl. I tell you, that dog is only fit for the Chinese place, what do you call it?

Dolores The Yangtze.

Noel Yeah. Sweet and sour naked lady and chips.

Dolores No, flied lice.

Noel Rice, Christ no. That's where I draw the line. Couldn't look at the stuff.

Ber Don't mind him, he had it only last week.

Noel Who did? Me?

Dolores No, the cat's aunt.

Noel Ah yeah Ber, that was after a feed of pints. That's different. I'd eat shite if I know I'm not going to remember it.

Cactus You're obviously not marrying him for his mind, Ber.

Noel We're only talking about the poxy dog, who said anything about getting married?

Cactus Oooops. Did I say something wrong? Am I not supposed to know, Ber? Sorry, sorreee.

Noel Supposed to know what?

Ber Don't mind her, she's talking through her arse.

Dolores It's lovely again today isn't it? We're haunted.

Noel Hang on a minute, just hang on a fucking minute.

Cactus Oh God. Sorry sorry sorry. It's all my fault. I just thought since you were engaged, that you had the ring and everything . . .

Dolores pinches Cactus's leg.

Ouch. What did you do that for? That hurt, you know.

Noel What load of shite have you been telling them? Answer me.

49

Ber Nothing Noelie boy. I swear. She's only making it up. Mind your own business you or I'll give you a proper dig.

Cactus You and whose army?

Noel catches Ber by the arm, almost lifting her.

Noel Ring? What fucking ring is she talking about? Do you hear me? What fucking ring? I bought you no ring.

Dolores Let her go you. Let my sister go.

Ber fumbles for the ring around her neck.

Ber Here look. It's only a stupid ol' thing I got myself. It's only mock.

Noel You dopey fuck, what did you do that for?

He reefs the chain from her neck.

Ber Ouch. The girls at work . . . sorry Noelie. I told them we were getting engaged.

He throws the ring into the field behind.

A bastard. That's all you are. Fuck you anyway.

He pushes her and she falls down the steps of the monument.

Dolores (*whispers*) The baby.

There is silence. Noel shakes his head, the others are stock still.

Noel Tell me I'm hearing things here. The what?

Nobody answers. Noel lights a fag and walks around in a circle. Ber edges her way back onto the steps. Dolores comforts her.

I said, the what?

Cactus The baby! Are you deaf or something? The baby.

Alright. Did you hear that?

Noel stares at Ber. She nods. Cactus is peeling the leaves off the wreaths.

Ber I think I'm up the pole.

Noel You are in your hole.

Ber I'm not sure yet like, I think I am though.

Dolores She's three weeks late, is it? And her chest is killing her.

Noel That's all I fucking well need. Jesus H Christ. Oh no, no no no, hang on a minute here. I get it now; you're only saying that so as to get married. (*laughs*) What kind of an eejit do you take me for? You can go and fuck yourself.

Ber Jesus Noel. I swear. I wouldn't do that Noelie. I am, really.

Noel You lying little pox bottle. I wouldn't believe daylight out of you. Sweet lamb of divine fuck. Even if you are, don't think I'm marrying any ol' flah bag who's after getting herself in trouble. Christ like t'would kill the fucking mother.

Cactus That's lovely, that is.

Noel And you, you shut your face if you know what's good for you.

Ber gets up and heads back to work, crying. Noel goes off in the opposite direction, shouting after her.

And you needn't think I'm going to waste my fucking time making bubble gum either. Fuck bubble gum. Do you hear me? I'm not having some bastaring Yank telling me what to do. They can stuff their jobs up their holes.

Ber runs after him, he pushes her away. She turns and

goes on her way to work. Dolores follows her.

Ber Leave me alone. Oh Jesus God help me. Leave me alone, will you. Just leave me alone.

Dolores comes back to the monument, near tears herself.

Cactus What a gutty boy. You know, the phone isn't even working. Dirty liar. Still, that was good hack wasn't it?

The wreaths are shredded.

(*Music: 'Wonderful World, Beautiful People' by Jimmy Cliff.*)

SCENE THREE

Dan has Cactus on his back and is running up and down behind the gate. Cactus has his rope and is slapping him on the bottom with it.

Cactus Giddyup Danti-dan, giddyup. Danti-dan, danti-dan, danti- dan dan dan.

He runs towards the gate. When they reach it she leaps off his back and onto the gate.

Naw, no use. You have to go faster coming up to it. Again.

She climbs back over the wall to him. He stoops for her to get on his back.

(*whispers*) Richard, take me to the hospital.

Dan straightens up slowly. She walks towards him trancelike. He's rooted to the spot.

It's James, Richard. He's fallen from his horse.

Dan doesn't react.

What's wrong with you, are you deaf or something? Is that it? (*She shakes him.*) You are aren't you? Can't even give someone a decent higgy back. Fat lot of use you'll be in the Wild West. That's if you ever get there of course. Only I know that. (*She flicks at his nose with her fingers.*) Love to know wouldn't you, nosey baa.

Dan does his best not to react, though she's obviously hurting him. She makes a lasso out of the rope and starts skirling it.

Dan Alright.

He makes to go under the bridge. She stops him.

Cactus No. Here. What are you afraid of? I told you, everyone does what I tell them to do. Did you forget? Hmmm? Did you? Come on, I haven't got all summer you know. Do it Danti-dan.

He kisses her, his arms stiffly by his sides. She thumps him to make him more active. He clumsily fumbles inside her shirt. She gropes in his pockets and down his trousers. Dan starts coughing and breaks away.

Dan I'm suffocating.

Cactus I told you to breathe through your nose. How many times do you have to be told everything?

Dan I can't, it's blocked.

Cactus Ah shut up will you, you little moaning minnie.

She grabs him, he pushes her away. She loses her temper.

Right. That's it. I'm going to ring the man this time. Definitely. I'm going to ring him and tell him. Then you'll be sorry. (*She heads towards the telephone box.*) I should've known you couldn't keep your word. The man's going to be real disappointed. No books – no money. No money – no Wild West.

Dan pinches his nostrils and tries to breathe through them.

Dan Hang on Cactus, hang on. I think they're after clearing.

Cactus They better be Dan. They better be. I'm warning you. (*She stands on the wall looking down at him, snapping the rope at him.*) You're sure Danti-dan?

He nods, she jumps down next to him and dances around him.

Dan When's the man going to give me the money?

Cactus Oh . . . ehm . . . let me think. When I ask him for it I suppose. So . . . you better watch it Danti. You better watch out, you better not cry, you better not pout, I'm telling you why . . .

She holds up a notebook and waves it in front of Dan. She kisses him ferociously. Gasping for breath, he separates.

Dan Here's Ber, coming over the bridge.

Cactus Do you know what? Kissing you is like kissing a holy water font. (*She kisses the notebook and shoves it in her waistband.*) You better watch out, you better not cry . . . see you later Danti and remember . . . (*She puts her finger to her lips.*)

She walks off towards the cornfields. Dan picks up his rope and is doing bucking bronco on the gate as Ber comes level.

Ber There's my boy. I'd've been better off with you than that other langer. I'll tell you this much boy, I'm brassed off with fellas, full stop. Don't ever grow up, do you hear me. It's cat, cat melojun.

Dan (*chanting*) Rolling, rolling, rolling, keep them dogies rolling, rawhide. Rolling, rolling rolling rolling, keep them dogies rolling, rawhide. Du du du du du du du . . .

Ber Will you quit that, you're giving me a pain in the brain. Fuck's sake . . . thanks. Sorry I nearly ate you. I'm in awful crabby form. Over Noel like, it's all off, but I suppose you heard that.

Dan shrugs. Some cars pass.

What's bugging you? Christ almighty, this place is gone mental altogether. Everyone has a puss on them over something.

Dan looks like he might cry.

Why aren't you talking to me? Where's your books, you should be doing them, shouldn't you? Look there's cars coming and all. What's up with you, love? There's a van, hurry up or you'll miss it. Dan.

Dan I . . . I don't have to take them all . . . the man . . . see . . . no ehm . . . Cactus is minding them. Is Noel coming back? Is he gone away for good?

Ber He'd be delighted to know someone's missing him. He's gone nowhere boy, he's hanging around with that shower by the grotto, drinking himself stupid. Stupider than he is already. Bad company, that crowd. Mammy is right for once.

Ber takes out ten fags. She offers one to Dan.

Go on, I'll tell no one. They'll hardly stunt your growth at this stage.

He sits with her on the bridge and takes a cigarette. She notices what looks like a love bite on his neck.

Come here a minute, show us your neck. Jesus. What's

that? What happened to your neck?

Dan shrugs and rubs his neck, then puts the rope over his shoulder.

Ah the rope, must be a burn off of the rope. I thought for a minute there . . . naw.

She takes her lighter from her bra and they light up.

Dan Can you play poker?

Ber Naw, ludo is my limit. (*reading the inscription on her lighter*) 'Light of my life', I ask you. A dirty louser, that's all he is.

Dan You must. I could teach you, then . . .

Ber He gave Eileen . . . what's her name, from in the back road?

Dan Hurley.

Ber Hurley, yeah, Eileen Hurley. Mrs Hurley's precious sliotar. He walked her home last night. All the ways from town.

Dan I have Cact . . . cards here and all, look.

Ber It won't last like. She's too grand for him, she even got honours in her Inter, and she's useless at jiving. You'd want to see her like, it's a panic.

Dan But Ber, listen. If you knew how to play he'd bring you with us. To the Wild West. Me and Noel are going, I'm saving up.

Ber Yeah, and I'm getting married. (*laughs*) And I didn't believe it when the teachers told me I was thick. He's a lying bastard Dan. (*throws the lighter away, near tears*) Don't believe daylight out of his mouth. Jesus, look at me, up the pole without a paddle.

She breaks down into tears. Dan gets panicky and upset.

Dan Ah Ber, Ber. Stop Ber. Will you stop. Stop. He'll come back for us. He swore. He said riding the range we'd be. Round 'em up and brand 'em. Rawhide, Ber.

Ber Don't you start. Thick as pig-shit plaited the pair of us. (*She hugs him.*) Sorry love, I'm grand again. Right so, are you any use at snap?

She takes the cards and starts to deal them. Dan grabs them back.

Dan Not snap, poker, I said. You have to know poker.

Ber Alright, alright. Jesus. Just don't ask me to remember what a trick is, or what do you call thems, suits. Alright.

Dan Our ranch is going to be called Fort Knox, you know. Come on, we have to go under the bridge.

Ber Ah Jesus, play if you're going to play.

Dan Here?

Ber No, I'd love to play in Tim-bloody-bucktu, only I've no car. Hand out the shagging cards or we'll never get anywhere. I'm worse, I'll be knitting next.

Dan deals, putting the cards into two ultra neat piles.

Dan One two, one two, one two, one two . . .

Ber Shut up counting if you're not going to go any higher than two, will you?

He finishes dealing, mouthing 'one two'.

Jesus, one two, one two. I though I was bad at sums. Now what?

Dan plays a number card, as does Ber. This happens a couple of times, then Dan plays a king.

Dan Now, you have to . . . you must kiss me. 'Cause it's a King, see. I'm the King and the girl must . . .

Ber That's a good one, Jesus. If I knew poker was this much hack, I'd've been at it long ago. (*She gives him a cursory peck on the cheek.*) Come here Dan, 'tisn't a ranch we'll be going to at all boy, but Las Vegas. Do I play again now, or what?

Dan Properly.

Ber What? How do you mean? Oh, it's your go, is it?

Dan (*getting upset*) No. You're supposed to kiss, I said, properly. On the mouth. Play properly.

Ber Poker or no poker, you're a bit young for that. Sure look at the trouble it got me into. A kiss is just a kiss, me eyeball. Come on.

> *They continue to play, like snap. Dan throws his cards down each time, in exasperation. There is a run of number cards.*

Dan We won't get in if we don't play by the rules. It'll be your fault then.

> *Ber has lost whatever interest she had in the game, and is picking nail varnish off her nails. Dan is getting a bit frantic.*

Play will you. Play for God's sake.

Ber Jesus wept bitter tears of mercy, ye haven't the patience of a worm between ye. All the bloody same. Here.

> *Dan plays a jack and Ber puts an ace on it.*

Dan You're supposed to wait, you're ruining it.

Ber Ah for feck's sake. Come on, two colouredy ones, what's that supposed to mean now?

Dan grabs Ber's hand and puts it on his crotch, he puts his hand up her skirt. Ber begins to laugh initially, then Dan starts to bang against her, trying to kiss her. She tries to get past him but he persists. She slaps him hard across the face.

You little bollix you. Don't you ever, ever, do that again. Do you hear me? Ever. Or I'll fucking well tear you to shreds. Jesus, Mary and Joseph. I'd tell your mother on you only I wouldn't know what to say to the poor woman. Who showed you that?

Dan shrugs, he's stunned by Ber's reaction.

I have a bloody good idea, you needn't bother protecting her.

Dan No one showed me. I made it up myself.

Ber You couldn't make a bed, boy, let alone make that up.

She walks off, dropping her cards as she goes. Dan slaps himself with the rope.

(*Music: 'Band of Gold' by Freda Payne.*)

SCENE FOUR

Dolores and Cactus are washing the monument. They have two buckets and are scrubbing with deck brushes. Cactus isn't exerting herself too much.

Cactus If she's blaming me over the wreaths, what did she make you wash it for?

Dolores She said I was to blame as well because I should have stopped you.

Cactus Fantastic. She should have been a scientist or something.

Dolores What's that supposed to mean?

Cactus Eh, that your mother is very intelligent, Dolores. Pity she's such an old bitch as well.

Dolores Excuse me, Cactus.

Cactus You're excused, Mrs bloody wash the monument. They were withered away. They're there since Easter.

Dolores That's not the point actually, they're a mark of respect to the dead. You wouldn't do it in a graveyard, would you?

Cactus Depends.

Dolores Flip's sake Cactus, you liar. You would not.

Cactus I said it would depend, alright. Do we have to do the sides as well?

Dolores And the back. When she says the monument, she means the whole monument.

Cactus Shut up will you, you're as bad.

Cactus sits and lights a cigarette. Dolores scrubs the inscription with an old toothbrush.

I hate to break it to you Dolores, but they're dead, there's no good in brushing their teeth.

Dolores Very funny, I don't think. Are you going swimming after?

Cactus No.

Dolores How come? The water's meant to be lovely today.

Cactus Just.

Dolores A quick one even. You never come down these days hardly.

Cactus So.

Dolores Well, what are you doing so?

Cactus That's for me to know and you to find out. Naw, I'm going to teach Danti-dan how to fart the National Anthem. Okay?

Dolores Get lost. Since when are you great with him, I thought you said he was a langer.

Cactus I never said he wasn't. He's an alright kisser though. Better than you, that is.

Dolores Pull the other one, it has bells.

Cactus Swear.

Dolores I don't believe you. Oh God.

Cactus Yeah, I taught him to play poker, with my rules though. He hasn't a clue. He'll do anything I tell him. Langer, is right.

Dolores Like what?

Cactus whispers into Dolores's ear. She is incredulous.

Oh mammy. And is it like . . . you know, white pudding?

Cactus Naw. More like a cocktail sausage.

Dolores Ah no. That's disgusting. Ah God, no. I don't believe you.

Cactus Come down after so, and we can all have a game of cards.

Dolores Sure he wouldn't let me. I'd be morto like.

Cactus It's grand. Only a bit of a laugh. He'd let you alright, if I told him to. Don't worry.

Dolores I might so, for a look like.

Cactus It's good practice. Better hack than swimming anyway. I'm sick of this. (*She flings her bucket of water at the monument.*) There now, we're finished.

Dolores She'll inspect it.

Cactus Fuck her.

Dolores Yeah. Fuck her.

Cactus About half past so?

Dolores Yeah. Okay.

Cactus goes off, Dolores tidies up.

(*Music: 'Let's Work Together' by Canned Heat.*)

SCENE FIVE

A phone is heard ringing, faintly. Ber is looking up and down the road.

Ber (*shouts*) Dolores. Dolores. It's working. It's ringing. Dolores.

Noel comes from the bridge end and stands watching her. She turns.

I thought I got the smell of Harp. Well?

Noel Water.

Ber You never lost it.

Noel What?

Ber Nothing.

Noel What's news?

Ber We're after getting the phone in at long last.

Noel And I thought that that was your drawers ringing. Well, it'll save me walking up to the mini-market if I want to talk to you. What's the number? Just in case.

Ber Eh, eight, seven . . . something. I don't know it off yet. We only got it in today like.

Noel That a new frock?

Ber It's a skirt, actually.

Noel You're after filling out a bit, are you?

Ber Must be all the Weetabix I'm eating.

Noel No, on top like.

Ber Bigger than Eileen Hurley anyhow, of course you'd know all about that.

Noel I'd say she never saw her own fucking chest, not to mind anyone else seeing it. She wouldn't give you the steam, that one.

Ber My heart pumps piss for you. I don't know what you're telling me for, I couldn't give a sugar about her.

Noel That makes two of us. Dozy cow nearly clattered me. I told her the joke about the two pencils. You know the one. It's eejity.

Ber No, go on.

Noel Ah you do. Why don't big pencils have little pencils?

Ber No, I don't know.

Noel Because they have rubbers on the end.

Ber laughs. They stare at each other.

Did you hear the news?

Ber Don't tell me, I'm pregnant.

63

Noel Ah Jesus no, I know that. No, I got a job above in the chewing gum factory.

Ber That's brilliant Noelie. I'm delighted for you.

Noel Brilliant? It's fan-fucking-tastic girl. You'll be mad after me now I'm loaded.

Ber That's what you think. I better go in and do the delph or she'll be out on her broomstick after me.

Noel Will you be around tonight?

Ber I might, then again I mightn't.

Noel I might see you so.

Ber You might.

Noel Right.

Ber See you so. Oh listen, if you see Dolores tell her I was looking for her. She's dying to have a go of the phone.

Noel She was up at the bridge, while ago with Dan. That poor fella's not the full shilling. He was going on about the Wild West, America. I hadn't a bog what he was talking about. I just said 'yeah yeah'.

Ber He's not as green as he's cabbage looking, I can tell you.

Noel That Cactus one is turning into a right little sex pot, isn't she? The go of her, trying to get me to go playing cards with them. Wiggling her arse and all. Fuck's sake.

Ber The brazen little bitch, she has Dolores at it now. I'll reef her out of it. Walk up along and I'll catch up with you, I have to put on my shoes.

She runs home. Noel dawdles.

(*Music: 'Sex Machine' by James Brown.*)

SCENE SIX

In front of the gate, Ber has Cactus by the arm. Cactus is holding a bundle of Dan's books. Noel is standing to one side.

Cactus Would you mind letting me go please. I don't know where they are. She's your sister, not mine.

Noel They were with you earlier.

Cactus So.

Ber So where are they? You better tell me or I'll break your fucking arm, I'm warning you.

Cactus I'm scared shitless.

Ber Jesus, but you're a bad piece of work. (*shouts*) Dolores. Dolores. Dan.

Cactus I told you, they're not here.

Dolores appears on the other side of the wall, followed by Dan. They both look dishevelled and guilty. Cactus is raging that they've surrendered but smirkingly brazens it out.

Ber Get out here, the two of you. (*to Cactus*) You lying little bitch you.

Cactus shrugs. They get over the wall. Noel starts laughing.

Noel She's the image of the mother when she's roused.

Ber Shut up you. What were ye doing? Come on. Tell me. What were ye doing under the bridge?

Cactus is rattled but silences them with a look.

Cactus God. Alright. We were playing cards, okay? Since when is that a sin?

Ber I know what kind of cards you were playing alright.

Cactus What would you know? You can't even add two and two without using the cash register.

Noel There's no call for that now.

Ber Come over here and look me in the eye Dolores, and tell me, were you playing cards?

Dolores comes closer, but doesn't look her in the eye.

Dolores Yeah.

Ber You filthy little scut you. Dan, is it the same rules as you showed me?

Cactus Don't mind her Dan, she has no right to be bossing you.

Ber Shut up you. Is it?

Cactus runs to the bridge and holds Dan's books over the river. Ber grips Dan. Cactus starts to wave the books.

Cactus Dan. Yohoo. Danti-dan.

Ber Is it Dan? Did she make you do that?

Cactus opens one of the books and reads mockingly.

Cactus Renault. Blue. CZT 520. 2.39. Lovely joined up writing and all, Danti-Dan. Zetor. Red and black. No number plate. 2.44.

Ber Stop tormenting him you.

Dan Leave my books alone. They're mine.

Dolores It was only french kissing, I swear Ber.

Ber You better tell me Dan, do you hear me? Or I'll call your mother down. You don't want that, do you? Then she'll send you away somewhere.

Noel Ease up girl.

Dan She said . . .

There is a splash as Cactus lets slip one of the books, exercising the only control she has left over him . . .

Cactus Ooops.

Dan No.

He starts to hyperventilate, on the verge of a panic attack. He tries to go to stop Cactus, Ber grips him and shakes him roughly.

Ber Go on Dan.

Dan Noel said you have to know poker. They're my statistics. She made me take . . . Lulu with her tits falling out. That's for a queen.

Cactus can't believe that Dan is spilling the beans. She desperately tries to deflect.

Cactus See. It's all your fault Noel.

Noel Christ like, I never said nothing.

Cactus Anything.

Ber Listen, I'm warning you, you better tell me what she made you do.

Dan is gulping for air. Cactus is frantic. She climbs onto the wall.

Dan She made me . . . made me take out my winkie. The man's going to give me money for my books. For Fort Knox. She was pinching it.

Cactus Liar, liar, pants on fire.

Ber Shut up, you filthy little bitch you.

Noel Christ al-fucking-mighty.

Ber Go on, Dan.

Dan She was minding them. Now they're in the river. They're all in biro even. She said if I didn't . . . kiss . . . she'd . . .

Cactus lets go of two more books, there's a splash. She retains one. Dan screams.

Cactus Oh sorry, they just slipped.

Dolores Flip sake Cactus.

Dan succeeds in breaking away from Ber, he lunges at Cactus trying to grab the remaining book. In doing so he pulls her to the ground. They roll around fighting like cats and dogs. Dan is extremely traumatised and viciously pulling Cactus's hair and clothing. Cactus lashes back, well able for him.

Ber Jesus, Mary, and holy Saint Joseph. You're just . . . an animal, that's what you are.

Cactus Takes one to know one.

Dolores Will I go down and try and get them out?

Noel I would, only I can't swim like.

Ber I'm telling your father on you. The poor child.

Dolores Will I Ber?

Ber goes to where the two are fighting and pulls Cactus off Dan.

Ber Come on love, you'll be alright. We'll get you more books.

Cactus Dan.

Cactus runs to the bridge, gets up on the gate and

throws the remaining book into the river. Dan lets out a blood-curdling roar, pushes Dolores out of the way and gets up on the wall. He leans across the capping stone and screams at Cactus.

Dan I'm telling on you, I'm telling on you, I'm telling on you.

Cactus Just shut up, shut up, shut up.

She tries to push him off the wall, he hangs onto the capping stone. With unmerciful strength she pushes the capping stone off the pillar. Dan and the stone disappear behind the wall.

Langer, you're not telling anyone anything.

There is a thud, then silence. Dolores looks from where Dan has fallen to Ber.

Dolores Oh God.

Ber and Noel join her, and look over the wall.

(Music: 'Wand'rin' Star' by Lee Marvin.)

SCENE SEVEN

Epilogue. A month later.
  Dolores is returning from swimming, through the corn field. Cactus is sitting on the gate.

Cactus Long time no see. Oh, you're still not talking to me either.

Dolores I'm not let.

Cactus God. Do you always do everything you're told?

Cactus offers her a cigarette. Dolores declines.

Dolores I gave them up, for swimming like. I'm training for the medals.

Cactus In the river?

Dolores No, the baths. I'm in a club now. How come you weren't at the . . . you know, the funeral?

Cactus (*laughs*) They wouldn't let me. Sure everyone's saying I did it on purpose. I suppose you are too.

Dolores No. I'm saying nothing to no one about it.

Cactus It's the County Council's fault. That thing was broken for ages. Something was bound to happen.

Dolores Yeah, I suppose. No, I don't think they own the wall though.

Cactus Did you end up touching his . . . you know what, at all?

Dolores That's desperate Cactus. How can you say . . . that's awful.

Cactus Only asking, Jesus. Listen, I heard Ber's getting married.

Dolores Next Saturday, yeah.

Cactus They're made for each other. Two beauts. And Dan's ma is making her dress.

Dolores She offered like. Couldn't say no.

Cactus She'll need yards of the stuff, I'd say. Ber must be out to here by now.

Dolores And ye're moving.

Cactus Yeah. Limerick. My father got a transfer. At least we'll be in a town though, not like this boring old kip.

There is an awkward silence. Cactus smokes.

I'll send on my address when I know it.

Dolores You better not. It's Mammy, she'd have a fit like. I have to go. My tea. It'll be ready.

Cactus If you gotta go, you gotta go.

Dolores See you so.

Cactus See you.

Dolores walks away. Cactus shouts after her.

Cactus Hey, Dol, Dolores, come here a minute.

Dolores returns.

Dolores What?

Cactus See you.

They stare at each other.

Music: 'Everything is Beautiful' by Ray Stevens.

Afterword

Danti-Dan took a relatively short time to write, relative
that is to the time it took me to get down to it. I was
commissioned in 1992 to write a play for Rough Magic
and for a year and a half I did an impression of a dog
getting into a basket, circling, circling. During that time I
worked on and off on an idea I'd had for some time. It
even had a title – *Mesa*. It involved children becoming
Magellan, da Gama and any other explorer you care to
think of, and them circumnavigating the globe on an
upturned table in their kitchen. To read it you'd think I'd
never been to see a play let alone been in one; it was an epic
sprawl. By Christmas of 1993 writing had become a chore.
I had a long talk with Lynne (Parker, Artistic Director of
Rough Magic), during which we decided that the best
thing to do was to put *Mesa* in a plastic bag, hide it, and
start again.

I booked myself into the Tyrone Guthrie Centre, an
artists' and writers' retreat in Co. Monaghan, and began
to think properly about what I did and didn't want to
write. Lynne had advised me to stick closer to home, to
write what I know. I took her literally and decided that it
would be totally autogeographical, set on the bridge
opposite the house where I grew up. Cork is divided into
two classes; the have yachts and the have nots. I knew I
wanted to deal with the latter, to explore lives of limited
aspiration and thwarted expectation, where ambition is
viewed with suspicion and the claustrophobic atmosphere
is at odds with the open landscape. Besides, I know
nothing about sailing. Writing a play set in the country
presented its own problems, the main one being that the

Irish stage is awash with them. I was determined not to have any auld fellas in brown coats on bikes, no valve radios tuned to Athlone, nobody carrying trays of tea nor rashers forever sizzling in the pan, and above all no nuns, priests or canons, in fact no clergy of any kind.

It's difficult in retrospect to remember what came first. Once I'd decided to deal with teenagers and sexuality, the characters of Cactus and Dan formed quickly. Girls of that age are very often presented as passive victims of men's behaviour towards them and I wanted to see what happened if the reverse was the case. I'd never bought into all of that sugar and spice stuff and was interested in having a female character with an unnervingly steady gaze and who appears remorseless. The action moves from horseplay to foreplay to catastrophe. From an adult point of view there may be a certain predictability about what transpires. This was intentional, the point being that if an adult had been present they would have seen what was happening and nipped it in the bud. The play is set in 1970 for a number of reasons, partly because that was when I was entering my teens so I knew the territory, and also because at that time you were sent out in shorts and sandals as soon as the school holidays began and didn't really go home until September. Innocence was presumed and no accountability was expected.

I was very conscious of avoiding nostalgia and sentimentality but was amazed when I saw the first run at how totally lacking in affection everybody was; it's as if any sign of gentleness would be taken as weakness. It's not that that wasn't the case but things have moved on from there. There used to be a joke about a Cork couple where the girl asks the boy if he loves her and he replies 'Of course I loves ya, didn't I flah you and buy you chips?'. But now go to any airport in the country and you'll see Irish people greeting each other with hugs and kisses. In public. We've come a long way.

Thanks are due to Bernard and Mary Loughlin at Tyrone Guthrie Centre, Annaghmakerrig. Finally, I would like to hugely thank Lynne Parker and Siobhan Bourke (General Manager of Rough Magic) for their unstinting encouragement, patience and for taking such a gamble on me in the first place. We were lucky enough to have the most ferociously talented, though ridiculously young, cast of actors we could hope to find. Above all, we enjoyed ourselves.

Gina Moxley
Dublin, 1995

A PICTURE OF PARADISE

Jimmy Murphy

Characters

Angela
Declan
Sean
The Lord

Act One

Darkness. A dark winter afternoon.

The sound of a glass smashing and a woman hauling herself through a window.

From a doorway we see the light of a torch frantically moving around. Footsteps.

A woman enters, **Angela**, *she is scared. She shines the torch around.*

Angela (*aggressive*) Who's there! (*Pause. A little frightened*) Is there anyone there?

Declan (*off*) Hurry up Ma!

Angela (*jumps*) Keep your voice down! (*She shines the torch around.*) Come out if there's anyone there.

Declan Quick, open the door and let me in!

Angela (*a final check of the room*) Come out I said!

Declan Ma!

Angela shines torch at photos on wall. She drops the torch with fright. It rolls around the floor. She picks the torch up and shines it over for a good look at photos.

For God's sake hurry, there's a million eyes burning a hole in me back!

Angela Hold your whist, will you! I'm coming!

(*Exits through another door.*)

She returns with her son, **Declan**. *They have some bags with them.*

Declan You shouldn't've smashed the window.

Angela Do you have to bring out the whole block with your roaring?

Declan Everyone's heard that glass smash. (*Tries to look around with torch.*) I don't like this Ma, we're taking an awful chance.

Angela If you don't take chances where'll you be?

Declan We'll all end up in a cell tonight!

Angela The Guards can't do anything about this.

Declan Breaking and entering!

Angela We're here now and no one's budging us!

Declan And what if the place is already given to someone?

Angela Possession's nine points of the law.

Declan We're not even known round here!

Angela They'll know me tomorrow!

Declan And then what?

Angela They'll all bake apple pies and call in to say hello! (*Sits on floor. Takes out some tablets.*)

Declan There was a time you wouldn't walk past here . . .

Angela Get me a drop of water.

Declan . . . wouldn't get on a bus here!

Angela Water! I'm parched.

Declan (*shouts*) Ma! . . . (*Pause.*) They don't like outsiders here.

Angela I'm no outsider! Born and rared round here me . . . your father too. (*Takes tablets.*) Water . . .

Declan A fat lot that'll matter when they 're even robbing oul grannies' handbags. (*Shines torch into kitchen.*)

Angela They won't get far on mine if they get it.

Declan returns with some water cupped in his hands. Angela drinks. A pause. They rest to let their nerves settle. Angela has a smoke.

Declan Four floors up! As big as Liberty hall, this kip.

Angela And we're in the penthouse suite. Now turn on the light till we have a look.

Declan No! We don't want to bring attention to ourselves.

Angela Would you rather we sit in the dark?

Declan The torch'll do us.

Angela For the love of Jesus Declan, would you just do as I say! The dogs in the street know about us now.

Declan shines torch to find the switch. It doesn't work.

Declan The electricity . . . it must be cut off. We can't stay if the elec–

Angela (*snatches torch and shines it at ceiling*) There's no bulb! Did you pack one?

Declan You never said anything about bulbs.

Angela You'd better try one of the rooms.

Declan I'm not going out there on me own!

Angela Afraid of the dark, too, are you?

Declan The torch'll do us till Da gets here . . . if he gets here.

Angela Agh, get out of me way, I'll look for one meself! You're useless!

Declan Give me the bloody torch. (*He exits.*)

*Angela lights up a smoke. Her hands shake. With the
match she looks around the room. Each time a match
goes out she lights another. After a moment Declan
returns carrying an old chair and a bulb.*

Got one! In the hall.

Angela Did you have a look around the place?

Declan There's one room open at the front . . . the stink of
it. It's no bigger than a wardrobe.

*He stands on chair and puts bulb in. He turns light on.
The flat is bare, some old photos on a wall.*

Jesus!

Angela What ails you now?

Declan Well . . . it's not what you'd call home from home,
is it?

Angela It'll do. (*Looks around.*) It'll have to do.

Declan (*looks at photos on the wall*) I thought you said it
was empty!

Angela D'you see anyone here?

Declan Then what's this?

Angela He won't be bothering us, God rest his soul.

Declan He's dead?

Angela Two weeks ago. The ESB fella found him . . . saw
him through the letterbox. He'd been dead for a week on
the floor.

Declan (*looks at floor*) A week!

Angela I seen it in the *Herald*: 'Old man dies alone.' That's
the place for us I thought. Squat in before the corpo give
the keys to someone else.

Declan What sort of kip is this when you can be dead for a week? Come on Ma, before it's too late.

Angela Where to boy . . . the streets? 'Cause that's all we've left!

Declan Are you sure the corporation have nothing?

Angela Two hours I waited in them offices yesterday evening . . . two hours. (*Looks away from Declan.*) A nine-month waiting list for a house or a flat. We're doing them a favour, if you ask me. If we didn't take this flat it'd be wrecked by a gang of yunfellas.

Declan Aunty Rita said –

Angela She said me and you were welcome to stay. Where's your father supposed to live? Back in that kip house in town?

Declan What did he go there for in the first place? He could've come with us, couldn't he?

Angela They never got on, your Da and Rita.

Declan He burns all his bridges! As soon as he moved into that place you should've warned him . . . told him to straighten himself out or else.

Angela He'd no choice. (*Playing the Samaritan.*) Look, your father's not well, Declan.

Declan He's gotten worse . . . wouldn't be supprised if he was on the wine too!

Angela It's all that bastard's fault . . . the swine he met in there, whoever he is.

Declan He's dragging us down Ma. (*Pause.*) And he's not the only one . . .

Angela It's me that's holding this ship together!

Declan You're doing a great job of it, aren't you?

Angela All the more reason for us to stick together!

Declan If we stick together we sink together.

Angela No, this is it, it feels ours! (*Gets up.*)

Declan It feels spooky!

Angela It's going to bring good luck this place, it's perfect. (*Sizes the room up.*) The sofa'll go nicely over there. And the oul cabinet will just about fit in that corner.

Declan Oul cabinet! Grannie's press . . . the only thing left worth money.

Angela Everything that was sold will be replaced. (*Kicks a bag at him.*) Now come on, see if there's a curtain will fit that window . . . there's a small one somewhere in the bag, shove it up in the kitchen, least people won't be able to see in.

Declan (*takes out a piece of material and enters kitchen*) We'll need a steam cleaner for this hole!

Angela A drop of Jeyes' fluid, that's all it needs. You'll be able to eat your dinner off the floor when I'm finished. (*Takes off her coat and rolls up her sleeves.*) I was thinking green.

Declan Green what?

Angela It wouldn't cost much to cover in here in carpet.

Declan You're gas, we've hardly the money to feed ourselves and you're talking about doing the kip up.

Angela You have to have a bit of comfort, you know. (*Starts to take a few things out of the bags: bleach, rags, air freshener, etc.*)

Declan (*returns to room*) Comfort . . . I think I remember that.

Angela The good old days, what?

Declan They weren't that long ago.

Angela Long enough to forget, son.

Declan That's what you'd love, isn't it? For us to forget about everything?

Angela If you stop to look back in the past you get stuck there. (*Starts to sprinkle some bleach around the floor.*)

Declan Well I can't, or won't forget! I'm the laughing stock of all me mates.

Angela Only oul wasters anyway, the lot of them. (*Hands him a pan and brush.*) Take up that glass off the floor.

Declan I haven't the neck to show me face around the street.

Angela I wonder how many of them are still tied to their mother's aprons?

Declan I pay me way. (*Enters kitchen.*)

Angela £20 a week out of your dole . . . sure that doesn't keep us in bread and butter! I'd say your mate in Bulgaria sends his mother home twice that for herself.

Declan What would you know? And it's Belgium!

Angela What is?

Declan Where he is.

Angela Well he's not there now. He called around to Rita's with a message for you the other day.

Declan He's home?

Angela He said he'd have called sooner but . . . but he didn't know where you moved to.

Declan What did he want?

Angela Just said try and give him a ring before he goes back tomorrow, go and have a drink.

Declan Tomorrow! He's going back tomorrow and you're only telling me now?

Angela That's three out of that family over there. It must be good whatever they're at.

Declan An Irish bar. His brother's opened one up. Four years labouring on the building sites of Germany and he's a publican!

Angela You see, you don't need school. Hard work, that's all. Though there's no hope of you ever doing the likes of that.

Declan You didn't tell him anything about here, did you?

Angela You've nothing to be ashamed of. (*Has a look around.*)

Declan I'm glad you think so. (*Looks at his watch.*) It's half three! What's keeping him?

Angela Don't worry, you'll be out in time for your . . . your *course*! Isn't the place is only up the road?

Declan It's not a course, not yet anyway. This afternoon's just an interview to try and get a place.

Angela Computers! What do you know about computers, what do you know about anything?

Declan Nothing, thanks to yous two.

Angela Waste of good money.

Declan Well it's mine to do what I like! Didn't I have to sacrifice enough to get it?

Angela No wonder you managed to save with the buttons you hand me up!

Declan There'd be no need for me to scrimp and save if I'd've stayed on at school.

Angela If you want to squander it all on a course just make sure you can still get your dole. I'm not going short.

Declan No, we couldn't have that, could we?

Angela (*takes out some things from a box. Sprays some air freshener.*) Is that glass going to clean itself up?

Declan (*returns*) But, after today it won't matter a curse. In twelve weeks' time I'll have completed the course in flying colours. A computer programmer!

Angela A computer programmer! You could hardly use the microwave!

Declan The docks, that's where I'll head, the Financial Centre, there's a million jobs in there . . . and one of them is going to be mine.

Angela Yeah, emptying ashtrays in their yuppie bars.

Declan D'you know how much a programmer can make?

Angela Just hurry up with that window before we freeze to death!

Declan Over a thousand a month! And that's just the start. Company cars . . . holidays – it's all out there Ma, you don't need to go away anymore. Them days are gone, all you need do is jump on the right bus.

Angela I know the bus you'll jump on if you get your fancy job.

Declan Would I do a thing like that? (*Looks out at veranda.*) No, this is something I should've done years ago. Let Noel Mills shag off to Belgium, let him live like a sardine. Oh his brother might've opened a pub, but at what cost . . . a family disintegrated all over the place,

87

girlfriends, wives, families all left behind!

Angela You weren't saying that last year when you were looking for the money to go with him.

Declan No more Fas courses, no more S.E.S. schemes. I'm taking hold of me own reins from now on.

Angela Is that right dreamer? Now, enough yap. Let's get this place sorted out. (*Pause. Walks around.*) You won't recognise this in a few days. You wait and see what it's like when I sort the furniture out, you'll be proud to bring anyone up here.

Declan Furniture . . . there'll be more furniture in a doll's house.

Angela I'll have a lookout for an oul telly, there should be no problem getting a robbed one in these flats, no problem getting the whole gaff done up with robbed gear.

Declan There's nothing stolen coming into this flat, d'you hear? We may be down but we're not savages!

Angela An oul telly wouldn't hurt!

Declan No!

Angela Get a telly in here for forty quid.

Declan Not as much as a toaster!

Angela A lovely colour one, remote control. Get a video too.

Declan We're starting from scratch, get one out by the week . . . the same with a washing machine, a fridge.

Angela (*sarcastic*) Of course! We'll get a new car too . . . and a microwave, dishwasher, a video, get them all out by the week!

Declan One piece at a time, until it's all replaced . . . all honestly!

88

Angela Please yourself! If you're happy living like a pauper.

Declan It'll take a while but we'll get back on our feet . . . the right way.

> *Angela takes a* Golden Pages *from a bag and throws it at Declan's feet.*

What's that?

Angela You can start with marking out some good restaurants.

Declan Bringing us out for our dinner?

Angela And look up some of them new hotels in town. Come Monday your Da's going looking for work again.

Declan (*laughs at the thought*) Are you having me on?

Angela What's so funny about that?

Declan Work! As what . . . a lockhard man?

Angela At least he's getting up off his arse and doing something to bring in a few bob, isn't he!

Declan And what am I doing?

Angela Day dreaming.

Declan Well you'll see. It's not me who's day dreaming, it's you!

Angela He's giving all that stuff up now . . . a new start.

Declan Who'd give him a job as a cook with the state of him! He's been that long out of work he couldn't boil an egg.

Angela Your father's got qualifications other men'd cut their right hand off for.

Declan He'll spend the rest of his days with a cap stuck on his head and a newspaper rolled up.

Angela It brought in money, didn't it?

Declan I seen him last week in town . . . begging, that's all he's doing? I had to pretend that I didn't know him when he called out me name.

Angela Begging! Your father's out trying to make a shilling and you call him a beggar!

Declan Parking cars! Did you ever hear the like?

Angela Look, just write down a few numbers and don't be annoying me!

Declan Let him write them down himself! (*Throws book down.*)

Angela You'll see, your father'll get us back on top while you're fannying around on your . . . your computers! He'll have us the way we used to be. All he needs is to sort himself out.

　　A cynical laugh from Declan.

And what's that supposed to mean?

Declan I found something in your purse the other day.

Angela What were you doing rooting in my purse!

Declan The day you told me to get the money out for a naggin of vodka.

Angela (*defensively*) That wasn't for me . . . it was for Rita.

Declan A handful of bookie tickets.

Angela They were old ones.

Declan With last week's date on them?

Angela (*pause*) It was just the one day.

Declan Over forty pounds' worth.

Angela I hadn't backed a horse in weeks.

Declan You said you were finished gambling, that's why we started handing over the housekeeping money again.

Angela I am finished! It was just . . . I felt lucky, that's all.

Declan Is that right? Well I was talking to Shay Farrell the other day . . . he saw you going into The Mint . . . another lucky day, was it?

Angela Tell him he needs glasses!

Declan Back at the poker machines too?

Angela It was probably his own mother, she's never out of the place.

Declan That was Wednesday . . . the day you said you lost the housekeeping.

Angela I showed you the hole in me coat pocket, didn't I?

Declan The day we had to eat carrots and onions for our dinner.

Angela There's good nourishment in vegetables.

Declan If you're a rabbit! Listen, if you're back at them machines I'm going to stop giving you me rent again.

Angela I only spent a few pounds for God's sake!

Declan I'm not going hungry. I'll buy the messages again, and pay the rent . . . if we get to pay rent!

Angela (*shouts*) I said I was finished, alright!

Declan How many times have we heard that? Jesus, was last month not enough for you?

Angela looks away from him. Pause.

You got enough warnings, more than me or him did!

Angela Declan, look –

Declan From March to September.

Angela Listen son –

Declan Seven pounds a week, that's all the rent was.

Angela I'd too many bills.

Declan Too many bills alright! Bookie and lottery ticket bills! (*Pause.*) Three hundred pounds. Jaysus, when was the last time you paid the rent . . . when Shergar went missing?

Angela Your Da . . . he just (*Pause.*) . . . he just stopped looking for work. I wasn't used to having no money.

Declan But it was alright if me and him went without?

Angela You'd begrudge me the only bit of enjoyment I have.

Declan Enjoyment?

Angela Well I'm a bit too old to take up aerobics! (*Pause.*) Look, this flat is a new start Declan, a new beginning, alright. Once we get our feet back on solid ground we'll be on the pig's back.

Declan We won't get on our feet this way.

From a bag he takes out a neatly folded cheap suit. Angela crosses over and looks out at veranda.

Angela Grand view from here too, what?

Declan If you like concrete. (*He starts to change his clothes.*)

Angela Look, at them mountains . . . who'd want to live out there, hah? Who'd want to pack up and head off miles away into a kip?

Declan What kip?

Angela This flat is perfect. Ten minutes from the old house. Everything we need within reach . . . the post office, the dole office, Crazy Prices up past it . . . the same old faces. It'll be as if we never left.

Declan (*joins her at window*) Can almost see the old house from here.

Angela turns away.

Look . . . (*He stares out.*)

There is a thump at the door. They freeze.

I told you not to turn the lights on!

Angela Shh! Don't make a sound. (*Peers through kitchen.*)

More thumping.

Stand up against this door with me! (*She leans her body tight against the door.*)

Declan The veranda, quick! Get out onto the veranda. (*He tries to open the door, it's locked.*)

More thumping.

Angela And what do we do when we get out there? Abseil down the block? Get over here quick!

Declan joins her. She runs into the kitchen and returns with a large piece of the broken window. She stands behind the door.

Okay . . . go on out and open it. (*She lifts the glass up over her head.*) Go on!

More thumping.

Declan What're you going to do?

Angela Open it slowly, then run back in out of the way.

Declan What if it's . . . what if it's Da?

Angela I told him to knock three times.

Declan Or the Guards!

Angela Just open the bloody door!

Declan I knew it . . . I knew something like this would happen. (*Pacing up and down.*) You wouldn't listen to me, would you . . . you never listen!

More banging.

Angela Am I going to have to do it meself?

Declan gets ready to go.

Sean (*off*) Angela! Are you in there?

Declan It is him!

Angela Jesus! (*Puts glass down.*)

Sean Are yous in there?

Angela Let him in.

*Declan exits. He returns with **Sean**, his father. He is carrying an armchair, with some boxes on it, and a small rug rolled up. He throws them down.*

Angela Are you brain dead?

Sean What now? (*Sinks into the chair breathless.*)

Declan Have you got the box with me shoes? (*Rummages through box.*)

Angela Three knocks, that was the signal!

Sean Three knocks on the window . . . but there's no poxy window there, is there?

Declan I couldn't force the lock so she smashed it. (*Looking through box.*) Did you bring me shoes?

Sean D'you know how much a pane of glass is, do you?

Angela Stick a bit of cardboard over it for the time being.

Sean Cardboard! We'll be like three ice cubes in the morning with that gale blowing out there! You may as well stick an advertisement outside on the stairs! 'Squatters, first turn on the left'! (*Looks around the place.*) Anyone bother yous getting in?

Declan Me shoes! They're not in this box! (*Looks in another box.*)

Sean I don't like the looks I was getting when we pulled up in the van.

Angela Tell no one nothing!

Sean Anyone in here ask me the time they can have me watch!

Declan (*pulls a shoe out*) Where's this other one?

Angela Anybody looks crooked at you stare at them . . . right into the eyes . . . d'you hear? Once we throw our weight around no one'll bother us.

Declan Me other shoe? Where is it?

Angela Don't ask me . . . I didn't pack it.

Sean Have yous got the lock changed?

Declan Lock?

Sean I told you, the first thing to do is change the lock . . . then we're the key holders! Have a look in that bag for it, will you, and get it done? (*Pause. Looks around. Sees photos.*) What's all this? I thought it was empty?

Declan This is a dead man's flat. Can you credit that? She brought us to a dead man's flat!

Sean What, he died in here?

Declan On the floor.

Angela Agh whist up the two of yous, you'd swear he was going to come back and haunt us! (*Pause.*) Well, what do you think?

Sean It's a rough spot you picked.

Declan Me good shoes were in this box . . . where's the other one? (*Looks in another box.*) Ah for God's sake! I put them in here, I know I did! (*Takes out a shirt and tie from the box.*) Jaysus, this is in a million creases!

Angela If it was that bad there'd be no one living here.

Sean Are you sure you want it?

Angela Amn't I here?

Sean Did you see the state of that stairway? The stink of piss all over it . . . seen a needle too, that's all we need, junkies for neighbours.

Angela It's either this place or me and Dec go back to Rita's and you go back to –

Sean (*shouts*) No! (*quieter*) Never again! I spent me last sleepless night there last night.

Angela Well then, get cracking, let's make our mark in here!

Declan But I have to find me other shoe. I have to get ready.

Sean Don't be minding your shoe, just get the stuff up!

Angela It's probably in the van . . . go on down and have a

look and start bringing the things up before the driver
starts looking for overtime!

Declan You better've not lost me good shoe, d'you hear!
(*He exits.*)

Sean There was no word off the corpo?

Angela (*changes subject*) We should have room for
everything.

Sean The corpo Ang, what did they say?

Angela (*takes out a curtain from a box*) Four hours I was
sitting in there.

Sean And . . .?

Angela Six months waiting list.

Sean Six months! What are we supposed to do for six
months?

Angela I'm not letting them tell me where I have to live!

Sean Would you not go back and ask them again . . . tell
them it's urgent . . . tell them how we've been living, how
I've been living?

Angela I'll be going back in alright . . . after I collect that
money today. (*Rolls out the rug Sean brought in.*)

Sean Money . . . (*despairing*) It will work, won't it, they
will take it?

Angela Who in their right minds would refuse hard cash?

Sean If they do take it, we'll be back in their good books,
won't we? Everything'll be even Steven?

*Angela picks up phone book and throws it to him. He
doesn't catch it.*

What's that for?

Angela I took it from a phone box today. Dec's going to give you a hand look for a few numbers.

Sean (*kicks it back*) Tear it up and light the fire with it, for jaysus sake!

Angela You said a new start Sean . . . a home, a job. You get back inside a kitchen, Jesus, there'd be no stopping you!

Sean There's good money in parking cars Ang, you wouldn't believe it. You just stand there and wait for them to come.

Angela But a proper job, you wouldn't know yourself with a proper job again.

Sean I made eleven pounds the other night! Eleven pounds in two hours . . . and that was on a bad night. The Lord says you can make twice that on a weekend!

Angela You'd make five times that in a hotel or a restaurant.

Sean All you do is wave your newspaper. (*Takes out a paper to demonstrate.*) 'A bit to the right . . . left, left . . . forward, lock hard . . .' That's all there is to it. Money for nothing.

Angela There's new hotels going up all over the city.

Sean The Lord says I'll have to get a cap too. Said I should pick one up in Francis Street market for a pound or two.

Angela The Lord, The Lord! To hell with The Lord! (*Shakes him.*) Are you listening to me! You'd easily get a job in one of their kitchens. (*Lets him go.*) You know you would.

Sean (*Pause.*) Had a great name as a chef in this town.

Angela All your old contacts . . . look them up.

Sean Could make a meal out of straw. Royalty . . . film stars . . . fed them all.

Angela You will try, Sean, won't you? You will get us out of this mess?

Sean Me hands . . . (*Holds them out. They shake.*) . . . look.

Angela (*takes his hands and rubs them*) That's just the cold.

Sean I couldn't cut butter. (*Looks down at himself, his feet.*) Look at me . . . I'm falling asunder.

Angela With your suit cleaned and a new hair cut you won't know yourself.

Sean I don't know meself as it is . . . and no one else seems to either.

Angela Here, look what I found. (*Takes a battered envelope from a box. Hands it to him.*)

Sean What's this?

Angela They must've got stuck inside the wardrobe. It fell out when we were moving it . . . go on, open it.

Sean (*opens the envelope and takes out some pages, looks at them*) It's like it was somebody else.

Angela With references like that, Sean, you could waltz in anywhere. (*Takes them from him. Reads.*) 'Highly recommended . . . honest and trustworthy. A valuable employee.' A fella'd kill for references like these.

Sean Ten years in that hotel and then torn down to build a shagging office block!

Angela There must be someone out there you could ring.

Sean No one knows me anymore! No one seems to remember me.

Angela You still have one or two contacts. Old friends.

Sean Too old . . . should've kept in contact . . . kept in touch.

Angela It's never too late.

Sean (*pause*) Oul Harry O'Connor's head waiter in The Ashbury.

Angela You taught Harry everything he knows.

Sean And 'member Terry . . . oul Terence Gough. Has his own place now! Up off Dame Street, would you credit that? What's he call it? The . . . the Cajun Hall! There was a photo of him in the paper a while back, he won some hygiene award.

Angela A phone call, that's all it'd take. (*Lifts up phone book.*)

Sean I could've swore I passed Harry last week in Nassau Street . . . I'm sure of it. 'Harry!' I roared across the street; 'Harry it's me . . . Sean Farrell', he looked back at me too, stared a while, I waved . . . then he walked on.

Angela He mustn't've recognised you.

Sean I mean I haven't changed that much, and me eyes are still good . . . it was him. I'd know his face anywhere, know his walk.

Angela It's hard to see in town nowdays with all the traffic.

Sean It's funny though, I thought I saw Declan the other day too, in South William St . . . but he didn't seem to see me either. (*Snaps out of it.*) I'll have to look good, mind you. Appearance – that's half the battle.

Angela I'll have you looking like a king.

Sean A proper gent in a suit, me.

Angela We'll have them fighting one another looking for you. (*Picks up phone book.*) Now what did you say his restaurant was called . . . Cajun Hall? (*Starts looking it up.*)

Sean (*takes phone book from her and puts it down*) Is there a drop of tea going while we shift the stuff up? The electric kettle is in one of the boxes.

Angela First things first! Then we'll get a fire roaring and send Dec out to the chipper. Get a couple of singles and a batch loaf. This horse I'd been following for ages was running in Limerick yesterday, nearly missed it in the paper.

Sean Where did you get money to –

Angela The few bob I'd put by for the van driver. I did a double with it yesterday on a horse called Home Improvements and another called Angie's Day, well, I had to didn't I?

Sean No! Ang. No, not again!

Angela (*laughs*) Home Improvements! It won! At three to one and the other at four to.

Sean You won? (*Adds it up.*) Sixty pounds!

Angela Well, not really.

Sean What d'you mean, not really? Five pounds at three to one is fifteen, fifteen at four is –

Angela I stuck twenty each way on a jockey I was following . . . I knew the horse was useless, knew it!

Sean Twenty each way! Jesus, do you never know when to stop?

Angela Still, there's the guts of ten pounds here.

Sean Ten! But –

Angela I bought a few scratch cards as well.

Sean Ah for –

Angela I got three stars.

Sean Great, stick them under the grill and we'll have them for our tea!

Angela D'you not see Sean? It's changing, our luck is changing. (*Picks up the phone book.*)

Sean Don't cod yourself!

Angela When was the last time I won on the horses? When was the last time I won anything?

Sean Never! You never won anything!

Angela A lucky streak, Sean, that's what I'm on, a lucky streak! The bad one is over! We're on the move, on the way up!

Sean Stop it!

Angela This place is lucky . . . can you feel it? (*Touches a wall.*) Feel the luck.

Sean grabs her and shakes her. She lets the phone book fall.

Sean Stop it I said, Angela! Stop it!

Angela bends down to pick up the phone book. It's on an open page. She looks at it. Pause.

Angela There . . . what did I tell you? (*Tears a page out of phone book.*) Look. The Cajun Hall.

Sean (*looks at the pages*) A fluke!

Angela Nearly a thousand pages in that book, and look
. . . a million to one chance! (*Hands Sean the page. Almost
an excited whisper*) A million to one! Mark my words
Sean, mark my words, this flat is lucky. You ring that man
today and see am I wrong! (*Exits.*)

> *Sean looks after her in despair. He looks at the torn page
> then puts it in his pocket.*
> *Declan enters carrying a mirror from an old dressing
> table. He sets it up against a wall.*

Sean There's no talking to that woman . . . no talking.

Declan This is ridiculous, Da. There's no sign of that
other shoe anywhere!

Sean It's there . . . it's there somewhere.

Declan (*starts to put on his good clothes, a shirt etc. He
stands in front of the mirror*) We won't be allowed keep
here Da.

Sean Isn't it empty?

Declan There's rules!

Sean And there's a nine-month waiting list, she was in
with the corporation again yesterday.

Declan A six months waiting list.

Sean Six, nine, whatever . . . it's still a hundred years
away.

Declan Well wherever we are on the waiting list we'll be
stuck right down at the bottom over this.

Sean No, the arrears. Once we've paid them back there
should be no problem staying here.

Declan Arrears? We've some hope finding three hundred
quid!

Sean Three hundred and sixty-four!

Declan May as well be half a million.

Sean She hasn't told you?

Declan Told me what?

Sean (*pause*) We get it today . . . four hundred.

Declan Are you out of your head! We can't even afford to pay the last loan never mind a new one.

Sean She's . . . she's going to another moneylender, Cahil won't lend her anymore. There's this other fella in Dolphin's Barn. Sits in the back of a car at Rialto bridge all day.

Declan Another one! You can't let her go to another one after what we've been through!

Sean The Merchant of Venice, they call him. (*excited*) If we pay back what we owe they might even give us our old house back!

Declan Well there's two hopes of that.

Sean That'd be great, wouldn't it? To walk back up that street with our heads held high.

Declan It's gone.

Sean Open the gate, stroll up the pathway, and waltz in the front door.

Declan (*shouts*) I said it's gone!

   Pause.

Sean Gone? It can't be gone!

Declan There's someone else living in it now.

Sean Ah no, there couldn't be, there couldn't.

Declan We've been gone nearly a month.

Sean (*sits down*) No Declan, say it's still there, say it's still empty. It's all that's been keeping me going.

Declan What did you expect . . . that they'd keep it for us? That they just threw us out till we came up with the cash and then let us back in?

Sean (*angry*) Nineteen forty-eight me Ma and Da moved in there! The first on the road.

Declan I walked past it the other day. I nearly walked into the house, forgot where I was. (*Laughs.*) They've stuck a little plaque on the gate, Glenvale. A satellite dish on the gable wall. A blue mini outside the gate and a pram in the garden.

Sean A horse and cart all the way in from a tenement in Charlemount Street. (*Rambles to himself.*)

Declan Him and his wife and a baby . . . they were all playing out in the grass.

Sean Why, why did they have to go and do that on us?

   Declan exits. Sean calls after him.

They would've got the money Declan . . . they would've got it. (*Goes over and looks out at veranda.*)

   Angela returns. She begins to sort some things out.

It's gone for good Ang . . . gone for good.

Angela What ails you now?

Sean Glenvale, they've called it.

Angela Will you get cracking! (*She rips open a few boxes.*)

Sean What are we going to do?

Angela What do you think we're doing here?

Sean If this doesn't work Ang . . . (*Stares out window.*)

Angela drops a large package on the floor.

Angela Well it won't work with you mowping around all day.

Sean Here, here, go easy with that! (*Lifts out a large parcel from a box. Then kneels on the floor and unwraps the parcel.*) I've a hammer in that box there, Ang, and some nails . . . give us them out.

Angela Leave it be Sean.

Sean (*takes out a picture and holds it up*) There you go. Our picture. (*Holds it up.*)

It is an old tacky picture of a tropical beach. He stands back and looks at it. He goes to the box and takes out the hammer and nails. He hammers a nail into a wall and puts the picture up.

Angela Take it down. Please Sean, I don't want to look at it.

Sean We'll get there yet Ang.

Angela Put it away . . . burn the bloody thing!

Sean And burn me promise?

Angela Twenty-six years ago!

Sean I'll still take you there . . . one day.

Angela Will I hold me breath?

Sean It'll still be there . . . those palm trees, the blue sea. And the sand? As white as snow . . . and as long as it's there my promise stands.

Angela They'll have cancer cured by the time you get me to Portmarnock, never mind paradise!

Sean (*grabs her and starts to waltz*) You'll look lovely in a grass skirt.

Angela Stop it!

Sean (*laughs*) A grass skirt and a garland of flowers.

Angela (*pushes him away*) Get away from me!

Sean Jesus, I'm only joking.

Angela You and your promises! It's all I ever got! Now hurry up and get the stuff in!

> *Sean, surprised at Angela, exits. Declan enters and looks at picture.*

I was hoping we'd lose that on the way.

Declan Go way out of that . . . you love it.

Angela I'm sick and tired looking at it. Twenty-six years hanging over the fireplace . . . the place probably doesn't even exist.

Declan Well, wherever it is, you'll never see it.

Angela I used to think I'd get there one day but –

Declan But I came along and ruined it all.

Angela I made the best of it . . . like I always do.

Declan A honeymoon baby?

Angela Honeymoon? A week on the Isle of Man. (*pause, close look at picture*) That's where he got that yoke.

Declan The Isle of Man? Big spender!

Angela He was hoping I'd settle for a few days in Rush. I wanted to see Scotland . . . we'll split the difference on the map, he said. The honeymoon suite at the Truscott Arms Hotel, Douglas. (*Laughs.*) Two separate beds stuck together. (*Pause.*) We were only kids, God love us. I was nineteen and your Da was twenty-one. (*Stares into the picture.*) The world was wide open to us then.

Declan And then I came along.

Angela You should've seen me mother with the calendar when I told her I was pregnant.

Declan Your first big gamble!

Angela Oh you were planned alright . . . just your father forget to tell me anything about it.

She unpacks one of the boxes. Pause.

Declan Ma . . . don't get another loan.

Angela It's me last one, Declan. I told him too, I said, 'I'm sorry Mr Cahil, but this is the last loan I'll be wanting off you . . . don't care whether you're vexed or pleased,' says I, 'but this is me last!'

Declan Stop it!

Angela He wasn't too happy when he heard that.

Declan Stop lying, will you! Cahil wouldn't give you a loan . . . you're gong to someone else!

Angela (*pause*) What are you worried about, you're not the one that'll have to pay it back.

Declan The other loan's not even half paid off.

Angela Don't mind the other loan. That fella won't find me in here. Mind you, I wouldn't have to do it if . . .

Declan If what?

Angela That course will cost a lot of money, and who's to say that you'll get on it? Say if it's full?

Declan Yeah, you'd ask me too, wouldn't you? You'd ask me for every penny of it.

Angela It's your money.

Declan That's right! Mine!

Angela A clear slate . . . that's all I want. If we start off with a clear slate with them they'll let us have here no problem.

Declan They don't want the arrears . . . the case is closed, we didn't pay the rent, they evicted us!

Angela Cash! That's all people care about nowdays. Once you've cash in your hands you can do anything. When I slap down the guts of four hundred quid you'll see them boys jump.

Declan We're barely managing as it is!

Angela Sure with your Da's few bob . . .

Declan Pennies and twopences! (*Exits.*)

Angela (*calls after him*) Well maybe if you got up off the sofa and got some work! Instead of throwing good money away on a course! (*Mutters to herself.*)

Angela opens a few more boxes. At the doorway a man appears. The Lord stands, silently, looking at her. He has an old busman's hat on his head, a rolled-up newspaper is sticking out of his pocket. When she sees him she freezes.

The Lord There you are so . . . (*Enters and closes door.*)

Angela Jesus! (*Backs away.*)

The Lord Cold oul night out, isn't it? Then again, it is November.

Angela (*calls*) Sean!

The Lord You'd want oxygen masks up this high.

Angela (*louder*) Sean! Declan!

The Lord Making yourself at home? (*Walks over and looks at photos.*)

Angela What do you want in here?

The Lord Rough looking shop from the outside, what?

Angela Who are you?

The Lord There's gangs of kids running around like a pack of wolves down there. (*Makes a howling sound.*)

Angela Who are you I said!

The Lord (*looks out veranda*) A roof over the head . . . you can't beat it.

Angela Me husband and son'll be back up in a minute! If you go now –

The Lord It's the foundation stone of everything . . . a roof. If you haven't got that . . . (*Nods out to the window.*) You get sucked in.

Angela I've no money . . . nothing!

The Lord Who said anything about money Angela? It is Angela?

Angela How do you know – (*She looks at the photos on the wall and then at him.*)

> *The Lord walks over to her and then around her. He stands behind her and smells her hair then runs his fingers through it.*

What do you want?

> *Sean enters. The Lord walks back.*

Sean You could've brought something up with you Lord!

The Lord I was . . . I was just getting acquainted with the missus.

Angela That's . . . that's him!

Sean And who did you think it was?

Angela That dirty looking yoke?

Sean Can you not be civil?

Angela What's he doing here?

The Lord I was asked to come and lend a hand, isn't that right, Sean?

Sean Eh . . . yeah, that's right.

Angela Creeping in like that and frightening the life out of me! He's no business being here.

The Lord And it's alright for you to come barging through the window.

Sean (*an angry whisper*) What are you doing here!

The Lord I thought you'd need a hand with –

Sean I told you not to come until –

The Lord Many hands make light work. We have to make sure we're in time to get our patch. (*to Angela, an attempt at dignity*) It's very hard to get a patch nowdays. Everyone's at it.

Sean He's discovered somewhere special, haven't you Lord?

The Lord A newly demolished listed building on the quays.

Sean Right in the heart of the city.

The Lord Should fit at least ten cars into it until they throw up another apartment block for the scum.

Sean Ten cars Ang, d'you hear! Ten cars at what . . . a pound an hour?

The Lord One fifty . . . there's a lot of demand for spaces in town nowdays.

Sean One fifty an hour, eight hours a day!

The Lord The best of the lot though is a good spot in the city, catch them coming out of the pubs.

Sean They're always more generous when they've a few drinks on them.

Angela That's the future for Dublin, car parks.

Sean The future, d'you hear, the future!

The Lord Forget fast food and Left Banks. Soon the whole city'll become one gigantic car park, there'll be work for everyone. (*Goes over and looks at the photos on the wall.*) The family album, what?

Sean Someone take them photos down . . . they give me the shivers. (*Rips some photos off.*)

The Lord Here! That's bad luck. (*Takes photo off him.*) That's someone's life on that wall.

Sean They're no good to him now, are they?

The Lord That's all that man had left.

Sean I don't want anything left of him here.

Angela Dec'll take them down and put them in a box or something.

The Lord Show a little respect for the dead! (*Gently takes the photos down.*)

> *They start unpacking. The Lord takes a bottle of wine from his pocket.*

Eh . . . the monks make it. For the throat . . . smokes have me killed. (*Takes a swallow.*)

Angela stares at him. She makes him uncomfortable.

Eh . . . anyone fancy a drop, there's a nasty chill out.

No reply. He puts bottle back.

Angela Is the furniture going to carry itself up?

Sean There's some stuff I left out on the landing, bring it in, will you? I'll follow you out in a minute.

The Lord exits.

Angela What did you bring him here for?

Sean I didn't bring him here.

Angela Then how did he know where we were?

Sean I must've told him. Anyway, the more help we have the quicker we get the stuff up.

Angela What'll people think if they see him with us? The stink off him would knock you out.

Sean Look, don't start, leave him be, I'll get rid of him later.

Angela We're bad enough without you bringing winos into the place.

Sean He's not a wino!

Angela He lives in a bloody doss house!

Sean A men's hostel!

Angela A kip!

Sean Wasn't it good enough for me for the last three weeks?

Angela You didn't have to go there, there was plenty of room in Rita's.

Sean I wasn't welcome there, thrown out after one night!

Angela Well you had to come in drunk and call her a whore.

Sean Well she is! Left to fend for meself over the bitch.

Angela Look, are you going to get that stuff in!

Sean What's the rush?

Angela D'you think I like having me life's possessions paraded up the stairs for everyone to look at?

Sean At least they'll see there's nothing worth robbing. Did you see them . . . gangs of them, all hanging over the balcony with their eyes hanging out.

The Lord enters with a mattress.

(*looks at Lord*) What ails you? (*Kicks mattress.*) That doesn't belong in here!

The Lord You're very jumpy.

Sean What do you expect? The middle of the day and us breaking into some oul divil's home!

The Lord (*takes a bottle of wine from his coat*) Here then . . . (*He offers Sean some wine.*) It'll calm the nerves.

Sean You know I don't touch that stuff!

The Lord (*to Angela*) Yourself, missis?

Angela (*looks at bottle, wipes her mouth*) What do you think I am?

The Lord Are you sure?

Angela (*a false laugh*) Put that away, will you!

The Lord Please yourself. (*Takes a slug.*) But wait till you're dying for a drink and haven't the price of a pint.

Angela I'm not that fond of the drink.

The Lord Did I say anything of the sort?

Angela Only take a drink when I feel like it, me. When I feel like it, that right Sean? (*Stares at The Lord drinking.*)

The Lord I remember the day I wouldn't dream of it either. (*Pause.*) But when you take your first swally . . . it hits you right there. (*stomach*) Second swally and the belly starts to warm up . . . third, fourth swally, you're on fire. (*Starts to shadow box.*) Wild horses couldn't stop you then, wild horses!

Angela (*wrestles the bottle off The Lord, shouts*) For the love of Jesus man will you put that bottle away out of me sight!

> *The bottle falls and spills. Angela is about to react and dive on it to pick it up but The Lord beats her to it.*

Sean What ails you?

Angela Get it out of here!

The Lord OK, OK . . . take it easy.

Angela Just hurry up and bring up the furniture!

Sean I'm going, alright!

Angela And take that bloody mattress with you!

> *Sean exits. The Lord puts the bottle away.*

The Lord I, eh, I didn't mean –

Angela Just get out of me way till I wipe it up! (*Gets a rag and mops it up.*)

The Lord (*looks at the photos on the wall*) A sorry sight, isn't it?

> *Just for a second Angela forgets herself and licks the wine from her fingers.*

(*catches her*) I said, *a sorry sight*.

Angela (*jumps. Undecided whether to talk to him*) He's no more worries now, wherever he is.

The Lord A horrible way to go, isn't it . . . on your own with no family?

Angela (*pause. Looks up at him*) You must have one . . . a family?

The Lord Everyone has a family.

Angela Kids I meant, a wife. You wear a wedding ring.

The Lord (*rubs his wedding ring. Pause*) My youngest'd be about the same age as your yunfella. (*Takes some photos from his coat.*) That's all I've left of them. (*Hands her the photos.*)

Angela Two girls and a boy.

The Lord Nora, Mary and Colm.

Angela They're the image of you.

The Lord (*hands her another photo*) That's me and her outside the GPO . . . remember the oulfella that used to hop out and take your photo? The night we got engaged . . . we were on our way to The Corinthian. (*Hands her another.*)

Angela This is a postcard.

The Lord Look closely.

Angela (*reads*) 'The Oval Ballroom . . . Bognor Regis'? (*Pause.*)

The Lord Can you not see?

Angela All I can see is some people dancing.

The Lord Yeah, but to what? Look at the band. The drummer . . . see?

Angela I can see an elbow.

The Lord And me shoulder, if you look closely.

Angela You . . . the drummer?

The Lord We were well known. So was I . . . The Lord of the Drums, that's what they called me. Used to do this - ten-minute solo at the end of the night. (*Sees a plastic bucket, picks it up and begins to tap it.*) Beat the drums alive . . . people used come just to hear those ten minutes. The Golden Chords . . . that's what we were called. You might have heard of us?

Angela I can't say I did.

The Lord Played in every Butlins on the map!

Angela (*hands him the photos back*) You've kept them up very well.

The Lord They're all I've left.

Angela Just photos?

The Lord If you've no photos you've no proof, have you? No proof you were here. (*Pause.*) Like that old soul on the wall. (*Puts the photos back.*)

> *Declan enters. He is now almost fully dressed but has a*
> *dirty pair of runners on.*

Declan Has that other shoe turned up yet? (*Sees The Lord.*) Who's –

The Lord You must be Declan?

Declan Ma! Who's this?

Angela I'll give you two guesses! (*Exits.*)

The Lord D'you not remember me . . . I was with your father last week. You, eh, you didn't seem to recognise him.

Declan If you're here to help there's a pile of boxes down there waiting.

Sean is heard calling him. The Lord exits. Declan waits for The Lord to leave. Looks at himself in the mirror. He holds out his hand as if shaking someone's.

How do you do? 'Take a seat.' Thank you. (*Sits down. He stands up again.*) How do you do? Declan Farrell. (*Takes out a sheet of paper. Reads.*) Maths . . . B. Irish . . . C minus, no C plus. (*Writes with a pen.*) English . . . B. Geography . . . D in Geography and History. Science? Say you didn't do science. (*Puts paper away.*) Sorry about the shoes but . . . Agh! My apologies for my appearance but – I know what you must be thinking about my shoes but you see – (*more frustrated*) But you see we got thrown out of our house last month, broke into another one this afternoon and lost me shoes in the meantime! (*Takes off his jacket and flings it.*) Agh this is stupid! Can't go looking like this!

He looks through some more boxes. Sean enters with The Lord. They are carrying a sofa.

Sean Stick it down here.

Declan Still no sign of it?

Sean It has to be somewhere.

Declan You're sure you touched nothing after I packed them?

Sean It'll turn up after everything's out of the van.

Declan It better. (*Exits.*)

The Lord It's a grand flat Sean.

Sean Haven't had time to look at it yet.

The Lord Two bedrooms, is it?

Sean I suppose. Why?

The Lord Just wondering, that's all. If all this works out you won't forget me, hah? You'll still call for me . . . do the bit of work with me?

Sean I don't forget me mates.

The Lord Yeah, mates, me and you pals, aren't we?

Sean And why wouldn't we be?

The Lord Maybe even . . . even stay the odd night here. You know, on the sofa.

Sean Eh . . . sure, of course.

The Lord And then again . . . if there was another room, one that yous weren't using . . .

Sean A room?

The Lord You know me, never get in the way. Yous wouldn't even notice me.

Sean Look Lord –

The Lord All I need is a hand up, a way out. The way mates would help each other.

Sean (*trying to find a way out of it*) Don't worry, you looked after me in there, showed me the ropes.

The Lord (*pause*) Haven't had a mate in years. Acquaintances alright, a fella you could tap maybe for the price of a bottle of grape or for a few smokes . . . but no mate . . . no proper pal.

Sean You never said . . . how you ended up in there.

The Lord Like everyone else in it . . . the blackest of bad luck.

Sean gets up and sorts out a few things.

I'd a grand life Sean, a fine big house, a shop and a lovely family.

Sean Had a fine house ourselves. (*Looks out window.*) Just up the way past the lights. Had this big old shed in the back, full of old paint tins and pots. Used to sit in it for hours pottering away.

The Lord I do go up and look at where the house was sometimes when I'm feeling low . . . stand at the bus stop across from it and stare.

Sean I'd give anything to be in that shed now.

A pause as they light some cigarettes. The Lord stares into the flame. He picks up the plastic bucket and starts to tap a rhythm.

What shop?

The Lord What?

Sean You said you had a shop. I thought you were in a band . . . a drummer?

The Lord The band was part-time, semi-professional. I'd me own business . . . a pet shop.

Sean A pet shop?

The Lord I'd two lads working for me while I'd be on the road. Rabbits, budgies, hamsters.

Sean What happened to it?

The Lord Wasn't much of a drinker them days, the odd gin and tonic after a gig. It was after they . . . after. (*Pause.*) I was on a binge one week after a gig in Kilkenny. A week and a half down there. Came back to open up the shop . . . (*Pause.*) When I opened the door a thousand flies flew into me face . . . and the smell. Nothing left of them but worms. (*Drinks some wine.*) I wasn't regular with the wages, the

120

boys got fed up not knowing what day of the week they'd
be paid and fecked off one afternoon. Locked up the shop,
the poor animals too. (*Pause.*) Didn't make much from the
sale after I covered the bills.

Sean The missus . . . she didn't like your drinking, that
why she left?

The Lord (*looks at bottle*) This came after. (*Pause.*)
Finished this wedding for a county councillor in Wicklow,
a big red neck bastard! (*Pause.*) Not a trace of them when I
came home?

Sean Vanished?

The Lord walks over to window and looks out.

The Lord Twelve years ago . . . that was the last I saw of
them.

Sean The dirty bitch! Doing that on a man, taking his kids
and disappearing like that!

The Lord She never –

Sean You shouldn't've given up looking!

The Lord I should've made more time for them.

Sean I wouldn't care how long it took, I'd find me kids.
Let her shag off if she wanted to.

The Lord Shouldn't've been on the road that much. It
wouldn't've happened if I'd've made more time . . . if
I'd've said no.

Sean What happened to the band?

The Lord After I lost the family I lost heart in everything.
Fell over the drums on stage one night . . . the boys sacked
me. (*Drinks some more.*)

Sean Jesus man, that stuff . . . it's only for . . . for –

(*Breaks off.*)

Angela (*returns struggling with an armchair*) Bad cess to you and your wine. Turning me flat into a . . . a doss house!

Sean Leave him be, you, will you!

Angela Let him do that carry on outside in the street! I'm trying to make a home in here.

The Lord Sorry missus, sorry. (*Exits.*)

> *Angela tries to organize a few things in the flat. Sean has a smoke. A pause.*

Angela Get away from him Sean, he's not your sort.

Sean (*a little annoyed, turns his back on her*) The Lord looked after me in the hostel.

Angela Last night was your last night in that place . . . let that be an end to it.

Sean What harm is he doing?

Angela I don't want him 'round us.

Sean I'd've gone down only for him.

Angela You should never've went there!

Sean I wouldn't've ended up there if it wasn't for you!

Angela You're changing . . . you can't see it but I can. Turning into a . . . a waster!

Sean (*raises his voice*) . . . wouldn't be here if it wasn't for you! Wouldn't be in this mess if it wasn't for you!

Angela Look at the cut of you . . . the stink of you!

Sean And whose fault is that? Twelve hundred pounds! Jesus Christ, I must've been mad listening to you!

Angela God curse the day you set foot in the kip!

Sean And while he's at it let him curse all the poxed horses you put money on . . . let him curse all the numbers between one and forty-two!

Angela (*starts to raise her voice*) You wouldn't have said that if it'd worked.

Sean You've me heart broke.

Angela . . . you wouldn't be saying that if I came home with a handful of fivers and tenners, would you?

Sean You need luck to win, we haven't an ounce between us.

Angela It was the only thing left to do, you'd no job, Declan'd none . . . the rent had got out of hand, one bill was coming after another.

Sean You and your brilliant idea! '. . . you never win on that yoke, if you do it's only twenty or thirty pounds.'

Angela It worked long enough, didn't it?

Sean Three bloody months, that's all! Three months of handy money and then what?

Angela A fluke!

Sean A twelve-hundred-pounds fluke! An out-on-the-side-of-the-road fluke!

Angela Didn't I nearly make it back?

Sean Nearly? Nearly made it back . . . a week's dole money on a horse that's still poxy-well running!

Angela It came second!

Declan I'd've ran quicker meself bejaysus! Bread and jam we had to eat for a week over the bastard!

Angela But if it had won . . . D'you not see Sean, if it had've won!

Sean If-if-if! The story of our bloody lives!

Angela By a nose . . . just by a nose, it lost! I should've done it each way!

Sean You should've just told them the truth and let them feck off!

Angela And have me throat slit?

Sean Or lied to them even, jaysus knows you're good at that!

Angela They'd have found out.

Sean All you had to say was that you forgot to do it that week, they wouldn't've checked, they never did before. Whatever happened it wouldn't've been as bad as this.

Angela (*pause*) It could work again Sean, I know it could.

Sean (*silence. Stares at her*) What?

Angela In here . . . in the flats, when we settle in.

Sean For God's sake woman!

Angela It could never happen again, think of the odds.

Sean Stop it Ang, please, stop it!

Angela A million to one, Sean, 50 million to one!

Sean We lost our home over that carry on.

Angela I know we don't know anyone here yet but we will . . . soon.

Sean Lost our life!

Angela Start with one or two of the women, tell them the last one I was in got five numbers up. (*Grabs Sean.*) Jesus Sean, by Christmas there could be twenty or thirty people in the group. Then by the new year start showing them the

124

old dockets . . . if anyone spots anything I'll just tell them that I got the dockets mixed up.

Sean (*breaks away*) Jesus Christ Ang, will you listen to yourself!

Angela There's enough people in these flats to make thirty, forty pounds a week!

Sean Two pounds a week, two pounds a week would've done you, the price of a packet of smokes. A pound a week even. Once you were making an effort to pay.

Angela I thought I could catch up . . . catch up with the bills.

Sean You made sure you'd enough for your horses and lotto, didn't you . . .

Angela And you never had a drink?

Sean . . . you made sure you'd enough for your poker machines and bingo.

Angela I never thought it would add up so fast.

Sean What about the warning letters they sent you, why weren't we shown them?

Angela Hadn't I enough worry trying to find money to feed ourselves never mind pay a moneylender? Enough worry trying to hold the family together.

Sean I must be mad coming here with you . . . must be out of me head. Not an hour in the kip and you want to start back at your old ways.

Angela Stop shouting . . . you're making a show of us.

Sean What do you care . . . you've no shame!

Angela Look who's talking. You'd rather sleep with filth and dirt than your own family.

Sean I had to go there, didn't I? Your poxy sister wouldn't let me set foot inside the house.

Angela If your own family wouldn't have you, you hardly expect mine to! You've made a holy show of us with your car parking, your . . . your mate! Who's nothing more than a tramp. Why don't you just shag off out and live with him if you're so fond of him? Hah, why don't you move in with him altogether . . . 'cause you're no use to me like that!

Sean Like this! (*louder*) Like this? Jesus woman, it's you that has me like this!

Angela Always looking for someone to blame, aren't you?

Sean I was a noble man, me!

Angela A liar, that's what I married!

Sean Head and shoulders among anyone.

Angela The tales you spun me, the promises you broke! I gave it all up for your lies, sacrificed everything so you could play the gentleman!

Sean (*shakes her and roars*) Look at us, we've nothing left, nothing more to gamble with! (*Kicks over the coffee table.*)

Angela As long as you can draw breath you can gamble, even if it's only to cross the road.

Declan (*rushes in. The back of his suit trousers is ripped.*) Jaysus Christ Ma! The thread . . . where's the thread?

Sean I lost me home, me pride – lost everything over you! And so has that poor bastard.

Declan I'm after ripping me trousers on a nail outside! (*Starts looking for thread everywhere.*)

Sean The only thing is he doesn't know why . . . doesn't know the truth!

Declan Give us a hand, will yous! I've to be out the door in two minutes!

Sean Tell him why we were thrown out of our house . . . go on!

Declan (*looks in mirror to survey the damage*) Look at me! I'm like an imbecile! I'll be a laughing stock . . . run out of it!

Sean Mrs Money here came up with this brainwave.

Angela It was a fluke Dec.

Sean We'd make a fortune, she said!

Declan Look, can we keep this for another time . . . I'm going to an interview with me arse hanging out!

Angela I never thought you'd win on that.

Sean Go on . . . tell him.

Declan (*shouts*) The needle and thread. Has anyone seen the needle and thread?

Sean Tell him I said.

> *Declan throws stuff out of the box, finds the thread and takes his pants off and begins to sew hurriedly.*

Angela It was a handy thirty quid a week . . . God knows we needed it. Just once, that's all, just the once we got four numbers up . . . a pound each was all we won.

Declan What am I going to look like at all?

Sean They were in a group, remember, her and the women off the road? Two pounds each week they used to put in every Saturday . . . she used to collect it and do the numbers.

Angela I had to do something, didn't I? Had to find money somewhere?

Sean We would've managed, like everyone else. But, no, you had to do that.

Declan What time is it? (*No answer. Shouts.*) What time is it I said!

Angela I was working nights cleaning an office. The staff, they used to do the lotto in there. They had as much luck as us. (*pause, nervous laugh*) I used to take their dockets out of the bin and bring them home and show them to the girls on the street, pretend they were ours . . . it was as simple as that.

Sean I told you to stop it, told you something would happen!

Angela I was coming out of the bingo that night . . . Maura Healy comes running over to me: 'Five numbers,' says she, 'we're after getting five numbers up!' I nearly dropped. I walked around in circles that night . . . walked for hours.

Sean Eleven hundred and eighty pounds!

Angela 11, 13, 34, 2 and 8. I'll remember them numbers till I die.

Declan (*stops*) You won?

Angela I couldn't tell them that I didn't do it . . . they'd've killed me. (*Pause.*) Seven of them. A hundred and sixty-eight pounds fifty pence each. What could I do? I had to go to a moneylender for the money.

Sean Over seventy pounds a week we had to pay back.

Declan You won the lotto?

Angela I would've managed it if I kept on collecting the money but your father wouldn't let me.

Declan When did all this happen?

Sean You shouldn't've paid them a penny Ang! Should've told them to shag off!

Angela And have me throat slit?

Sean Like shagging paupers we had to live.

Angela Weren't we blessed it wasn't the jackpot?

Declan This is what all this mess is over?

Angela You should've let me keep on collecting it.

Sean And now she wants to start the same carry on in here!

Angela Don't you see . . . it's all a gamble. All you need is to click once, that's all, click once and you're made for life.

Sean You've gambled our lives away.

Declan (*finishes sewing. Tries trousers on and looks in mirror.*) Agh this looks ridiculous!

Angela Your lives? It was you that lost your job.

Sean You that gambled that poor bastard's future.

Angela Look at him! You'd think he was going for a job with the circus!

Declan What?

Sean Don't mind her, you'll do. Just don't bend down.

Declan Do I look alright?

Sean Go on . . . hurry.

Declan You'll be alright till I get back?

Sean Can you not fasten a tie. (*Fixes his tie.*) Now away with you, go on.

Declan (*pause*) Yous'll be alright here?

Angela What do you think!

Declan Right then, I'll see yous later. (*Takes a roll of money out, counts it then exits.*)

Angela (*calls after him*) Hurry straight back! This place has to be sorted out.

Sean You could've at least wished him luck.

Angela For what? A job that's not there?

Sean You turn me stomach, d'you know that!

The Lord (*enters*) That's about the last of it . . . just an armchair.

Sean Leave that down and come on!

The Lord But –

Sean Come on I said.

Angela You stay where you are!

Sean I've had enough of your nagging for the day!

Angela I've to go and get the money.

Sean And you want me to go with you and hold your hand?

Angela It'll be cash.

Sean You know where to stick it, don't you!

Angela And what about here? The window . . . all the furniture?

Sean This was your idea . . . you sort it out.

Angela Hold on Sean, you can't leave me here on me own.

The Lord There still a few things down there Sean.

Sean Are you coming or what?

The Lord Sean . . . you can't leave her like this.

Sean gets his coat and puts it on. Exits.

I'll eh . . . I'll better go with him so. (*Exits.*)

Angela Go on you pig! Off to the pub. Only waiting on an excuse, that's all. Go on . . . doss out on the streets all day, that's all you're good for. (*Runs out the door after him.*) Just don't expect me to sit in here all day, d'you hear! I've things to do as well you know! (*She enters the kitchen and returns with a glass of water then sits and takes some pills.*) Good for nothing bastard! (*Shouts.*) The pair of yous! I'm always the one left to sort things out, amn't I! (*She starts to arrange a few things. Then stops and throws an item across at the wall.*)

Suddenly there is a loud banging at the hall door. Angela leaps up.

Sean? Sean is that you?

More banging.

Sean . . .? (*She gets the piece of glass. Is about to open the door. The sound of a door crashing. Angela screams.*)

Lights out.

Act Two

About half an hour later.
   The exterior of the block of flats.
   A broken and battered car stands to the side.
   Bits of the furniture and clothes etc. are scattered, some pieces broken.

Angela (*looking up to flat*) Stop it . . . please! Please! Don't smash that! Please – (*Ducks as an item is thrown.*)

   An item is thrown down from the flat. The kids cheer as it lands and breaks.

No, No! Please! Can you not see what you're doing? You're smashing it all . . . everything!

   Another item is thrown over.

I didn't mean to hurt anyone . . .

   A box of clothes is flung down.

Will yous not wait till me husband comes back? Just leave it out on the landing till I get someone to collect it.

   More things are thrown over.

(*turns to another block of flats*) Jesus, will someone not talk to them, will someone help me! Please, I know you're there, I can see yous twitching behind your curtains.

   An empty can is thrown at her. Cheering as it hits her.

Kids (*chanting*) Out-out . . . Squatters out!

Angela Get away yous bastards . . . go and leave me be!

More jeering from the kids.

(*cries out*) For the love of jaysus is there no one out there!

Another item is thrown over.

Please, somebody! They're destroying everything.

Kids (*more jeering*) Out, out, squatters out!

Angela Can yous not leave me in peace! (*Throws something at them.*)

The sound of kids squealing and running away.

Voice (*on a balcony in the distance shouts down*) Go on you oul targer, go back to where you came from!

Angela If you go back to the sewer you were rared!

Voice If anyone's squatting here, it'll be one of our own!

Kids (*the sound of them taunting again*) Out out . . . squatters out!

Angela (*trying to pick up some things*) Sean, Sean, Declan!!! The curse of jaysus on yous, where are you?

Kids (*mocking her call*) Sean . . . Declan!

Angela Cowards! That's all yous are. Yous wouldn't be doing that if me husband and son were here!

Something else is thrown at her, it hits her.

(*cries at them*) Will yous not leave me alone!

More jeering.

What have I done on yous at all? (*Looks up at the flats.*) Try to put a roof over me head . . . try to make the best of a bad thing? And this . . . me own stock . . . this is what I get from yous?

The jeering dies down.

133

Where do I go tonight, what? Where do I get a night's sleep?

Silence.

Yous haven't thought of that have yous? Oh you've brave men in your . . . your '*Neighbourhood watch*'! Brave men indeed. Throwing a family out of their home like that! Well don't worry about us, d'you hear? We'll be alright . . . it'll take more than scum the like of you to keep us down! (*She packs a few things into a bag and walks off to the left. To the flats.*) Oh it's a fine kip this, and yous are welcome to it! Letting an old man starve to death on his floor!

The sound of the kids jeering her in the distance until it fades away.

From the right Declan enters. His pants are back in the torn state. He stops. Looks at the furniture then walks on. He stops and looks closely at it then looks up to the flat.

Declan (*quietly*) Ma . . .? (*louder*) Ma! Jesus, no! No! (*Looks up.*) Ma . . . Da! (*He looks around at the debris. Then runs up to the flat calling his ma. After a few seconds he returns.*) Where are yous . . .? (*Runs around the stage looking for them. Louder.*) Where are you Ma!

He picks up one or two things, a confused few moments; should he gather things up, go to the flat . . . What's going on? He runs off in the direction of the kids.

Come back . . . c'mere for a minute. What happened . . . what happened to the woman in the flat . . . (*Fades out as he exits.*)

The lights fade. An hour or so has passed.
Sean and The Lord enter. They have some bottles of beer with them in a bag.

The Lord (*stops. Sees the stuff*) What's all this?

Sean goes over. Starts rummaging.

Anything decent there?

Sean Oul junk, that's all.

The Lord (*finds an overcoat. Tries it on*) What d'you think?

Sean Check the pockets.

The Lord (*takes off coat*) Not a penny. (*Throws it away. Picks up another jacket, tries it on.*) I like this one. (*Twirls around.*) A grand fit.

Sean Well, I better go up and face the music, are you right.

The Lord You went looking for work, she can't give out over that!

Sean I should've rang him, shouldn't have gone in like this.

The Lord Not to worry, my car park in town . . . that'll see us right.

Sean Shouldn't have gone looking like this . . . like a . . . a – (*Stops. Looks at Lord.*) That's odd . . . (*Looks closer at the jacket.*) I've a jacket like that . . . Jaysus! (*Runs at Lord.*) Get that off! (*Tries to tear jacket off The Lord.*)

The Lord Here, hold on!

Sean Get it off you!

The Lord Let go!

Sean Get it off you I said!

The Lord Hold on, I got it first!

Sean It's mine that overcoat! (*Tears the coat off him.*)

The Lord There's plenty others!

Sean What's going on? (*Looks up towards the flat.*) It can't be! It can't! (*Starts to pick up bits and pieces and examine them.*)

The Lord What ails you now?

Sean Jesus, Mary and Joseph! (*Roars.*) Angela!

The Lord Keep it down will you?

Sean Ang, where are you . . . Ang – Declan! (*Runs around picking up bits and pieces flinging them away and picking up more.*) What's after happening?

The Lord What are you on about?

Sean All this stuff – it's ours, mine!

The Lord But all yous is . . . (*Looks up to flat.*)

Sean Look, at the sofa . . . the coffee table. The cabinet . . . where's me mother's cabinet? (*Pulls a sheet off to reveal the broken cabinet.*) Oh no . . . it's destroyed.

The Lord Jesus Sean, are you sure?

Sean Me good shoes . . . (*Takes out a piece of paper from a shoe.*) The bit of cardboard I stuck in to keep the rain out!

The Lord Oh no . . . what are we going to do now?

Sean We, what d'you mean we?

The Lord That flat was the leg up I needed.

Sean Look, you're weren't –

The Lord I told it was bad luck tearing them photos off the wall. Now what are we going to do?

Sean Maybe it was gurriers. Bastards got in through the window! It might be safe to go back up?

The Lord Here . . . (*Looks around.*) They might be still around . . . waiting. We better be going!

Sean Come on where!

The Lord We've got to find somewhere else.

Sean I'm not going to go and leave me life lying out on the street!

The Lord Before it gets too late.

Sean Yous bastards! (*Shouts up at flat.*) D'you hear me, yous didn't have to do this! You've left us with nothing, nothing! (*quieter*)

   The sound of the kids jeering him.

(*shouts at them*) I was there first . . . it's mine that flat! Mine!

The Lord (*shakes Sean*) Are you trying to get us killed!

Sean Maybe there's something wrong . . . maybe she got mugged with all that money?

The Lord What money?

Sean We owe the four hundred in back rent.

The Lord Maybe you should ring the hospitals?

Sean Ring the bookies! That'd be more like it. Ring the bingo halls!

The Lord She could be lying in a hospital somewhere with her face black and blue!

Sean Jesus! What if she's got the money and given it to the corporation!

The Lord She'd hardly give it to them after this.

Sean She was to go and collect it and give it to them . . .

she mightn't even know about this.

The Lord Oh jaysus!

Sean Maybe she didn't . . . maybe she knows, please God let her know! That money . . . we'll have to book into a B&B for the night with it.

The Lord A B&B!

Sean There should be a phone book around, I'll get a number of somewhere near and ring up. (*Starts looking for the phone book.*)

The Lord What do you want to go wasting good money on a B&B?

Sean Shouldn't cost much, a few pound, that's all. (*Finds a phone book. Look through it.*) Hotel . . . B&Bs . . . (*Tears out a page.*) Money for the phone . . . I need money for the phone!

The Lord Who in the name of jaysus'll let you stay in a B&B in that state!

Sean And have you any better ideas?

The Lord Another flat Sean, we've got to get another flat!

Sean Look, what's all this 'we' stuff?

The Lord A way out Sean, a way back. (*Looks around.*) There must be another empty kip around here, there has to be. Come on . . . we'll find one and break in. Have everything ready for the missus when she comes back. (*Starts to gather some things up.*)

Sean Hold on, hold on! This is stupid . . . there are no other flats left. If there is they've been burnt out. And you couldn't come with us even if there was!

The Lord What?

Sean I never said you could stay with us.

The Lord But . . . but I thought we were mates.

The sound of the car screeching. The sound comes closer. The lights of the car blind them for a moment. The kids are heard cheering. Again.

Kids Here, Granda . . . give us a smoke!

Sean (*looks around*) Here, yunfella! Did any of yous see a woman . . . a woman on her own?

Kid (*off*) She's around the corner giving Macker a gobble!

All the kids laugh.

Granda! Granda!

Sean She moved into the top flat today.

Something is thrown at them. He runs after them.

The Lord Leave them be Sean!

Sean Bastards. (*Walks back among the debris. Sees the picture.*) No! (*Gets onto his hands and knees and tries to pick up the bits.*) It's ruined . . . destroyed!

The Lord Jesus man, be careful, you'll cut yourself.

Sean Paradise . . . it's in smithereens!

The Lord It's only an oul picture.

Sean Give me a hand Lord, give me a hand pick up the pieces!

The Lord It's wrecked. And so will we if you don't get going . . . come on. (*Drags him up.*)

Sean Here! There's a light on in the kitchen.

They look up.

That was the flat, wasn't it, the one on the left?

The Lord There's a new pane of glass in it too. And curtains! It's not gurriers, whoever they are.

Sean Are you right? (*Runs to leave.*)

The Lord (*grabs Sean back*) You can't go up there . . . if they did this what'll they do to you?

Sean I can't just stay down here.

The Lord The law of the jungle, Sean . . . this is their jungle.

Sean (*knows he's right. A pause*) Then you do it.

The Lord What?

Sean Say you're looking for someone . . . for the oul fella that used to live there.

The Lord You have another thing coming if you think I'm going next or near that flat.

Sean You're just enquiring, say.

The Lord I'll be enquiring over that balcony!

Sean Then the two of us!

The Lord I'll keep me feet on the ground, thanks very much! And so will you if you know what's good for you.

Sean (*shouts*) Bastards! (*Throws something up to flat.*) Hard men . . . waited till we were gone!

The Lord (*grabs him*) Are you trying to get us killed!

Sean What am I going to do? (*Pause. Stares at him.*) If I go back there it's the end.

> *The Lord forces some clothes into his arms. Sean throws them down and grabs The Lord.*

I have to wait . . . wait for Ang.

The Lord You don't know that she'll come . . . she might have been and left.

Sean I'm waiting!

The Lord Till when . . . the cows come home? (*Looks at watch*.) If we've nowhere to go we'd better go back and book in for the night.

Sean You know the way home.

The Lord And what about our patch, have you thought of that?

Sean You know what you can do with your patch!

The Lord If we lose that Sean!

Sean What use is that to me now?

The Lord Once you lose a patch, it's gone for good. (*Pause*.) Come on, before it's too late.

Sean Too late for what?

The Lord I have work . . . and a roof over me head. Are we going to throw that away as well?

Sean That carry on might be good enough for you, but not for this boy! (*Pause*.) Only went there because I had to, that's all. (*Looks around*.) But there's no going back, never! You can go where you like, but I'm out of there . . . free.

The Lord Free, is it? (*Gestures around*.) Some kind of freedom.

Sean I'm not going down, d'you hear me! Not going down!

The Lord You're just scared, that's all. Scared if you go back there you might never leave.

Sean Are you mad!

The Lord I watched in there, saw how you took to it, maybe not for the first few days, but after a while you seemed more at home there than I did.

Sean I couldn't get out of the place fast enough!

The Lord Got to know the ins and outs; who to touch for a smoke . . . the price of a pint.

Sean (*grabs Lord and pushes him to ground*) That's a lie, d'you hear, a lie!

The Lord gets up. He laughs at Sean.

I hated the bloody kip! The smell, the people . . . I couldn't stand it, not like you. You blend in in there, part of the furniture. You'd sleep on a pile of shite if you had to!

The Lord You think I like the way it is . . . think I like roaming the streets as if I was born there . . . raised there?

Sean Why don't you get out of it then, why don't you pick up whatever pieces you've left and get out of it?

The Lord Living in a hostel mightn't be much to you, parking cars mightn't be much . . . mightn't be much to anyone. But it's a life . . . the only one I have.

Sean You just want me to go back there, that's all, go back and get sucked in like you did!

The Lord (*shouts at him*) I had a life before this, d'you hear me . . . a life better than yours! A life better than anyone in there! A house! A car! You name it bucko and it was on my shelf!

Sean sits down takes out a bottle of beer and opens it. He drinks it back in one go. He takes another out and opens it.

Sean I'm just . . . just not able for this carry on, wasn't made for this carry on! (*Gets up and walks around.*)

The Lord Who is? You think this is a career move!

In the distance the sounds of the kids playing.

I thought at this age I'd be sitting at home taking it easy . . . playing with me, me . . . (*Looks to where the kids were jeering them.*) . . . grandchildren.

Sean Have you any –

The Lord How could I have any grandchildren?

Sean I meant cigarettes.

The Lord (*gives him a cigarette. Pause*) An hour . . . that's how much I missed them by . . . one poxy hour.

Sean Who?

The Lord If I'd've left on time I'd've been back in time to . . . to . . . We were playing that gig in Wicklow, a wedding. I'd promised her I'd drive straight home after it. (*Pause.*) This eegit, the big thick muckah that got married, came backstage for a photo with the band, then wanted to buy us a drink. (*Pause.*) Just one drink, that was all I said I'd have . . . just the one. Two hours went by before I looked at me watch. (*Pause.*) I was pissed drunk. The weather was bitter that night . . . black ice everywhere on the road. (*Pause.*) She used to light the gas fire before going to bed to heat the house for me after the long drive back from the gigs. (*Long pause.*) I remember the fire engines passing me at Islandbridge, three of them. I was stopped at the lights at Knockmaroon hill and could see flames leaping up into the sky, clouds of black smoke and sparks bursting up into the air. (*Pause.*) The flashing lights of the ambulance and fire engines had me dizzy as I drove up to the house. A Guard stopped me and told me there was no traffic being let through. (*Pause.*) He smelt the drink off me . . . kept me in the car while a breathalyser was got. When I got out of the car to give him me name and address I saw a roof blazing . . . our roof. All the neighbours were out with blankets over their shoulders. 'You drunken bastard', I heard someone shout. (*Pause.*) One of the kids . . . must've been Nora, left a teddy bear near the fire. 'Teddy Johnson', that's what she called him. (*Pause.*) That's what they said was the cause of it. (*Takes out the photos and looks at them.*) Nothing left of them but ashes.

Sean Jesus man! You . . . you never told –

The Lord I've played that gig in me head a million times . . . each time that thick asks us in for a drink I smash his head in . . . I make it home just in time.

Sean I . . . I – (*Unable to speak anymore.*)

The Lord Yeah, like everyone else, you thought it was the drink? (*Pause.*) After that day I lost heart. When you lose that . . . (*Pause.*) it's all over.

Sean (*blesses himself*) God bless their little souls.

The Lord Two of the kids, Colm and Mary. They . . . they must've been holding each other while the fire raged. That's how they found them . . . in each other's arms . . . welded together. (*Pause.*) They buried them that way . . . wrapped in each other's arms.

Sean Your wife too?

The Lord All buried under a big granite boulder in Palmerstown.

Sean If I'd've known – I didn't mean –

The Lord All the men in that hostel . . . there's lives behind them beards, boy, tragedies under them overcoats.

Sean (*sinks into a chair*) And I thought I'd troubles?

The Lord The bastard Guard charged me with drunken driving. Everyone turned on me . . . said if I'd've been home it wouldn't've happened.

Sean There was no one you could go to . . . relations?

The Lord Wasn't even given a sofa to sleep on. That's how I first stayed in the hostel . . . got a flat a few weeks later, tried to pick up the pieces . . . but I drifted back.

Sean Would you not try and get a little flat of your own again? Get out of that place and get back on your feet.

The Lord Oh I've tried, God knows I've tried. I thought this way out.

Sean You don't know Ang.

The Lord A fella has to try.

Sean An oul flat of your own and you'd be grand.

The Lord Wait till you try and get a month's rent in advance . . . and a deposit.

Sean No! You gave in . . . but I won't.

> *The Lord picks up a plastic bucket and starts tapping a rhythm on it.*

No sir! I'll get us back up and running. (*Gestures around him.*) This lot . . . a slip up, that's all. A rough patch, we all get them. But you watch, I'll have us back up there, you watch.

The Lord Your mate, what's his name?

Sean What mate?

The Lord The 'restaurateur'.

Sean (*angry*) He just doesn't remember me, that's all.

The Lord The Cajun Hall! Did you ever hear the likes?

Sean Sure how could he, I haven't spoken to him in years.

The Lord I wouldn't let any one man handle me out of a building the way he did.

Sean (*tries to salvage some pride*) He's not me only mate! See, I've got respect in this game, Lord, reputation. You know I once prepared a banquet for Jack Dempsey and Movita. Called me out and got the guests to applaud the meal. Then gave me a signed photo of him . . . 'To Sean, thanks for a wonderful meal . . . Jack.' The boss hung it up on the restaurant wall with all the other photographs for all to see. You wait . . . you wait and see. I'm a new man in a suit, me. You watch . . . when I ring me other buddy, Harry O'Connor! (*Claps his hands.*) 'Sean, me oul flower' he'll say, '. . . long time no see!' He'll have me in his kitchen the next day, mark my words.

The Lord Would that be the same fella that wouldn't even rec you in Nassau Street last week?

Sean I was on the other side of the road.

The Lord laughs.

Sean (*turns away*) Like I said . . . new man in a suit, me.

The Lord You stick by me Sean. Cars . . . they'll see us right.

Sean I'll hit every restaurant and hotel in the city . . . I'll get us back up, have us the way we were. Three meals a day and a good suit for Sunday! With my references I'll march in anywhere. They're like your photos . . . proof! Proof that you worked, that you were something.

The Lord There's no road back.

Sean There is boy . . . and I'll find it.

The Lord I've walked every street and alley in this city looking for one . . . all you find are closed doors.

Sean With references like mine there'll be no closed – (*Pause.*) No!

The Lord What now?

Sean (*starts to rummage in the debris*) A brown envelope . . . look for a brown envelope! (*Panic.*)

The Lord A what?

Sean Everything's in that envelope . . . everything I was . . . I am!

The Lord What are you on about?

Sean Me references! Look for them. (*Sean finds the envelope. Pause. He lifts up a soggy envelope, torn and battered. He takes out the sodden references.*) Sweet Jesus!

The Lord Are they all ruined?

Sean That's it now. (*Falls back into a chair.*)

The Lord Maybe you can get them . . . (*pause*) . . . restored?

Sean What proof have I now? What's there to tell them the man I was?

The Lord Pieces of paper, Sean, that's all they are.

Sean (*page by page he throws them away*) The old Jury's in Dame Street . . . 1968. The Green Rooster . . . 1972. The Hibernian Hotel . . . '74. (*Throws the rest away.*)

The Lord (*lifts up Sean*) Come on Sean . . . before it gets dark.

Sean (*shouts up to flat*) Think you can do that with a man's life!

The Lord We'll come back in the morning and get the rest of it.

Sean (*shouts*) I'm not going down without a fight, d'yous hear! (*Runs off.*)

The Lord Sean! For God's sake Sean, don't go up there!

> *The sound of a stolen car in the distance. It gets closer. The lights of the car blind The Lord. The car revs up as if it were about to run him over. Dazzled with the lights he backs away. It screeches off in another direction leaving the Lord drained.*
> *Angela enters from behind. She is distressed.*

Angela You . . . you're bad luck you! What are you doing here?

The Lord Mrs! What's happened, are you alright?

Angela Where's Sean?

The Lord Is the youngfella not with you?

Angela Look at it . . . all me furniture, smashed to bits.

The Lord What happened Angela?

Angela The sofa, the curtains . . . all ruined.

The Lord (*calls out*) Sean! Sean, she's here!

Angela Where is he . . . is he alright? (*Calls.*) Sean!

The Lord He's gone up to the flat.

Angela No! Get him back . . . the bastards! They'll murder him!

The Lord (*calls*) Sean, will you come down!

Angela Where did he go on me? Why did he leave me like that? (*Pause.*) What are we going to do? We've nowhere for the night.

148

Sean Ang . . . Angela is that you? What happened, what did they do?

Angela (*runs to him and beats him*) You bastard you! You bastard! Why did you leave me like that?

Sean Did they harm you love, did they hurt you?

Angela Why did you run off on me? (*Breaks down.*)

Sean hugs her.

Sean I'm sorry pet, I'm sorry.

Angela You were only two minutes gone when they came.

The Lord Who did it?

Angela A family from the other block. They said the flat was for somebody else . . . one of their own, a daughter or something.

Sean Why did you open the door to the bastards!

Angela Open the door! They kicked it in on top of me. They must've been waiting for you to go. (*Snaps at him.*) Why, Sean, why did you leave me on me own to face all that! (*Pause.*) The bastards! They kicked the door in on me and dragged me out. (*Runs and beats him.*) Why did you go Sean, why did you leave me?

Sean Declan! Where's Declan? (*Picks up a piece of wood.*) Let's see them drag me out by the hair.

Angela (*drags him back*) There's a gang of them.

Sean Are you right Lord?

The Lord Are you not listening to the woman? A gang!

Angela (*walks among the debris*) What are we going to do with it all?

Sean (*throws wood away*) And you think I have any

answers? (*Pause. Picks up a bit of his references.*) Me
references. (*Throws them up in the air.*)

Angela The job! Did you ring the job?

Sean Won't have much of chance with them ruined, will I?

Angela I bet he was glad to hear from you, what? Bet you
he –

Sean (*overlaps Angela*) He threw me out.

Angela . . . said start Monday!

Sean Him and a waiter.

Angela I told you he'd – (*Stops.*) What did you say?

Sean I thought he was joking. 'It's me Terry . . . Sean . . .
Sean Farrell.'

Angela You went? Went like that?

Sean I kept waiting for him to break into his laugh . . . but
he just looked at me, stared.

Angela You waltzed in like a tramp and expected the man
to entertain you?

Sean I'm still something you know!

Angela No Sean, say you got a job!

Sean In front of everybody . . . marched me out.

Angela No, Sean, no, you didn't!

Sean Look at the cut of me . . . I couldn't get arrested!

Angela (*pause. She starts to cough*) Water . . . I need a
drink of water. (*Takes some tablets from her bag.*)

The Lord There's none . . . only this. (*A bottle of beer.
Hands it to her.*)

Sean Least we won't have to give the corpo the money now.

Angela takes the tablets with the beer. Walks over to some debris. Lights up a smoke. Kicks what's left of the picture.

Angela The curse of jaysus on that picture!

The Lord starts to drum at a bucket.

Sean You did get it, didn't you?

Angela (*looks at him*) I never mean to do it . . . you all know that. I never mean to do it.

Sean The loan . . . did you get it?

Angela If only I hadn't seen the paper . . . but it was staring me in the face.

Sean Listen to me! Have you got the money? I have it all planned. A B&B, look for that phone book. (*Starts looking.*)

Angela This big headline . . . it jumped right out of me. I was sitting behind this man on the bus . . . he had the paper open. '*A picture of paradise*'.

Sean What she on about? (*Finds phone book.*)

Angela I couldn't help it, I tried to ignore it, but it wouldn't go away. I kept thinking of the wedding present . . . the picture . . . our picture. I thought it was an omen . . . a good luck sign.

Sean Angela!

Angela I looked up the paper and studied its form. A dead cert. (*Sits down.*) We would've been made for life.

Sean You didn't do it (*quietly*) . . . you didn't spend it? Say you didn't do it . . .

Angela We could've lived like kings.

Sean No! No Ang! (*Grabs her handbag.*) Where is it! Where's the money?

Angela He was coming nowhere then all of a sudden his white nose bobbing up out of the group . . . he passed one horse, the jockey lashed the whip into him . . . he passed another, then another, two fences to go and he passed three more! (*Stands up.*) Just one more horse between him and the winning post. The jockey crouched down, they were neck and neck. (*Starts to whip an imaginary horse.*) He lashed out with the whip! It drew blood, I'd swear it, he belted him so hard. The roars in the bookies . . . they could hear us in Chepstow. The two of them charging away for the finishing line. (*Pause.*) Then he did it . . . he took the lead and romped passed the post.

Sean (*throws her bag away*) Sweet Jesus!

Angela When he passed that line all our troubles were over. 8 to 1. Two hundred pound I'd on him . . . 16 hundred pounds. (*Laughs.*) I had it spent in me mind. Carpet for all the rooms, a new telly, fridge, I'd dress meself in Arnotts . . . the boys too. A big heavy coat each for the winter. (*Pause.*) I was on me way over to hand in me slip when I heard it on the intercom.

Sean (*Shakes her*) Did you do it all, did you do it all?

Angela Stewards' inquiry. Illegal use of the whip.

Sean How much have you left?

Angela I had to try and win it back . . . didn't I . . . had to stay? But I couldn't go . . . couldn't get out. I kept thinking the next one . . . the next race I'd win it all back.

Sean (*shakes her*) Is there anything left!

The Lord Stop it man, you're hurting her.

Sean pushes her to the ground. She is crying.

Sean Forty-five pounds a week to some moneylender and not even a roof over our heads!

Angela He's not getting a penny back of his loan! Let him come looking for me too . . . he won't find me up there. (*Nods towards flat.*)

The Lord Look . . . I'll give it a try. There has to be another empty flat round here, so what if it's burnt out, can't you shove all this stuff into it for the night?

A pause, they look at him. He runs off.

Sean And me thinking there wasn't any lower you could drag us down and you come up with a trump card. Well you wanted paradise girl . . . here it is!

Angela We would've been rich, love . . . made for life.

Sean Just this once we had a chance . . . a real chance, and what do you do?

Angela I'll make it back . . . make every penny of it back, you watch. (*Gets up.*)

Sean We're always in sight of the finishing post and bang! You pull another trick out of the bag! (*Pause. Kicks bits of the debris.*)

Angela There's another moneylender in Bluebell . . . I can go to him on Monday.

Sean (*starts to ramble*) I thought with the money we could book into a B&B for the night. (*Starts to pack a few things.*) Then rent a flat in town till we got things straightened out. Now . . . it's back to square one.

Angela (*grabs him*) Me sister's . . . we'll go to Rita's.

Sean You and Declan, you're alright . . .

Angela One more night won't kill you.

Sean I'm not going . . . I'm not going back there.

Angela And tomorrow . . . tomorrow we'll go into the corpo.

Sean What the use? You said there's a six months' waiting list, didn't you?

Declan enters. He stands and looks at them.

Declan Six months! Nine months! I don't think she knows herself. Do you Ma?

Sean Declan . . . we're gone son, finished.

Declan You don't know the half of it!

Sean She's after gambling every penny on a horse!

Declan It gets better. I don't suppose you know anything about this? (*Shows a letter to Angela.*)

Sean A picture of poxy paradise.

Angela No, Declan, no! (*Tries to take letter.*)

Sean What's that?

Declan Me Ma's great at hiding things . . . aren't you?

Angela Tear it up!

Declan When I came back and found all this I got a bus straight into Wood Quay . . . tried to stop her handing over the money to the corpo before it was too late. (*Pause.*) You weren't down there for even four minutes yesterday, last week or any other day!

Angela Please Declan, you don't understand.

Declan They knew you alright . . . I'll give you that much. In fact they sent you a letter two weeks ago, to Rita's.

Angela We'd never've managed out there Sean!

Sean What letter?

Angela I thought if I'd've said no that they'd give us somewhere else . . . somewhere near home!

Declan Such a row I had in there. I said me mother's bad . . . but she'd never do a thing like that. (*Pause.*) So he went off and got me a photocopy.

Angela We couldn't move out there son! You wouldn't like it . . . none of us would.

Sean Let me see that! (*Takes letter. Reads it.*)

Angela A kip, that's all out there is!

Declan A six-month waiting list!

Sean Jesus Christ, Angela!

Declan They offered us a house two weeks ago.

Angela (*snaps back*) They offered us a shack!

Declan A second chance!

Angela In Ballyobair? Have you any idea what Ballyobair's like?

Declan A real chance!

Angela Tallaght, Sean. Did you ever hear the likes?

Sean A new home . . . they offered us a house and you turned it down?

Angela The bloody Famine started in Tallaght!

Declan A new beginning.

Angela You always refuse the first offer, everyone knows that!

Declan We could've made a fresh start out there, put everything behind us.

Angela Stuck out on the side of the Wicklow mountains, that's not a start, it's an end.

Declan But you never told us . . . never gave us a chance.

Angela One mistake, that's all, one mistake and we're to turn into the Beverly Hillbillies.

Declan And now look at us . . . The Flintstones!

Angela How was your father supposed to look for work stuck out there . . . how were both of yous? It'd cost yous a fortune in bus fare if yous got a job, cost us all a fortune in bus fare.

Declan We didn't have to go through all this, squatting, moneylending. All along there was a house waiting for us.

Angela If you want to go out to Tallaght, good luck. (*Throws some coins at him from her pocket.*) There's your bus fare.

Declan It's wasn't as if it was the jungle!

Angela Who would we know out there, what? We'd be strangers . . . out on our own!

Declan Like now?

Angela You don't understand . . . I thought if I turned it down they'd offer us somewhere else . . . somewhere where we knew.

Sean A home Ang . . . you turned a home down!

Angela But Sean –

Declan Who cared how far away it was? Who cared what it was?

Angela We're still in one piece aren't we, still got our heads above water!

Declan You call this one piece?

Sean There's no getting up from this.

Angela We have Rita's!

Declan A sofa and a few cushions on the floor?

The Lord Listen, I think I'd better go and leave yous to it.

Declan Well I won't be putting up with it anymore.

Angela D'you know what . . . do you? It's not men I have around me but monkeys! Not an ounce of guts between yous! I've held this family together for nearly thirty years.

   Declan laughs.

Yes, thirty years with no help from anyone.

Declan Put on another record.

Angela You, you long streak of misery! You've been a weight around my neck from the day I conceived you! And if it wasn't for that drunken bastard there that wouldn't've happened!

Sean Shut up, shut up you vulgar bitch!

Angela Not a week married and me life was over!

Sean You wanted a child.

Angela But not nine months after I married!

Sean Don't talk like that in front of him.

Angela Maybe after two years . . . three even, maybe then start a family. But I wanted to enjoy me bit of freedom away from home.

Sean I did you a favour taking you out that house.

Angela We could've gone Sean . . . on our two wages . . . we could've saved and seen paradise! We could've done lots of things . . . but no. One drunken night and wallop!

Sean I gave you the life of Reilly.

Angela The life of Mother Reilly maybe! When all the families on the street were off to Blackpool or Courtown what did we get?

Sean Sure wasn't everything you needed in Dublin, hah?

Angela The shame of it. Every summer holiday I waited, hoping, wishing you'd come home from work and tell us to pack.

Sean Break your back working just so you could throw all your money away on 'Kiss-me-quick' hats and candy floss!

Angela You'd no mention of taking me to paradise!

Sean Hang on to his money, that's what the wise man does.

Angela So in the end I found me own.

Sean (*glares at her*) Hell, that's what you found!

Angela (*laughs*) I only went in to get out of the rain. I was waiting for a bus one day, a 78a came and it was full, not another one for twenty minutes. (*Pause.*) You should've seen it . . . lights flashing, bells ringing and the clink . . . the clink of coins belting out onto the silver bowl when someone would hit a jackpot. (*Pause.*) I got two pounds' worth of tenpences and picked a machine. I'd only put three coins in when I won. Three bells! A fiver. (*Laughs.*) I think ten 78s had gone by the time I remembered where I was. (*Pause.*) Seventeen pounds I had in the pile of coins in front of me. I carried them over to the till in me jumper.

Sean One win, that's all, one lucky strike and you were had for life!

Angela First thing the next day I was back in there.
Brought back me winnings. That day was better than the
first. Was playing two machines at a time . . . the bandit on
the left and a poker machine on the right. I couldn't get the
money in quick enough! (*Laughs*.) Three bars . . . no one
ever got three bars on that machine a woman said . . . well
I did. It cost me nine pounds but when they came up the
coins gushed out, they came out that fast that some of
them spilt out over the edge and across the floor . . . I'd
bend down to pick them up only to have more spilling over
the edge and rolling all over the place. (*Pause*.) Did you
ever see fifty pounds in ten-pence pieces? Did you ever run
your hands through a mountain of money that high? There
was men and women there that stopped playing just to
look at me! I was a hero, a champion! It was like I'd
broken in a wild horse that others had tried before me and
failed. (*Laughs*.) I was clapped on the back, me hands
shook, people were called from the other end of the hall to
look at the machine with its three bars sitting across the
middle line. I felt like one of them hunters standing over a
dead lion in the jungle!

Sean (*sarcastic*) Oh weren't you the great woman!

Angela There was no stopping me after that day. Horses,
dogs . . . two drops of rain falling, I couldn't lose.

Sean Then all your luck ran out and left you high and dry
and us with you!

Angela Who could have luck married to a whinger like
you! I'm surrounded by . . . apes, monkey boys. I'll tell you
one thing Sean Farrell, I may have brought us down but I
did it to try and keep us up!

    Declan starts to pack some clothes.

What are you doing?

Declan You always said I was too old to be tied to your apron strings.

Sean Your interview, did you get it?

Declan Well I won't be under your feet any more!

Sean They didn't turn you down?

Declan Turn me down? Well after I walked in looking like Coco the jaysus Clown I had to sit with over forty people. All in suits, all with their CVs, their . . . their certificates, references . . . all willing to cut off their right hand for a place! And what had I got, what was my trump card? (*Throws the bit of paper he had earlier up into the air.*) Nothing. I've no leaving cert . . . no inter cert!

Sean But what matter is that? Haven't you the money to pay your way?

Declan For all it's worth! Places were limited, they said. So they were giving them out in descending order . . . with the apes last . . . they wanted to make sure they'd no dunces in the class!

Sean But your money's as good as anyone else's!

Declan (*shouts at Angela*) Six months, Ma, six months was all I'd left at school.

Sean The money! Then you've still got the money son?

Declan You burst into the class and dragged me out . . . me books still open on the desk. Next morning I was handed me bus fare and a corned beef lunch.

Sean Three hundred pounds, was it? Sure we're sound, we're made!

Declan Brother Michael even came to the house two days later . . . showed you me exam results.

Angela A chance of a job . . . what was I supposed to do?

Sean Where's that phone book gone to?

Declan Washing plates in a kitchen! That's what you call a job?

Angela You start at the bottom, everyone starts at the bottom!

Sean (*starts looking through book*) Light a match Lord, I can't see.

Angela You would've moved up the ladder if you stuck at it!

Declan To what . . . sweeping the floor?

Angela You made a show of your father doing that . . . he begged his boss to give you that job!

Declan Like I begged you to keep me on at school? (*Packs some clothes.*)

Sean (*rips a page out*) Here we go . . . one down in Parkgate Street . . . we're made. (*Sees Declan packing clothes.*) There should be a big bag under that pile somewhere. Stuff me and your mother's clothes into it.

Declan I'm going Da.

Sean Try and fit as much as you can into it. With a bit of luck there'll be something left here for us to collect in the morning.

Angela Going where?

Declan I rang me mate after all.

Sean Rang who?

Declan Noel Mills . . . the fella whose brother's running a pub. I'm going to be a barman.

Angela (*laughs*) Barman! You couldn't pull a muscle!

Declan The money for the computer course'll do me to get set up in Belgium.

Sean Belgium? What's he talking about?

Declan I'm getting out Da . . . while I can.

Angela Belgium . . . you'd get lost in Henry Street?

Sean You . . . you're running out on us. To . . . to Belgium?

Declan (*takes out an airline ticket*) Row 16, seat d, eight-thirty flight to Brussels. I've just booked it.

Sean Hold on Declan . . . your money, we need your money!

Declan So she can blow it on something else? Look around Ma. . . maybe there's something you can bet on. Maybe there's two flies buzzing around this pile of shite!

Angela Go on . . . leave the sinking ship.

Sean You can't run off Dec . . . you can't! The money you had for the course . . . lend it to us. Just for the night son, just till we get on our feet!

Declan Da . . . please.

Sean But you have to son, you can't turn your back on us.

Declan (*pause*) I'm sorry.

Sean Jesus Christ Declan, look at us, we're on our last legs . . . you've got to help us.

Declan D'you ever hear that story, the one about an experiment with two monkeys, a mother and her baby? A man at the interview told it to us today, he wanted to know which kind of monkey were we.

Angela What's he shiting about now?

Declan They put the two chimps into this glass room with a metal floor and began to heat the floor. Slowly they raised the temperature and the monkey, holding its little baby, began to lift one foot up to give it a break from the hot floor. They raised the heat up more until the monkey was dancing from foot to foot. (*Pause.*) Then they raised it up again, it was now so hot that the monkey began to scream. It couldn't take it any more so it placed its baby on the floor and stood on it, protected itself from the metal floor. Self preservation . . . that's what they were trying to explore, how far would an animal go to save itself, what would it sacrifice just so it could survive. You'd never think they'd ask you questions like that at interviews, would you?

Angela (*too proud to beg him to stay*) Go on, shag off to wherever you're going, you and your stupid monkeys. We'll manage without you!

Sean Declan, no!

Declan walks away. Sean grabs him back. Falls to his knees.

Declan Please Da, don't, let me go.

Sean I'll do anything, son, anything not to go back there!

Declan (*breaks free*) Let go of me, will you!

Angela (*almost about to give in*) You'll be back . . . a week, that's all I'll give him . . . a week, and you'll come crawling back, crying for me to take you in!

Sean I'm on me knees to you son . . . on me knees!

Declan (*holding back tears*) I'm sorry Da . . . I'm sorry.

Sean Angela . . . do something!

Angela (*gives in*) Declan! We can still take the house

Declan . . . on Monday. Could tell them we didn't get the letter until today. (*Runs after him.*) It was sent to your sister's and she forgot to give it to me! It's not too late, it's never too late . . . one more gamble boys . . . the last one. (*Stops. Calls louder.*) If they don't give us the house then they'll have to give us somewhere. Wherever they give us we'll take it. (*Pause. Stares after him.*)

Declan Like I said . . . if we stick together, we sink together. (*He walks off.*)

> *Angela stares into the darkness. Sean lights a cigarette. There is the sound of a stolen car braking in the distance.*
> *The Lord returns. Badly shaken. He is wet all over.*

Sean Well . . .?

The Lord Bastards! They . . . they threw it over a balcony at me . . . piss!

Sean No flats empty?

The Lord No. Eh . . . I suppose we should . . . we should be getting to work?

Sean Work! You want me to park cars after this?

The Lord If we don't work tonight what'll we do for money? (*Takes off his coat and shakes the wet off.*)

Angela Come on. Start gathering it up.

Sean You can gather it up yourself.

Angela I'll start with the clothes you –

Sean Are you deaf!

Angela When that's done I'll go to Rita's and you can go –

Sean It's that easy, isn't it? I just disappear off.

Angela One night, that's all.

Sean And what about tomorrow night, and the next?

Angela Look, you've no choice.

Sean Have I not?

Angela And where else are you going to run off to?

Sean I'm not going down . . . (*Points to The Lord.*) I'm not going down that road! Not going under! (*Starts to back away as if terrified by the sight of The Lord.*) I'm going home!

Angela What do you mean, home?

Sean That shed is mine!

Angela What?

Sean Built that shed with me own hands.

The Lord What's he on about?

Sean (*grabs The Lord*) They can throw me out of me house . . . but not the shed.

The Lord Are you all right man?

Angela You can't go back to the house!

Sean I bought them bricks, that wood . . . put them all together!

Angela Will you get a grip man!

Sean They'll have a heart . . . somebody has to have a heart.

The Lord Sean, you'll be arrested!

Sean They won't even know I'm there. In and out over the back wall.

Angela Get back here you, d'you hear me!

Sean I'm tired . . . I have to sleep. (*He pauses for a moment then runs off.*)

Angela Sean! Sean come back! (*Runs after him. Then stops.*) Get him back, quick, before he gets into trouble.

The Lord Jesus man, have you lost your mind?

Angela Sean . . . for God's sake, Sean!

The Lord (*calls*) Our patch . . . we'll lose our patch! If we lose that Sean . . .

> Silence. Angela watches him go. She wraps a blanket round her shoulders.

Will you not go after and get him Mrs?

Angela Let them go, the pair of them. Let them see what it's like with no one to mother them.

The Lord (*looking after Sean*) He doesn't understand . . . no patch and you're finished!

Angela (*pause. She takes out her tablets*) Give me a drink.

The Lord (*calls*) Our patch Sean . . . what about our patch, our way back!

Angela Give me a drink I said, something, anything! (*Starts looking.*)

The Lord (*lower*) If we lose that Sean . . .

Angela (*shakes him*) More, there must be more, must be more beer!

The Lord Not a drop left.

Angela Buy some . . . run across to the pub.

The Lord Haven't a tosser.

Angela You must have something.

The Lord (*takes out a wine bottle*) There's always the oul grape.

Angela Get that away from me!

The Lord There's grand heat in wine.

Angela (*lifts up some bottles to drain*) There must be a drop somewhere!

The Lord (*takes a mouthful*) Agh, that's the man. The heat won't be long getting into me now.

Angela searches her pocket. Nothing there. The Lord gets on his knees and starts to pick up the coins Angela threw at Declan. Angela snaps them off him.

Angela Another fifty pence, that's all . . . ten bob and I've enough for a can!

The Lord picks up the plastic bucket again. He starts to drum slowly at it with a wooden spoon.

The Lord Get up out of that and have a drop!

Angela You must have a few pence on you!

The Lord That's my line.

Angela I'm parched. (*Picks up some cans and drains them.*)

The Lord A drop of sweetness. (*Pours some down his throat.*)

Angela (*stares at him, wipes her mouth*) A drop wouldn't kill me, hah, just to warm me up?

The Lord You'll be like an oven soon . . . be roasting.

Angela Just for the cold, mind you.

The Lord That's the boy for the cold alright.

The Lord walks over to Angela. He lifts her head back

*and pours some wine into her mouth. She drinks it. The
Lord takes some more. Angela laughs and pulls his hand
with the bottle back. He pours it into her mouth again.
Angela grabs the bottle of wine and starts to drink. She
coughs and splutters, it dribbles down her chin, she
wipes her mouth then drinks again. She stops. Looks at
The Lord and laughs nervously.*

*In the distance we hear the sound of the stolen car
again. Screeching and hand-braking. As the car turns,
the light from headlamps tears across the stage.*

The Lord We'd better get out of here soon.

Angela Tomorrow! Tomorrow I'll go back into them,
explain it all.

*The Lord goes back to the basin. The drumming gets
faster and faster. Angela coughs again.*

The Lord Slowly girl, slowly, that's it girl . . . go on, lower
it back. Feel the heat now?

The wine dribbles down Angela's body. The Lord yelps.

Angela They'll give us the house when I tell them the
story, won't they Lord? They'll give us another chance!

The Lord They'll give you whatever you want.

Angela Everything'll be alright then.

The Lord (*yelps*) I never lost it, what? I never lost the oul
drumming!

*Angela is more comfortable with the wine now. The
Lord laughs.*

Angela Once we get a roof over our heads we'll be on the
pig's back!

*He drums with one hand and swipes the bottle and takes
a slug.*

Angela swipes it back. She has the bottle pointing to the sky as she drinks with a ferocious thirst.

The Lord That's it . . . throw her back, all the way! Now you're learning! Yee haa!!! You're on the pig's back now, girl . . . on the pig's back now!

The Lord is away in a trance, playing on the bucket. The rhythm builds up and up until it is about to explode. Silence. Lights out.

Afterword

It's a common sight everywhere nowadays. The young man on the corner selling *The Big Issue*; the drunk, tattered and torn, waltzing up and down the street, a can in one hand, the other aimed at your face; the guy with an old bus man's cap, a size too big sitting on his head, and a newspaper rolled up, waving you forward to a parking space in an alley. They have become such a common sight that they are almost part of the furniture of the city. Who are these people? Where do they come from? They couldn't always have been like this, could they? Surely they had a life, a family, kids maybe, a job, a home, a flat? But somehow they lost it all. They lost their footing and fell just outside the picture and have remained there, caught in a web, unable to climb back and continue on the journey with the rest of us. Some may have taken that step intentionally, but the play is about those who didn't. It's a look at some of these people just before the final fall into the gutter, from where the road back is a million miles longer than the fall.

The question, if indeed plays are to pose questions, is: could a fall like this happen to any of us? And the answer is probably no, which is the same answer any unfortunates on the street would give if asked the same question a year or so before their fall. The play tries to show the lives behind one of the many faces now populating the alleys and doorways of our cities. A son, caught between finding a life of his own and trying to save what's left of his mother and father's; a down-and-out trying to get back on the roundabout; a man, looking at himself withering away, and trying hard to hold on to the past; and a mother, left with the burden of trying to hold everything together.

As all this is going on Dublin is changing. It is almost unrecognizable from the city it was five years ago. The Quays, once one of the city's biggest embarrassments, seems to sprout a new apartment block every week, old dead streets have come alive with fashionable cafés, restaurants and bars. With the end of the century around the corner, Dublin is hurtling towards it in fourth gear. Along this new expansion something has to give way. There will be a price to pay for this change, the natives are getting restless, finding themselves being pushed out further into the suburbs, their ancient corporation flats being revamped and sold off to become part of 'The Muesli Belt'. The *new* Dubliner, stretched out in his or her pad, might know how to order a smoked cod and chips in Burdock's or tell you where Capel Street is, but bubbles burst and gravy trains run out of gravy . . . but that's another play.

Jimmy Murphy
Dublin, 1995

GOOD EVENING, MR COLLINS

Tom Mac Intyre

Characters

Michael Collins
Moya
Kitty Kiernan
Hazel (Lady Lavery)
Dev (Éamon de Valera)
Squad Man A
The Captain
Arthur Griffith
Wee Johnny Lavery
plus assorted extras

The piece is for eight actors, one of them female.

Setting
Minimalist, essentials to be conveyed by lighting and
soundtrack. These basics: a piano, a table, a few chairs, a
chaise-longue.

Good Evening, Mr Collins was first performed at the Abbey Theatre, Dublin, on 5 October 1995 with the following cast:

Michael Collins Brian F. O'Byrne
Moya/Kitty Kiernan/Hazel Lavery Karen Ardiff
De Valera Pat Kinevane
Cathal Brugha/British Intelligence Officer/Arthur Griffith/Wee Johnny Lavery Mal Whyte
Shaw/Captain Simpson Sean O'Neill
McKee/Squad Man Sean Campion
Squad Man/Irregular Charlie Bonner
Squad Man/Irregular Tim Ruddy
Musician Conor Guilfoyle

Directed by Kathy McArdle
Designed by Barbara Bradshaw
Lighting by Nick McCall

Act One

SCENE ONE: PROLOGUE

Dev *tours the auditorium, declaring in subdued but firm tones:* 'The good news is: The majority has no rights whatsoever – none. Ponder that. Ponder that now . . .' *Dev now into the playing area. He pauses, allows a smile for the house.*

Dev Welcome . . . (*and exit Dev*).

> **Moya** *on, thirty-plus, cigarette-holder, smoking. She settles on a* chaise-longue.

Moya First time I've followed a man across a sea. A small sea – but still, the waves . . .

> **Collins** *on, as if he owned the place. Makes straight for the drinks cabinet, and he's busy fixing drinks for both.*

How'd you get in?

Collins Let myself in – being badly brought up.

Moya Out there long?

Collins A bit. Spotted a detective on the way. (*Beat.*) Sit down, won't you – and you in your own house?

Moya (*demurs*) In due course, Michael . . .

Collins You're bigger stannin' . . . What in God's name are you doing in this country, Moya Lewellyn-Davies?

Moya London bored me. I took leave. Irish leave. Besides, I wished to assist in the events here shaping.

Collins Taking shape.

They lift glasses to toast.

Collins The Republic –

Moya The Republic –

Collins, half-sitting on a table mid-stage, takes up a textbook she's been studying.

Collins *Tá mé . . . Tá tú . . . Tá sí . . .* Ever hear of the answer Good Queen Bess got when she asked for an example of the strange language spoken by her savage subjects westward – *D'ith damh dubh ubh amh ar neamh* – A black bull ate a raw egg in heaven . . .

Moya The view from Whitehall.

Collins flipping pages from textbook.

Collins Here's one for you: *Tá sí mar tá sí agus níl sí gan locht* – translate –

Moya She is as she is –

Both – and she's not without fault.

Collins (*quizmaster*) *Bocht*?

Moya Poor –

Collins *Nocht*?

Moya Bare –

Collins *Tocht*?

Moya puzzled.

A class of a catch at the heart – from an access of feeling . . .

Moya You experience that often? *Tocht*?

Collins Far too busy.

Moya Have a care . . .

Collins strolls, more and more relaxed.

And the firm – 'Irish Products – Limited'?

Collins I'm always hopeful.

Moya Use this place as you will.

Collins I aim to. Furry Park . . . 'Furry' . . . Fine name, fine holding.

Moya It attracted me instantly.

Collins The holding? The name?

Moya Both.

Sexual buzz. They view each other, warming to it.

Collins That bastard –

Moya What bastard?

Collins *D'ith damh dubh ubh amh ar neamh* – I'd love to drive a shovel up his arse.

Moya Are you vengeful, Mr Collins?

Collins Yes – but for a reason. (*Parading now.*) I need room. I haven't enough room. As matters stand. And to make enough room, I may have to exercise vengeance. So I've been –

Moya – nursing it –

Collins That's right – for quite some time – and, at the moment, it's nearing what they call 'match fit' . . . (*Beat.*) 'Our revenge will be the laughter of our children' – somebody wrote.

Moya Can you see your children?

Collins (*feckless*) No.

The two kiss. She takes off his tie.

Moya Now you're coming out of yourself –

Collins Into myself –

Moya And – not wishing to rush you –

Collins I can't be rushed –

Moya I know –

Collins Nothing if not methodical –

Moya As befits a book-keeper –

Collins And qualified accountant –

Moya It's just that I'd like to show you the house . . .

Collins (*teasing*) Didn't you show it to me the last day?

Moya Not everything. I'd never be that gauche.

Collins More to be seen?

Moya (*exiting*) A great deal more . . .

SCENE TWO

Heavy winter light . . . Church bells.

Collins I feel for a spy as I would for a dangerous reptile.
No crime in detecting and destroying their like. For too
long they've had immunity. That was our defeat. Not any
longer. They have killed without trial. We pay them back
in their own coin.

 Squad Man A *appears* –

SMA Aimes and Bennet lined up in the hall and shot.
Saunders was half-way through a window. We plugged the
bastard. (*Exits.*)

Squad Man B *appears –*

SMB Our four asleep, two with women. By firing-squad in the hall. Felt sorry for them. Prayed for them at Mass. (*Exits.*)

Squad Man C *appears –*

SMC We had four to get. Shot one in his pyjamas out the back garden. Other three lined up on the landing. (*Exits.*)

Squad Man D *appears –*

SMD Got three in their beds, clawin' for revolvers. The fourth had a girl –

Collins Where are McKee and Clancy? (*The question is repeated and again repeated, eventually it's a shout.*) I know the snivellin' whore's get who turned them in . . . (*In the course of this speech, Collins will go for Squad Man D in coarse fury, throw him to the floor, stalk the space, threatening anything in his path.*) . . . Jesus Christ of Almighty didn't I tell you a thousand times that little get Ryan should be sent on a long holiday or more to the point put under but fuck the bit of you would listen to a word I was saying, informer slopping out of his ears, leaving tracks after him, I know they're gone, it's in the room, the smell of clay, there they are looking at us, look at them and tell me I'm not seeing things, scorch-marks bullet-holes boot bayonet back of the truck and shat on before delivery to the Mortuary what's left of them . . .

Collins takes Squad Man D and hurls him out of the space.

That was the worst time. Nearly the worst. We went to the Mortuary Chapel and clothed them in their uniforms. Touts everywhere. And to the funerals. Touts, detectives, troops. We buried the two of them. Two of our best. (*Beat.*) Last time I was with McKee we talked – and shook hands – like we knew in our bones it was the last time . . .

Lighting change to convey flashback, and **McKee** *is in the space.*

I had another row with Cathal today. He's a type comes rushing straight at you but you can't dislike him. Even when he's at his worst, he's so himself.

McKee But your man Collins, you can dislike him?

Collins Certainly. Lots do.

McKee He's not 'so himself'?

Collins He's several selves –

McKee Fighting with other?

Collins Non-stop – bumping into other – and other people – doesn't come rushing straight at you – too many of him, poor divil.

McKee Any cure at all?

Collins Keep collisions to a minimum, best that can be done. (*Beat.*) Now that fella McKee –

McKee That Jackeen – to be seen everywhere, like the bad weather – what's he at?

Collins He's himself. He's the whole cloth. I'd go to hell and back for McKee.

They view each other, tenderly. The two embrace.

We have to do something about these gentlemen . . . (*Taking out a photo, giving it to McKee.*)

McKee 'The particular ones' . . . Them or us . . .

Collins You'll be in charge, all right?

McKee When you give the nod.

They're brooding over the photo.

Collins Wouldn't wish them on the neighbour's child, would you?

McKee We'll put manners on them, never fret.

Exit McKee.

SCENE THREE

Summer light, Kitty on. In tennis whites, with the gear. Collins and Kitty instantly into mime of wild tennis. Collins puts a stop to it by a wild swing which drives the 'ball' out of sight.

Kitty Why'd you do that?

Collins To rise you, Kitty Kiernan –

Kitty I need to be 'ruz'?

Collins I like teasing you –

Kitty To keep a distance?

Horseplay between the two. Kitty breaks from that.

There's a cruelty around your mouth.

Collins swoops on her again, mock-savage.

Collins I suppose I'm a bit of a savage . . . (*The two sit.*) I'll marry you though.

Kitty Men marry, women select – bear in mind. I'll pick a man when I'm good and ready.

Collins Just so's you know – I aim to get hold of you. I love you.

Kitty Why?

Collins I don't know. You irritate me. An irritant. So I have to deal with you. And I don't know you. And you won't enlighten me. So I'm left skimble-skamblin'. And I love the state of skimble-skamble in your vicinity. Therefore I love you. Which was to be proved. (*Beat.*) Finally, you've the right ideas. And you're from good ould stock.

Kitty (*rising to stroll*) Always a help . . .

Dev appears, in tennis whites. Collins will register him, lightly, Kitty not at all. Dev prepares to serve (mime), serves.

Voice off Deuce –

Dev (*assertive plus*) Advantage, Dev – (*Exits.*)

Kitty I believe I'll marry a bank-clerk – who'll be a manager by thirty.

Collins You'd shoot him on the honeymoon. The whole thing would have been a waste of time. And ammunition. Don't.

Kitty Politics bore me.

Collins Great – I get fed up with politics, often. All I want then is the quiet of the country, day like today – with you.

They're sitting together again.

Kitty Bit of a poet?

Collins Given any encouragement – all I seek is encouragement.

Kitty And that beautiful woman in your life?

Collins A friend.

Kitty In great need?

Collins She's there to help.

Kitty Has the right ideas?

Collins Right.

  Hiatus . . . Teasy gestures.

Ever tell you who's my favourite saint?

Kitty The Archangel Gabriel? Doubting Thomas?

Collins Saint Paul. The record of misbehaviour –

Kitty You find that –

Collins – appealing –

Kitty Have you thought of what happened after? Your mascot saint –

Collins Rose in the world, out of the world, got a halo –

Kitty Turned into a notable sourpuss and snarly-gob –

Collins Not my future –

Kitty Present?

Collins You wouldn't want me tame, would you?

Kitty Doesn't arise. Anyway the question is other.

Collins What other?

Kitty Several others. In a way, they – engage me – for the moment – but I'm not really a 'for the moment' person – that's the flaw in the –

Collins Ointment?

  Enter Squad Man A. Nod for Collins.

(*to Kitty*) McKeown's down the road –

Kitty To be sure.

Collins Back in an hour –

Kitty No, you won't –

Collins Or less –

Kitty When it suits –

Exit Collins and Squad Man A. Kitty stands there. Puts out her tongue – con moto *– in the direction of Collins's exit. Exits.*

SCENE FOUR

Dev on, wearing mortar-board and academic gown. Carries books, chalk-box, so on. Speaks to the audience as to a class.

Dev (*referring to book*) Machiavelli's *The Prince* . . . (*Goes on parade.*) Young men going into politics enquire – 'What should I read, Dev?' I reply – 'Read this. Study it. Absorb it.' What's it about? Discipline, in my opinion, discipline.

Collins, impudent pup of a pupil, arrives, slinks to his seat.

Collins Sorry I'm late, sir –

Dev (*fury*) No, you're not – you were born to be late, it's in us. I remember at primary school the fool teacher every morning used to turn back the clock one hour so's the pupils could be on time. We're always late – late at Kinsale, late at Aughrim, late for the races, the only thing we were on time for was the Famine.

Flip: Dev sweeps upstage, busies himself at whatever will function as makeshift blackboard.

(*writing*) Niccolò Machiavelli – his prime concern? His

constant theme? The new Prince, the new man, the one who has come from no background – but whose look is (*writing*) *Revolution* –

Collins (*for the audience*) Now d'ye mind!

Dev What of him? What of the 'new man'? This – (*coming downstage to his class*) page 57 . . . 'He should not stray from the good' – very well, he should not stray from the good – but – (*back to the text*) 'He must know how to enter into evil when necessity commands'. Why? Very simple. Because (*back up to the blackboard*) there is the question of (*writing*) *the final result*.

Collins (*for the audience*) Now yer thrashin'!

Dev Who wins? To whom the spoils? Ponder that. Ponder that now.

Collins (*sings, impudent/debonaire*) I'll sing you a song of peace and love . . .

Dev joins in, merrily collusive, and, for good measure, dancing the while.

. . . Whack fol-de-diddle-deedle-do-di-day/ To the land that reigns all all lands above/ Whack fol-de-diddle-deedle-do-di-day . . .

Song and dance dropped – like that – and pupil and teacher now fighting each other vocally.

Dev He also said – the good Niccolò – he also said – 'Make yourself feared – not loved' – and, a related maxim, 'There are no good laws without powerful armies to enforce them . . .'

Collins (*hand up*) Please, sir? Please, sir? Please, sir? Is it true that on your recent visit to the United States as Great Leader of the Tribe – ours – is it true that you spent most of your time devotedly fucking your devoted secretary?

Dev (*wisp of a smile, coming downstage*) I am no Prince. I am the new man. On my tour of the United States I was made a Chief of the Chippewa Nation. At that moment I felt a Prince. In these parts, I gather the matter was cause for mirth.

Collins Arrah, don't be sayin' that now –

Dev (*beatific by the blackboard*) The Chippewa Elders gave me (*writing*) the name 'Dressing Feather' –

Collins Dressing Feather –

Dev Nay-nay-unga-bee –

Collins Nay-nay-unga-bee –

Dev Nay-nay-unga-bee –

Collins (*pupil in revolt, exiting*) – pray for us and protect us –

> *Dev pursues the pupil, pounces, and beats him about the lugs – Flip –*

Dev Ambush and assassination are not helping our cause abroad –

Collins No, they're helping it here –

Dev I am in a position to know –

Collins And it's here we win or lose –

Dev Now for your own situation –

Collins Chief –

Dev My feeling is you can be most useful to us in the United States –

Collins Regular reports to be submitted –

Dev – to me or my secretary –

Collins How is she?

Dev Thriving. We'll confer before your departure –

Collins Ye long whore ye –

Dev Which should not be delayed –

Collins Ye whore's melt of a long whore –

Dev We shall be happy to advise you on conditions over there –

> *Collins winds Dev up – and exits – as Dev passes into his reminiscence glow.*

You will find our people wonderfully supportive. From New York to San Francisco, from Montana to Florida, they gave without stint. The rich brought silver and gold, the poor votive candles, cries of 'Failte, failte . . .' I recall one evening in Butte, Montana, sometimes called 'The Richest Hill on Earth' – this, as many of you will know, because of its celebrated copper deposits. It was winter, snow everywhere, and more expected – 'The white hurricane', so called . . . The organisers had booked the largest hall in the city, it (*exiting as he declaims*) was ordinarily used for ice-skating and related winter activities . . .

SCENE FIVE

Cathal Brugha *on. Little man, reefer jacket. Agitated, marching up and down.*

Brugha Would you not agree – this is a straight question – would you not agree that, as Minister for Defence, my views on, say, the question of ambushing should be taken into account? Am I out of order in seeking to establish – merely seeking to establish – that my views on this matter be taken into account?

Squad Man A has come on.

SMA But – there's overlapping, Cathal –

Brugha Thank you.

SMA Mick is Finance –

Brugha Thank you.

SMA – but also Director of Intelligence –

Brugha And Director of anything else he has a mind to direct. But while I remain Minister for Defence I intend to see to it that – as in all other Departments – the line of command remains clearly defined.

Collins on, upstage.

I am – I say it again – against ambushes as at present conducted. I say we should call on the enemy before opening fire.

Collins That wouldn't be an ambush, Cathal.

Brugha No, Mr Collins, it would be a fair and square fight it out, nothing squalid or back-alley about it – and if we can't have it that way, let's do without it.

Collins (*insolently holding to upstage position*) So – let me get it right now – you're advising me – to advise the men in the field – to advise the enemy before they open fire – letter or telegram or just walk up and tell them, ideally that, is it? Why don't we invite them to a candle-lit dinner while we're at it?

Brugha Mr Collins, leave the candles out of it –

Collins I take back the candles –

Brugha If I happen to be manager of a candle factory, that's neither here nor there.

Collins I take back the candles –

SMA He takes back the candles –

Brugha And another matter –

Collins *J'écoute* –

Brugha Concerning the shooting of spies –

Collins The Vermin Eradication Act – yes?

Brugha As Minister for Defence, I am now putting you on notice that in all cases, note that *all* –

Collins (*gesture to Squad Man A*) *All* noted –

SMA (*pencil and notebook out*) *All* noted –

Brugha In *all* cases I require fully documented proof of guilt to be provided –

Collins (*nod to Squad Man A*) In triplicate –

Squad Man A again active with notebook and pencil.

Brugha So as to be in a position to assure any future Commission of Enquiry that I – as Minister for Defence – and those in charge of Intelligence – and the men in the field – at all times acted in accordance with the generally accepted rules governing hostilities.

Collins I'll tell you what we'll do, Cathal, we'll have to set up a meeting.

Brugha And the sooner the better –

Collins now positioned by a table mid-stage, face-to-face confrontation imminent.

Collins We'll have to set up a series of meetings (*Collusive nods to Squad Man A who's busy with the notebook.*) – in fact, why don't we set up a Commission of Regulation while we're at it – and expand that, if needs be, to a run of

Committees – and if they can't unravel the feecha-foocha, we'll convene a special session of –

Brugha (*fury*) Mr Collins –

Collins I will not have my men –

Brugha *Your* men –

Collins – fight a war – and a dirty war at that – under the banner of *After you, Claude – No, I insist, Cecil* – and I won't have the drunken yella-livered spies of this generation given room to send our men to the grave while we assemble triple-plated documentary proof that they are what they are and they can't be anything else. We'll have a GHQ meeting on the matter next week – and I can tell you now what the vote will be.

Brugha Don't be too sure, Mr Collins. There's a few of us not yet on bended knees before The Big Fellow. *Feicimíd a bhfeicimíd.*

> *Exit Brugha. Collins – Squad Man A an appreciative spectator – lights a candle, mimes pouring two glasses of wine . . .*

Collins Listen, Cecil, old chap, could we talk about ambushes for a minute – how would your lads be for next Tuesday evening, eight o'clock or thereabouts, the bridge below the town, if that's convenient . . .

SMA Eight-thirty?

Collins Good man. Evening dress optional. Cheers!

SMA Cheers! (*They mime a mocking toast.*)

> *Squad Man A, grinning, exits.*

SCENE SIX

*Reduce lighting to candle's light or close to that. Collins
seated at the table, broody. Takes out a notebook,
methodically makes an entry. Removes a page from the
notebook, lights it at the candle-flame, lets it burn away.*

Collins We live in the hour of the body or the lash: who'll
yield first? Just got word the old family place was burned
down, house, out-buildings. 'Selective Reprisals', the
papers call it. My brother says they'd have burned the
seventy acres only they'd other houses awaiting the torch. I
loved that place – everyone, no doubt, says that – but it *was*
special. Everyone says that too . . . The barn . . . I think of
that barn a lot . . . Hay, swallows, a ladder hanging on a
wall – the longest ladder in the world it seemed to me, too
long ever to be used, maybe it was just there – for example
. . . Once when I was (*gesture*) that size, I was playing in the
loft with the sisters . . . I was brought up surrounded by
women – an oul wan told me once – *That'll always stand to
you* . . . But the loft, the floor of the loft, this particular day,
was covered with flowers. I can see them yet. There we are
playing garden of an afternoon. There was this trapdoor at
one end of the loft, and nothing would do me but find it –
even if I didn't know I was searching for it . . . I rambled my
way to it – the foxglove looking at me, the clover smelling,
the daisies basking, the buttercups shiny – and, the
trapdoor somehow not fastened – I'm gone, fifteen-foot
drop to the stable below. A lap of hay was all that saved me.
It wasn't, they said, supposed to be there – but it was. I was
asked once – What do you believe in? A lap of hay, I said.
May it always be there for you, was the wish came back.

Flip –
    *Lighting change, musical backing, and lunge to the
phantasmagoric. Kitty sweeps on, with hurling-stick.
Douses the candle, and belts it off the table.*

Kitty When they burned our place, I saved the silver –

Collins What has you here?

Kitty sweeps upstage to join Dev who has appeared.

Kitty Kitty Kiernan, Granard grass widow –

Dev What's a grass widow?

Kitty Available for grazing, you astonish me –

Collins *(advancing on them)* Get out, get out, get out –

> The *(English Army)* **Captain** *arrives downstage, crosses
> the space doing 'The Lambeth Walk'. Dev whirls Collins
> downstage. Kitty and The Captain into Hands-Knees
> and Bumps-a-Daisy.*

Collins *(pointing to The Captain)* Who's that bastard?
(Freeze on 'bastard'.)

Dev Your very good friend, The Captain –

Collins Who is he, I'm asking?

Dev On your payroll, *a stóir* –

> *Mayhem resumes. Kitty and Dev into song-and-dance
> routine upstage – 'Who were you with last night? The
> Captain is interrogating Collins downstage left.*

The Captain What's this about a grass widow, Mick?

Collins What the hell's a grass widow?

The Captain On the look-out for grazing, old chap –

Collins *Define the term*, will you?

The Captain On the hunt for grazing, man –

> *The Captain roughly propels Collins cross-stage, left to
> right, Collins increasingly in a spin.*

Collins Let them graze her – (*Freeze on 'graze her'.*)

The Captain (*lunatic/intense*) The girl needs minding, Mick –

Collins Have ye any manners, the lot of ye –

Break freeze.
Kitty, Dev and The Captain, in sync, produce black handkerchiefs, and – top-speed – mime flash-photo of Collins, one only. And exit Dev and The Captain. Kitty is now on the table mid-space, dancing teasy rumba-style. Collins – in panic – on his knees by the table.

Are ye drunk on sherry or what? Come down oura that? *Ye know I can't dance –*

Kitty not interested, simply ups the ante, but brief. She drops her black veil/hanky on Collins's head/face, and exits at speed. Collins left lying on his back, head/face thus covered.

LINKING CAMEO

Collins as at bottom of Scene Six.
Enter **Gunman**, *frail*, à la dérive.

Gunman Our three snorin'. Two with women. Locked up the women. Fenlon, Bell, Corrie. There on the landing. Bell in his pelt. Asked could he have a dressing-gown.

And exit Gunman.

SCENE SEVEN

Collins I said to the doctor, 'There's something atin' me'.

'Curds and whey', says he, 'Little Miss Tucket. Never fails.'

Moya on, with glass of curds and whey – which she presents to him.

Moya Drink up now, like a good boy. (*Beat.*) I haven't cracked you.

Collins (*sipping*) Do I have to be cracked?

Moya You're not whole until some woman cracks you.

Collins (*grimacing over the medicine*) It'll have to wait.

Moya (*addressing him from a distance*) Till you find the nerve.

Collins Why so sure I don't have the nerve for that?

Moya A lot of boy in you yet, Meehawl.

Collins I wouldn't listen to a word you were saying if you weren't an older woman – I've this thing in me about learning.

Moya You're a scholar?

Collins No – I like picking things up –

Moya – and putting them down.

The grimacing/sipping continues, Collins milking that score to the maximum. Moya approaches him, with intent.

I've this picture of you – you in a room full of shadows – you're in there, that big right shoulder pinned against the door – but there's one heading for you who'll waltz through the door – and woe betide.

Collins Just like that?

Moya She'll know all your weaknesses – far in advance.

Collins How so?

Moya She'll have met you before – some other life.

Collins What'll she look like?

Moya Beautiful.

Collins has been positioned on a chaise-longue: *Moya joins him on it.*

Collins More beautiful than you?

Moya She begins to interest you?

Collins Beautiful women – women – interest me. What'll her feeling be towards me?

Moya Merciless.

Collins Jesus . . . How can I protect myself?

Moya Let up the blinds, open the windows.

Collins Then what?

Moya Talk to her – know her –

Collins Then what?

Moya Then you'll be – what's that phrase you have – then you'll be 'leppin' out of your skin'.

Collins I can't wait.

Collins finishes the curds and whey, licking the glass to the dregs. Broody pause. Collins's strong hand bends the handle of the spoon back on itself. He dumps glass and spoon. Reflects.

You're the real thing, Moya, the real thing.

Tired child, he rests his head on her lap. Momentarily, she caresses his head.

Moya I have this weakness for the virginal in grown men. It'll be the death of me, no doubt. (*Beat.*) Some day I'll write a book about him – telling all – almost all. Gunmen – I can see their frowns – I could name them – will call, suggest I throw it on the fire. And I will – throw it on the fire. *Sin an saol*, as we say, *sin an saol*.

SCENE EIGHT

Enter Dev as raddled pianist – and to the piano. Begins – and continues – to play tinkle-tankle Christmas tunes.

Collins Hard to bate The Gresham for a bit of a *do* . . .

Waiter and waitress on – a table is set, drinks served. And Squad Man A and Squad Man B are on also.

SMA Mick, can we go – now you've made your visit?

Collins (*feckless/effusive*) Christmas – the goodwill, the music, the hubub-bububub!

SMA The touts, the detectives, the military –

Collins (*dismissive*) Arrah –

Collins – now possessed of a blackthorn stick and a glass of whiskey – lugs Squad Man B downstage centre. (Squad Man A seated uneasily at the table.)

(*to the world*) Peace on earth – 's go *mbeirimid beó ag an ám seo arís* . . .

SMB (*under duress*) *Saol fada* . . .

Squad Man B sits. Collins, wielding the stick, is into his party piece. Dev working away at the piano. Squad Man A and Squad Man B resigned to their fate. While not unappreciative of the rich colours loose in the Collins recitation.

Collins To Meath of the pastures from wet hills by the sea/ Through Leitrim and Longford go my cattle and me/ I hear in the darkness their slipping and breathing/ I name them the by-ways they're to pass without heeding . . . O, the wet winding roads, brown bogs and black water/ My thoughts on white ships and the King of Spain's daughter . . . O, farmer, strong farmer, you may spend at the fair/ But your thoughts you must turn to your crops and your care/ And soldier, fine soldier, you've seen many lands/ But you walk two by two, and –

The waiter arrives, whispers a message in Collins's ear.

Collins Thanks –

Exit waiter. Collins and the others compose themselves. An armed **Soldier** *appears, and a man in civvies who's clearly an* **Intelligence Officer.**

Soldier Merry Christmas, Gentlemen –

Collins and the others reciprocate.

And a Happy New Year, Gentlemen –

Collins And many of them –

Soldier Many many of them –

Collins (*brazen*) Bás in Éireann –

The Soldier moves to frisk Squad Man A and Squad Man B. The Intelligence Officer focuses on Collins. He frisks Collins, commences interrogation.

IO What might your name be, Sir?

Collins John Grace –

IO Fine wholesome name –

Collins Not the worst, Officer –

IO Occupation, Mr Grace?

Collins Company Director.

IO Company name?

Collins Irish Products – Limited.

IO What's this, Mr Grace? (*The frisking has yielded a notebook.*)

Collins Personal notebook.

IO (*inspecting closely*) 'Rifles', Mr Grace? For Irish Products – Limited?

Collins (*inspecting in turn*) 'Refills', Officer, 'Refills' –

The Intelligence Officer studies his man.

IO Nature of your business, Mr Grace?

Collins Importer – pens, pencils, erasers, that sort of thing –

IO (*enhanced rigour*) Sit down, please, Mr Grace –

Collins sits, happy to oblige. The Intelligence Officer has taken out a photo. Studies closely Collins's face in reference to it. Hands the photo to Collins.

Ever come across this prime ruffian in your travels, Mr Grace?

Collins Who have we here, Officer?

IO That gentleman familiar to you, Mr Grace?

Collins views the photo with 'solemn purpose'.

Collins That's Mick Collins –

Simmering pause.

IO You know Mr Collins, Mr Grace?

Collins Bumped into him once at a race-meeting, Officer –

shouldn't be on the loose – for what my opinion's worth –

Renewed intense scrutiny from the Intelligence Officer. Collins insouciant.

IO Business lively these days, Mr Grace?

Collins Well – considering – yes – I'm always hopeful . . .

The Intelligence Officer smiles – almost . . . Collins, debonaire. The Intelligence Officer returns the notebook: Collins returns the photo.

Soldier (*holds up a whiskey flask*) Confiscated property, Sir, *Tullamore Dew*, he says –

SMA (*brave sally*) Quoth the raven, Tullamore!

IO Edgar Allan Poe – I suppose he's bloody Irish too?

Collins On the mother's side, Officer.

Soldier Like to try it, Sir?

The Intelligence Officer has a swig.

IO Like a bog on fire – try some, Mr Grace?

Collins takes the flask.

Collins Happy Christmas, Officer – (*He swigs.*)

IO (*exiting*) Happy Christmas, Mr Grace –

Soldier (*exiting*) 'Quoth the raven, Tullamore!'

Two beats, say –

MC/SMA/SMB 'Tullamore!'

And Collins and Squad Man A in a bout of wrestling – Waiter and Waitress rushing to clear the table – Squad Man B, perched on a chair, giving a running commentary on the bout . . . and CUT –

SMB Cork bet an' the hay saved!

Collins and the others stroll from the space, dissolving (almost) into ghosts as they do.

Dev alone at the piano. Finishes the tune. Stands, collects his music, sips from a glass of whiskey which has been brought to him during the scene. Puts the glass aside.

Dev *Beidh me ar ais.* (*Exits.*)

Act Two

SCENE ONE

*Collins on, uneasily resplendent in his new uniform of
Commander-in-Chief. The whiff is of military dictatorship.*

Collins 'We'll have to hammer these fellows' is one way of
putting it. There's another way — and a better — 'The
safety of the nation is the first law. We shall not rest until
we've established the authority of the people of Ireland in
every square mile under our jurisdiction'.

Dev (*arriving upstage*) We'll see about the jurisdiction —

> *Dev settled stage left. He's in makeshift uniform. Sits on
> a three-legged stool, interests himself in eating a
> sandwich and slugging milk from a naggon bottle.*
> *Hazel has come on upstage right: speaks from that
> position.*

Hazel First time I met him I said – I've seen you coming
towards me this while back – *the most wanted man* – I
wanted to meet the most wanted man . . . Having met him,
what I wanted to happen, knew would happen, happened
. . . (*She joins Collins mid-stage.*) Can I be Governor-
General, General Collins?

Collins The job's yours, Lady Lavery –

> *They kiss, caress, the temperature is sexual obsession.*

Hazel It's not so much the job – it's the house. I love the
Vice-Regal Lodge – the park, the deer, the trees –

Collins I hate this life, Hazel. We've all run amok. We
sleep and wake in shambles – look at us, smell us – we're
all tusks, loose in the head – amok, amok –

Hazel *You* have not run amok. Your opponents split the Army, and went into revolt. You did everything possible to avoid blood-letting. *You* are meeting your responsibilities, *they* are running amok. And will – until they are thoroughly subdued.

Dev *Feicimíd a bhfeicimíd* –

Collins I need you to talk like that. (*Flip.*) I could be a stockbroker in New York this minute. Eight years ago the family nearly had me on a boat to the States, it's true –

Hazel America's loss, my gain –

Dev I wanted you to go to the States –

Collins I had the ticket in my hand, Hazel . . . Not me. Is this me?

Hazel (*in full stride*) Well, it's at any rate where you've landed . . .

> *During this speech, Collins will cross to Dev for a slug of milk . . . the naggon bottle is boldly offered, boldly taken.*

And if life has taught me anything, it's that – one way or another – where we've landed is where we desire to be. *You* desire to command. A weather I relish. To obey? To disobey? To obey – and disobey? To counter-command? An incomparable pastime – wouldn't you agree?

> *Collins – semi-circling the upstage area – on his way back to Hazel, repeating over and over in drugged fashion – 'Hazel . . . Hazel . . . Hazel . . .' Now they're together again in a sensual haze.*

Collins Did I ever tell you the Irish for 'Hazel' – 'coll- c-o-l-l . . .

Hazel (*it's a purr*) 'Coll' . . .

Dev The mother was a Coll –

Collins Also, in Irish there's a tree for every letter. Hazel goes with the letter 'c' –

Hazel Hazel goes with the letter 'c' –

Dev *Tá an ceart aice* –

Collins And 'hazel' also means 'poetry' – all this surprise you?

Hazel No. Yes. No. You're the first man to articulate it for me, that's all –

Collins (*flip*) When this is over I want to go away – to Connemara, say, learn Irish properly –

Dev Time for you –

Hazel I'll go with you. I can paint The Twelve Pins . . .

Collins (*flip*) Hazel, Hazel, how do we put an end to this?

Hazel Why, win the war – at speed – surely?

Collins You mean kill off my closest friends – one by one, that's your prescription?

Hazel Either you kill them or they kill you – it's the world.

Collins We want blood blood blood – nobody's sane any longer, nobody –

Dev I'm perfectly sane –

Hazel (*icy/pragmatic*) Michael, pursue that line and we're lost – we go under, vanish.

Hiatus . . . Wavering.

Collins Your letters to me are being intercepted, by the way –

Hazel What then? I stop writing you?

Dev – for the audience – flourishes a handful of letters, opens one, gives himself to absorbed reading of it.

Collins No, I need your letters. We'll get hold of the hero responsible.

The two embrace hungrily.

Lady Lavery –

Hazel Yes, General Collins –

Collins You know I'm an engaged man –

Hazel Kitty Kiernan, General Collins, is engaged to you –

Collins Correct –

Hazel And you are engaged to Kitty Kiernan –

Collins Correct –

Hazel But – as I understand the matter – not fully engaged, General Collins, not fully engaged.

The two exit, urgent. Dev gazes after them.

Dev He'd tip the crack of dawn, wouldn't he? As for M'Lady, if God made them he matched them.

Gathering his belongings, Dev wanders in the direction of their exit point. Takes out his binoculars, smiling, playful/louche. Trains his binoculars on their tracks. Lowers binoculars, contented. Exits, à loisir.

SCENE TWO

Arthur Griffith *wanders on, a tired fifty to sixty, pensive/wan.*

Griffith (*he's been humming to himself*) I love music. Do you know *The Bartered Bride*? Nobody has much regard for Smetana nowadays but he had his followers. (*Beat.*) Arthur Griffith, Prime Minister – partially retired. I've been in and out of hospital, safe a place as any these times. Not that I'm for shooting . . ., I'll die tying my shoe – or shaving . . . How do I know that? I don't. Just an intelligent guess.

> *Fiddles with his specs, straightens his tie. Takes out an envelope, reads.*

'To be opened after my death' . . . (*Taking slip of paper from envelope, he reads.*) 'Let the people stand firm for the State being founded. It is their national need, their economic salvation. Love to the Irish people and to all my colleagues and friends.'

> *Puts envelope and note away.*

All the Irish people? As the bombardment to drive the new rebels from the Four Courts commenced, I stood on the roof of Government Buildings and cursed De Valera. I flung my fists at the sky and I cursed the man. It isn't De Valera. It's something else – let out – voracious – rampant –

> *A working-class* **Woman** *on, pleased to recognize, almost congratulate Griffith.*

Woman Mr Griffith –

Griffith It won't be long –

Woman It's winding up?

Griffith Soon it will be over.

Woman Official-like, Mr Griffith?

Griffith What?

Woman Official-like?

Griffith That's the long and the short of it.

A fugitive Irregular – youthful – races into the space,
pistol in hand. Griffith and the Woman stand frozen.
Two armed heavies appear in close pursuit, open fire,
the fugitive goes down, killed, body picked up, and
lugged off.
    Griffith and the Woman immobilized for several
beats. Then they go to the spot, kneel, and pray. Griffith
back downstage. The Woman exiting.

I sent a note to the 'Commander-in-Chief' – last week was
it? – asking if Cabinet approval had been sought in the
matter of certain 'Special Squads' again active in our
streets. A reply is awaited. (*Beat.*) A reply is awaited.

Enter a Free State patrol, captain and soldier, armed.

FS Captain (*saluting*) Mr Griffith, Sir –

Griffith Captain –

FS Captain We'll be happy to drive you to Government
Buildings, snipers active around here –

Griffith Thank you, I'll be fine –

FS Captain Sorry, Mr Griffith, I can't take that
responsibility.

Griffith 'Responsibility'?

FS Captain You know what I mean, Mr Griffith –

Griffith You mean you'll arrest me if I don't accept your
kind offer?

FS Captain Mr Griffith, our job's to provide security —

Griffith Yes –

Whistling phrases from Smetana, Griffith allows the
patrol to lead him away.

SCENE THREE

*Kitty on – and on something of a high – wearing bathrobe
and carrying night-clothes which she tosses wherever. She
turns the table on its end to provide a make-believe mirror.
Positions herself before it. Towelling her hair.*

Kitty Michael . . . Meehawl . . . Mick . . . Mickeen . . .
Send a message to say you're on your way . . . Granard,
nothing strange in Granard, same old come-day go-day
. . . I've just had a bath. Am looking my best. And if you
were here, General Collins, you would not be safe, not one
bit of you . . . But since you are not here . . .

> *She flings off the robe, now wearing just knickers and
> bra.
>   Dev has come on, in academic gown, wearing the
> Chippewa head-dress and smoking the Pipe of Peace. He
> settles stage left, close to Kitty.*

– let us imagine you are – and delighted to see you . . .
(*Selecting now from the night-clothes.*) You've come just in
time – as you can see – like it was planned, really (*Donning
a pair of flowery peach pyjamas.*) – to find me in my daisy-
bells, as they say in Belfast . . .

> *The Captain arrives. He's wearing a smoking-jacket –
> but full length – and his military cap. And he's smoking,
> wielding a cigarette-holder to good effect. He settles
> stage right.*

The Captain (*purr*) En déshabillé –

> *Kitty models the outfit for the pair, in particular for Dev
> – the closest.*

Kitty Now – I know you're not that interested in fashion –
and you've much on your mind – but what do you think –
Switzer's best – I've been keeping them a surprise – like

them? (*Still to Dev, and extending a leg.*) Like to feel the silk?

Dev does, touch of the lubricious.

It's like – what? – the touch of your hands – when you're at home with yourself – and me . . . Thank you . . . That's Number One outfit . . .

The Captain Beautiful job, Kitty, beautiful –

Dev *Tá sí galánta* –

Quick change for Kitty into a pair of dark blue pyjamas. During which Collins arrives (in uniform), and settles uneasily in the lee of the upturned table.

Kitty (*chatting while she changes*) You'll notice a certain grace of movement – *if* you notice a certain grace of movement –

Cue for Dev and The Captain to exchange positions.

– that's from Miss Magenni's dancing-class . . . I promised her, by the by, I'd teach you to dance . . . So you've been warned – General Collins is going to dance –

Collins Is he though? Is he?

Dev He's going to dance –

The Captain An invitation –

Kitty He may not refuse – I thought – when I was spending my money – why not variety? – and there's a side of me that's dark blue – a gipsy told me at the fair of Balladuff – what do you think?

The question is addressed to Collins – who's now standing stage right, a removed figure.

Collins Bit severe.

Kitty Severe tripe –

Collins I take it back –

Kitty Thanks – what is it then?

Collins Grand – it's grand . . .

Kitty You excel yourself –

The Captain Regal, Kitty, regal . . .

Dev Comely –

Collins I wish to Christ you wouldn't take me up wrong all the bloody time.

Kitty (*mid-stage, approaching Dev, stage right*) Bit of mystery to it. Slubbed silk, I'll have you know. You'd want to dance in this –

> *Whom will she pick? She teases Dev, sweeps past Collins, arrives at The Captain. Chooses him, they dance briefly, she dismisses him in mid-step, goes on about her business.*

I can see you prefer the flowery peach – (*Now removing outfit two and donning the next, a cream nightie, clearly special.*)

> *Collins is now mid-stage, leaning on the upturned table, resolutely* dégagé.

That's all right, I don't take offence – I'm this evening in the height of good humour – because you've arrived – surprise visit – out of the blue of the summer evening – stars in the bog-holes, dew on the grass, which reminds me, we'll go for mushrooms in the morning –

Collins I'm going for no mushrooms – I'm shagged –

Kitty It has to be done –

Collins Take Dev, why don't ye – or the gallant Captain
Tongue-Hanging-Out –

Kitty No – *you*, Meehawl, you and I – and *that's that*, as
you'd say –

Collins That's that –

The Captain *Fait accompli* –

Dev A pleasure deferred, Kit –

> *Kitty steps on to a chair, arms extended towards the
> three.*

Kitty 'You see me, Lord Bassanio, where I stand' – Aunt
Kate used to say that every day of her life – God knows
why . . . (*Pause.*) I like this one best . . . You agree?

> *No nods: they simply stare.*

I knew you would . . .

> *She stands there on the chair, bit lost, hands drifting
> about her body . . . Fragile beyond fragile . . . Stretch to
> max.*

(*Coming out of that, off the chair, addressing the chair.*)
Well? What are you sitting there for? Gawkin'? In shock or
what? (*She wanders downstage.*) The killing, Meehawl,
what's all the killing about? For Ireland? For us? For you
and me? Cathal Brugha dead in O'Connell Street, and
Harry Boland gone and two young fellas from here shot in
Dundalk and everywhere shooting and killing and nobody
knows and nobody cares which side is which . . . The
killing . . . (*Pause.*) Let them not kill you anyway, love . . .

> *She goes, gathers her things, goes to Collins, takes him
> by the hand, and makes to exit.*

And now – I'm taking you to bed – you'll touch me with
that touch of your hands and I'll teach you to dance – but

don't forget the mushrooms – tired or no – you must pluck
them with the dew still on them, then they're – did you
ever hear said – 'the sweets of the morning', love, then
they're 'the sweets of the morning' . . .

She leads Collins off.
*From 'I'm taking you to bed', Dev and The Captain
have had, respectively, the Pipe of Peace and the
cigarette-holder raised – 45-degree angle – in salute to
the 'Bridal Pair'.*
Exit Dev and The Captain.

SCENE FOUR

*Space drab, anonymous; could be a back room
somewhere. Enter Squad Man A and Squad Man B in
shiny, new – slightly uncomfortable – free state army
uniforms. They hang about, restive.*

SMA I thought these bastards were to be here ahead of us –

SMB Maybe their safe-conducts didn't work –

SMA Blow the fuckers out of it. I've no stomach for this
palaver.

Two men wearing the dishevelled gear of **Irregulars**
arrive.

Irreg 1 Where's this fella?

SMA On the way –

Irreg 1 I saw the day he was punctual –

SMA He's on the way –

*Collins arrives, in full uniform. Tension. Collins spots a
cork lying somewhere. Picks it up, flicks it impudently
into the face of Irregular 1. The latter picks it up, flings it*

213

*back in Collins's face. The tension buckles. Free-for-all
wrestling commences . . . That's over.*

Collins All right, Tom, let's talk.

Irreg 1 What do you want to hear?

Collins How can we stop this?

Irreg 1 Not of our making –

Collins Let's not waste time –

Irreg 1 Have you proposals, Mick?

Collins Yes. Confront facts. The Castle has fallen. The
necessity is we must pull together and put the country on
its feet.

Irreg 1 I took an oath to The Republic –

Collins I don't give a tinker's tuppenny fuck for oaths –

Irreg 1 So we gather. I respect my oath to The Republic. I
won't swop it for a semi-Republic and an Oath of
Allegiance to His Majesty.

Collins Majesty me arse – His Majesty without His
Majesty's forces is a fiction –

Irreg 1 Not to me – and I'll tell you why.

Collins Go on –

Irreg 1 Because every last bone in my body remembers my
treatment at the hands of His Majesty's forces when I was
taken at Bandon, myself and Harte, you remember?
Remember what became of Harte?

Collins Are you asking me to take responsibility for every
casualty of the war? I can't do it – no one could. From the
first day I did everything possible to see that man got
proper treatment. Nothing to be done. Nothing. Nothing.

Irreg 1 I know. Nothing.

Collins What do you mean – 'I know. Nothing'?

Irreg1 They left nothing of him. Just a lump. Of nothing. Like lots were left lumps of nothing. Fighting for The Republic that's now just another lump of nothing.

Collins God damn and blast you, you're not here to talk, you're like the rest. Why can ye only look through and past me! Did we never meet before?

Irreg 1 You might swear we did. Has The Strong Man forgotten who organized us, supplied us with the guns and ammo, drove us to the limit, kept us going in the black days –

Collins Don't fret. My memory's better than most.

Irreg 1 In that case what are you at, Mick Collins?

> *Abruptly all four in the space are looking at Collins as traitor. He stands accused – and is brushed by self-accusation.*

Collins I'm trying to start – to *start* – a country. Ours – in case you've forgotten. I'm trying to organize an Army, a Police Force, an Administration. I'm trying to stop the killing. I'm trying to see a way through.

Irreg 1 To power. Power, Mick. The Republic is bigger than any of us – it'll see Dictators come and go – it's indestructible, a vision, a dream –

Collins Also a corpse – corpses –

Irreg 2 Some of them in fancy uniforms, maybe –

Collins Corpses from here to Kerry. And ye want it, can't have enough of it, can ye?

Irreg 1 (*exiting*) Stick tight to your cosy quarters, Mick –

Collins See these men to their escort – Slán –

Irreg 1 *Agus beannacht –*

Irregular 2, exiting, flings back –

Irreg 2 Don't come near West Cork, Collins. Come west, you'll not go east.

Several beats.

SMA (*exiting*) Shoot the bastards without trial.

Pause. Collins marooned upstage, back to the audience.

Collins Remember the Bandon business.

Bleak nod from Squad Man B.

At one stage they had them against a wall, firing-squad handy. 'Hold up that Union Jack, salute it.' Tom refused. They beat him to pulp all over again. Poor Harte held it up long enough for a photograph. Then he collapsed. Babbling. *God Save The King.*

Pause: Squad Man B's extended hand has Collins's cap on offer. It hangs there: any takers? Collins takes it . . . Dons it.

Collins Tom looking well, didn't you think? (*Exiting.*)

SMB Never better.

Squad Man B exits.

SCENE FIVE

Dev on, immaculate evening dress, Dev as concert pianist. He goes to piano, con brio, Chopin selection. The piano music will continue throughout the scene, volume varied as necessity dictates.

Collins and Moya on. Collins in distress, angry. Flails his cane against whatever target's convenient.

Collins Who arranged all this? Who'll forgive it? Who'll forgive it? Who'll forgive it? Who'll forgive it?

The two settle downstage right, seated.

I didn't tell you – poor Cathal Brugha – came to me in a dream the other night . . . I seldom remember dreams – I won't forget this one . . .

A ghost Brugha has appeared, upstage right.

There he was, wearing his Volunteer uniform – torn, scorched, blood, dust . . . Another Cathal though . . . Another Cathal . . .

Brugha Mick, I'm sorry – sorry for the hard words —

Collins *(facing audience)* Cathal –

Brugha Sorry for the hard words, Mick –

Collins Cathal, what are we at? What's going to happen to us all? *(Pause.)* He wouldn't answer, like he didn't hear the question even –

Ghost figure retreating, gone.

I woke. A sack of sweat. First encounter with a ghost. Far as I'm aware. What's that mean, Moya?

Moya There's a bit of forgiveness in the world –

Collins The two worlds . . . *(Pause.)* Came to talk to you about Hazel . . .

Moya Yes, darling Hazel . . .

Collins I eat, drink, think, feel Hazel. She's the same – to listen to her. Times I think we want to consume each other.

Moya I know one who escaped – an English Army officer a few years back. He simply stood up and walked away.

Collins He wasn't hooked –

Moya An exercise in will-power –

Collins Will-power?

Moya Or maybe – like Odysseus on that island – someone gave him the magic herb – and that was his protection.

Collins Simply stood up – and walked away . . . (*Pause.*) You gave him the magic herb – didn't you? When he was in the grip . . . Give me the magic herb so.

Moya You have to be ready for it. (*Rising.*)

Collins (*rising in turn*) Say prayers for that – (*Beat.*) Remember away back there at the start of the war, when we were all young and innocent . . . One night out here in Furry Park – a night like this – you came up with the phrase – 'No more lonely scaffolds' . . . I was going on about the men over the years who'd been left to die on their own, how the defeat of the people showed in that – and it must end – and we saw to it – it did. (*Beat.*) Now I'm the one on the lonely scaffold. If I get free of it, you'll be the one to thank – I know that.

> *They hug companionably. The two now making to exit.*

Moya, what happens to women the likes of Hazel?

Moya Like the rest of us – maybe a bit earlier – they stretch out and die.

> *For several beats, the two stand looking out into the audience. Both exit.*
> *Dev at the piano now to the fore. Moves majestically to the 'Polonaise' (say) climax. Then downstage to take the applause. Milks it. It strengthens, becomes an*

ovation for the leader. Dev's right hand rises in response.
Ruler, he moves away from his beloved people, exits.

SCENE SIX

Cold outdoor light. Two sentries on patrol. The
Intelligence Officer strolls on. Comfortable peacetime air.

IO Remember me? Cathcart – British Intelligence, that
Christmas Day in The Gresham . . . A story to tell my
grandchildren – I'm already telling it. You see – curious
thing Counter-Intelligence – there was that moment when I
knew – and he knew – it was this thing of shared
knowledge in a hot situation – it was even sexy, don't mind
saying that, it really was – something in a phrase he used
brushed me – I've forgotten the phrase – but it brushed me
– and there we were, knowing – and next thing I'd let him
go . . . Why? I don't know – you can't answer questions
like that . . . In a riddly sort of way, you're given leave to
thus behave . . . By whom? Cock Robin. Jack-O-Lantern,
Lady Godiva. Take your pick. Lady Godiva . . . Lady
Godiva . . . Next time, naked on her naked charger, she'd
as likely say – *Blow him to bits!* (*Beat.*) History . . . Rum
business 'istory . . .

Exit Intelligence Officer.
Collins on, uniformed, wearing greatcoat. And Dev
on – as priest, light overcoat over his soutane. The
sentries wander to and fro. Collins and Dev
perambulate, tied by symbiosis.

Collins I'm for Cork Sunday. Tour of Inspection. We're
winning the war – but it's important to boost morale.

Dev You understand you'll be shot.

Collins My own countrymen won't shoot me –

Dev The general understanding is they'll shoot you first, then disembowel and quarter you.

Collins Spare me your lurid imaginings.

Dev *Our* lurid imaginings.

Collins What do you want?

Dev Will you be frank?

Collins Maybe.

Dev You're sick of it –

Collins The rigmarole of my life.

Dev You're certainly not going to shoot yourself?

Collins No.

Dev None of your – intimates – are going to shoot you?

Collins No.

Dev I'm not going to shoot you.

Collins No.

Dev We enjoy each other too much.

Collins *Touché*.

Dev And therefore a Tour of Inspection – visit the heart of what's left of the resistance – go down like a hero – doing your duty –

Collins – for King and Country –

Dev Hazel will miss you –

Collins No, she won't . . . (*Beat*.) I'll be back in town next week, she'll be my first –

Dev Port of call –

Collins If you wish to put it that way –

Dev No offence. Extraordinary woman.

Collins She consumes –

Dev Those limbs –

Collins Where they'll take us I've no idea.

Dev You're appointing her –

Collins I *have* appointed her –

Dev Governor-General, I meant –

Collins It's irrevelant –

Dev Don't go morose again now, people are beginning to talk –

Collins About what?

Dev The sty. In your eye.

Beat.

Collins Let's slip around to Hazel's –

Dev Later. Let's settle this first –

Collins Settle what?

Dev Cork – the Tour of Inspection – do you come back walking – or in the timber?

Collins I'm always hopeful.

Dev That's what I like about you – you love the bullet just grazing your forehead.

Collins Let's go. We've had our chat.

Dev You're unhappy with it?

Collins It has its savours.

Dev That's more like it – could you manage a smile – a quote and a smile – the old form –

Collins 'If we do meet again, why then we'll smile' . . .

Dev Thank you.

Collins Just thought of something –

Dev You forgot to make a will? The orchids for Hazel? The daily note to Kit? Speak –

Collins One day during The Terror I sent a few of the Squad into a hotel to get rid of a certain British Intelligence Officer who was doing us harm. Going up the stairs, the lead man sees coming towards him an armed opponent. My fella opened fire – a mirror shattered – he'd fired at his reflection. (*Beat.*) He's not the same since. (*Beat.*) Which, I suppose, is to be expected.

Dev The symmetrical in you is taking – your feel for completion, is it? Tell me another story.

Collins Certainly –

Dev Cheerful one this time, please –

Collins Cheerful story?

Dev If you don't mind –

Collins Ever hear the one about the Wickla man?

Dev waves him on.

The Wickla man came down from the hills – first time ever – and into a shop. His eyes got stuck on an antique of sorts, oval-shaped, delf. 'What's that?' The shopkeeper took a look at him. 'Jever hear tell of a mare's egg?' 'No . . .' 'Well, that's a mare's egg. Leave it by the fire for nine months, it'll give you a fine foal.' 'Christ, I'll take it.' Off he goes carrying 'the mare's egg'. Back up into the hills.

About a mile from home, being tired, he puts it by the side of the road to rest himself a minute – and doesn't it roll off down the slope – breaks into bits – same breath, a fine jack hare jumps up from behind a bush and away like bejaysus. 'O, Christ me misfortune', says the Wickla man, 'If you'd only come full term the divil himself wouldn't catch you.'

> *At his own inimitable pace, Dev moves into paroxysms of silent laughter. Collins is tickled.*

Well?

Dev Well well well . . .

Collins There you are –

Dev We'll meet soon enough.

Collins I suppose . . . Slán . . .

Dev *Agus beannacht –*

> *Exit Collins.*

He's fucked, isn't he? Don't blame Dev. But, rely on it, he will be blamed.

> *Exit Dev. Exit sentries.*

SCENE SEVEN

Summery garden light. Birdsong. Enter Collins stage right, Hazel stage left.

Hazel You look like an ogre in that greatcoat. I believe I'll do a drawing – 'Ogre, with newspaper'.

Collins Hazel –

Hazel Sir –

Collins I can't handle you –

Hazel You've being doing very well, I should have thought.

Collins After today I don't see you – and that's that.

Hazel Fine. Leave.

Collins Listen to me. I have nothing to do except kill my friends, set a date for my wedding, attend funerals. Are you telling me I should have breakfast singing, fuck you three times a day, and be the Laughing Boy of all the ballads?

Clear song of the wren audible.

Hazel The wren. A particular friend. My favourite bird's the redwing. Winter migrant.

Collins Did you hear what I said?

Hazel At the risk of repeating myself – and I like to think of myself as a connoisseur of surprise – moments come when a man has to wipe out his friends or suffer the alternative. Your wedding arrangements are your own business. Funerals – am I to blame? As for fucking me three times a day – I love the eternal accountant in you – the relish evident on both sides suggests to me, at any rate, considerable commitment in the endeavour.

Collins I'm being choked –

Hazel Who's choking you?

Collins I feel like a Mafia boss. I wash too much. Woke up the other nights, my dream was a vomiting cock.

Beat.

Hazel You're right – in a way – Hazel as problem. If not the problem, she may stand for the problem. Fine. You dismiss Hazel – you cry *Halt* to an extraordinary meeting – and then what?

Collins I catch my breath. I look about me. I go on with my life.

Hazel 'Mick and the women' –

Collins I do what I have to do –

Hazel Not on your own – you're stuck with your nature, with what they all say of you – 'Mick and the women' –

Collins Stop writing my epitaph, Lady Lavery –

Hazel Walk off down the road, you still have to deal with Hazel, some Hazel – you have to deal with your own nature –

Collins I don't know my own nature –

Hazel Learn it –

Collins That's what I want to do. I have to be alone to do it. You're sucking me dry, Hazel. This bitch of a country is sucking me dry. I'm a walking corpse in a land of corpses. All I can smell is my own clay, your scent, and the stink of mortuary chapels.

Hazel You know your trouble, Michael? You don't want to get married. It's banal.

Collins My trouble is . . .

Pause. Collins wanders upstage left, adrift, desolate.

My trouble is I want to lie down. I have a cradle story. It's about falling through a trapdoor as an infant and being saved by a lap of hay. I've always believed in that lap of hay. The bother is I don't any longer. It's gone. Blown away somewhere.

Extended pause. Hazel approaches him.

Hazel Don't vanish. You know I adore you. Besides which, we're meshed. If ever a pair were meshed, it's

Michael and Hazel . . .

Several beats. Silence in the garden.

We've sent the wren away –

Collins We have?

Hazel Can't you hear – the silence?

Beat.

Collins Come back, ye little get ye . . . (*Now to Hazel.*)
Dreoilín, we call him . . . (*Pause.*) Come back, will ye – if
ye don't pipe up I'll gut ye for Christmas –

Exit Collins, firm of step, in his fashion.
Hazel in the space alone, serene . . . Exit Hazel.

SCENE EIGHT

*A painter, **Wee Johnny Lavery**, comes on. Bustle of work
about him. Smock, brushes, easel, so on. Upstage of him:
departure resonances. People come and go, suitcases,
various bits and pieces which echo motifs of the play. Dev
is seated upstage, close to the piano. He has a ledger, busy
writing his account, the chronicle of his stewardship.*

Wee Johnny Wee Johnny Lavery – I'm the painter –
unabashed – I paint the living and the dead. Painted the
Cardinal the other day. Said I made him look like a
monkey. He *does* look like a monkey. Little old man with
round shoulders and his head stuck forward. I had the
greatest difficulty seeing his eyes. Eventually, I say – 'Your
Eminence, I haven't seen the colour of your eyes.' He
looked up. 'They're grey, Your Eminence.' 'No', he
returned, 'they're black – or perhaps they're gone grey
with the years.'

Kitty at his elbow. She carries shopping items, and a bunch of flowers.

Kitty – Wonderful to see you –

Kitty You painted him, didn't you?

Wee Johnny And will again –

Kitty What'd you call him – 'A pasty-faced Hercules'?

Wee Johnny What would you have me call him – 'Hercules with his feet up'?

Kitty Where is she? Where is she?

Wee Johnny Everywhere, Kitty, *everywhere*, EVERYWHERE!

Exit Kitty. Wee Johnny is busy sketching whatever catches his eye.
   George Bernard Shaw *on, and downstage to address the audience.*

GBS GB Shaw – you knew I'd appear – period piece – *au contraire* – indefatigable disturber of the peace! (*Turns to Collins – who has arrived.*) Do what I did – leave the country, leave them to it –

Collins I'm about to. Don't you know I'm going to be shot?

GBS How does that feel – if it isn't a macabre question?

Collins How does it feel? I agree to circumstance. (*Beat.*) You blasted writers are all the same – you're already composing your paragraph on the death of Mick Collins – written all over you – dreepin' off you –

GBS Give it a try?

Collins You have the floor –

GBS Right . . . Let's see . . . Yes . . . 'So . . . So tear up your mourning – and hang out your brightest colours in his honour . . . And – and let us praise – let us praise God that he had not to die in a – in a snuffy bed –'

Collins 'Snuffy's' good, that's good – *snuffy* –

GBS 'In a snuffy bed – of a trumpery cough' –

Collins 'Trumpery'!

GBS 'Weakened by age – and saddened by the disappointment that would have attended his work had he lived' – how's that?

Collins You'd weep – if you'd the tears handy.

Exit Shaw. Collins drifts upstage to Moya who awaits him.

I just caught that cold fish Shaw composing his speech on the death of Mick Collins –

Moya He told me I'd the mouth of one with stories to tell.

Collins Will you tell them?

Moya Everything –

Collins Shatter the icon?

Moya Nobody loves an icon –

Collins But everybody wants one – funny –

Beat.

Moya Going down the country?

Collins Going down the country. Tomorrow. Is tomorrow Sunday?

Moya (*nod*) Are you wise?

Collins No. Just busy.

Moya (*exiting*) Well, you'll be among your own, won't you?

The departure traffic has been continuing – at varying intensity – throughout the scene. Wee Johnny engages Collins.

Wee Johnny You know why Hazel married me? Said I reminded her of Harry Lauder – (*warbling/manic*) 'I belang to Glazgee, dear auld Glazgee toun/ There's somethin the matter with Glazgee for it's goin' roun' an' roun' . . .' I'll tell you this, General Collins, if you don't know it already. My life is my painting. Hazel's life is life itself – she must have her hand on the very pulse of it or she aches.

Collins nods, ghost-like. Squad Man A – passing through – tosses Collins a blackthorn stick.

SMA 'I hear in the darkness' –

Collins downstage left, moving stage right as he recites. Hazel has come on downstage right.

Collins I hear in the darkness their slipping and breathing/ I name them the by-ways they're to pass without heeding/ O, the wet winding roads, brown bogs and black water/ My thoughts on white ships and the King of Spain's daughter . . . O farmer, strong farmer, you may spend at the fair/ But your thoughts you must turn to your crops and your care/ And soldier, fine soldier –

Waiter (*arriving*) Mr Collins, you might care to know, the Military are in the hall –

Waiter delivers glass of whiskey to Dev upstage, exits. Collins to Hazel: they kiss passionately. Wee Johnny busy sketching.

Collins With you I never know how to end a kiss –

Hazel May you never learn . . . Let me see you . . . (*She studies his face closely.*) Where are you now?

Collins With Hazel. I'm here. With Hazel.

The Captain makes a brief appearance stage left: in smoking-jacket and military cap, sipping from a demitasse.

Hazel You'll be all right?

Collins I'll be fine.

The two – lover gait – walk upstage. Hazel exits; Collins left alone, his back to audience. Collins swivels his head – slowly – leftward to view the audience. And – adagio – turns his gaze upstage again.

Dev closes his ledger, downs his whiskey, waits. Wee Johnny is still for the moment. Collins – moving as if gone from himself – turns and proceeds to a chaise-longue *downstage right, stretches himself on it.*

Swiftly now: soldiers on, candles, we're looking at Collins lying in state. Dev: an impassive face on offer for the audience. Wee Johnny: active as never before, easel, oils, don't anybody get in his way.

Kitty – in mourning – enters, goes to Collins, kisses those lips . . . and moves back. Wee Johnny – flash of irritation at that interruption – resumes work.

Fade.

Afterword

When I was in my early teens I found Piaras Beaslai's two-volume biography of Michael Collins in the book-case of my teacher parents. The climax to Beaslai's account – a summer evening, a lonesome road, the hero's bloody death – left me quivering. I knew then, instinctively, that Collins would be with me for a long day. What I didn't know was the common nature of my experience. Collins was a storm, and still around.

The house I grew up in was not, as it happened, a 'Collins house'. De Valera was frequently mentioned. His picture was in my mother's scrap-book, a caption convenient which referred to 'the felons of our land', Pearse and McDonagh were there also, Collins notably absent. And my grandmother had a fraught sense of De Valera as *The One*, warning me on a memorable occasion 'not to be spakin' like that about De Valera, you'd niver know when you'd have yer hand in his mouth'. The biography in the book-case was an unconscious talisman, a muffled icon; De Valera lived, De Valera ruled.

And De Valera was getting to me because, even as a young lad, I had an intuitive awareness of the cheerless tyrant in him, and, intimately linked, a perfervid feeling for the Cavalier in Collins, the impudent *enfant gaté*, the degree to which he was – perilously – 'a child of the mother'. In this implicit contest, obviously, the slain hero had the advantage. Time busied itself enhancing his halo – while De Valera slowly turned to stone, limestone, blue limestone. And yet: leaving death and the calendar out of it for a moment, Collins, I knew, would always have had my handshake. Why? He had the magic.

Wandering confusedly into the world, I was careful to bring the Beaslai biography with me. Not long after, however, in a penurious hour, I lugged the two volumes to a Dublin book-shop and sold them so that I could buy, on the spot, the standard two-volume *Chekhov* collected stories. The deal had a lick of guilt. The exchange was necessary, the guilt wasn't. Chekhov would bring me closer to Collins, just as the Collins music has led me to Chekhov. The one was the other. Both had the stink of life.

Inevitably, I wrote a short story in which Collins figured. Not unnaturally, it was titled *The Great Sword*. I'd come on a master-mechanic from the Armagh bible-belt. Of stout planter stock, he'd fallen – hopelessly – for Collins. He had no difficulty envisioning a Second Coming – Collins at the centre – a shimmering event which would put matters right on this island: 'This could be a grand wee country if it was one, if it was made whole . . .' He believed – and you loved him for it – that anything was possible and, indeed, given the slightest encouragement, dandled anthems to the 'wee lovely limitless word *all*'. The pair of us spent long summer evenings with Collins purring beside us like trapped lightning.

It will be evident that Collins and I were 'followin' one another around'. And now I began to hear – as they started to surface – stories long submerged which had to do with Collins's *Don Juan* side. And I began to make connections between the *Don Juan* exploits and his legendary deeds as leader of the armed struggle to expel the British. Surely the two had to be of a piece? Just as surely as he bristled conflict. What was the name of his shadow? Consideration of these questions brought me to the composition of *Good Evening, Mr Collins*.

I have a story to commemorate the venture. I was in the consulting room of my local GP, female. She enquired casually, as people will, 'Writing anything at the moment?' 'A play about Mick Collins.' She studied her thermometer. 'Ah, yes,' she sighed, 'Mick and the women'. The folk remember. And the folk forgive. My barrow-woman in

Moore Street declaimed only the other day – 'Why wouldn't he be spreading it around? When he had it? To give?' *Sin é. An togha fir.*

My last Collins story – for the moment – goes like this. In the deeps of writing the play, I was roused from sleep one night by a clap of thunder. Every stone in the house turned over, settled. Stillness again. Next morning, I enquired. My companion had heard nothing. No one in the townland had heard anything. Fine. What I'd heard, I'd heard. And it didn't surprise me. Collins was – is – the *coup de tonnerre*, the *coup de foudre*. If you're dealing with that kind of energy, expect a visitation. A nod in your direction, yours to interpret.

In Ireland, where story-telling persists, we tend to remember people for words uttered, a particular sentence, a phrase. There's a terse sentence associated with Collins. Keep in mind the time in which he flourished, the battle-time, 'the Terror', the body or the lash . . .

– How're things going, Mick?

(*Allow one beat, debonair.*)

– I'm always hopeful.

Find there the man's courage, laughter, his fallible longings.

Tom Mac Intyre
Dublin, 1995

PORTIA COUGHLAN

Marina Carr

For Dermot

Characters

Portia Coughlan, thirty
Gabriel Scully, fifteen, Portia's twin, a ghost
Raphael Coughlan, thirty-five, Portia's husband,
has a limp
Marianne Scully, fiftyish, Portia's mother
Sly Scully, fiftyish, Portia's father
Maggie May Doorley, mid-fifties, Portia's aunt,
Marianne's sister
Senchil Doorley, sixty, Maggie May's husband
Blaize Scully, eighty, Portia's grandmother
Stacia Diyle, (the Cyclops of Coolinarney), thirty,
Portia's friend
Damus Halion, thirty-five, Portia's lover
Fintan Goolan, thirtyish, barman of the High Chaparral

Setting
The play is set in the Belmont valley in the midlands. The
stage must incorporate three spaces: the living room of
Portia Coughlan's house, the bank of the Belmont river,
the bar of the High Chaparral.

Music and songs had not been decided upon when this
volume went to press. Anyone considering staging the play
should contact the author's agent. (See p.iv for address.)

Time
The present.

Glossary

Lewin	=	Popping out of
Naggin	=	Dram or tot
Cines	=	Coins
Talche	=	Talk
Thinche	=	Think
Yar	=	Your
Wache	=	Week
Lave	=	Leave
Grake	=	Greek
Bilt	=	Belt

Act One

SCENE ONE

Two isolating lights up. One on **Portia Coughlan** *in her
living room. She wears a nightdress and a sweatshirt.
Dishevelled and barefoot, she stands staring forward, a
drink in her hand, curtains closed. The other light comes
up simultaneously on* **Gabriel Scully,** *her dead twin. He
stands at the bank of the Belmont river singing. They
mirror one another's movements in an odd way,
unconsciously. Portia stands there drinking, lost-looking.
Gabriel sings. Hold a while.*

 Enter **Raphael Coughlan,** *Portia's husband. He has a
limp. He stands there unnoticed by Portia, watching her,
car keys dangling, portable phone. As soon as he speaks
Gabriel's song stops and lights fade on him.*

Raphael Ah for fuche's sache.

 Portia turns to look at him, looks away, takes another drink.

Tin a'clache i'tha mornin' an' ya'are ah ud arready.

Portia Though' you war ah work.

Raphael Ah war.

Portia Cem bache ta chick an me.

Raphael Noh especialla. (*Holds up brandy bottle,
examines level, looks at her.*) There's dishes i'tha kitchen as
hasn't seen a drop of waher this weeche nor more.

Portia So.

Raphael An' tha kids, ya didn't drive thim ta school in
thah geh up ah hope.

239

Portia (*lighting a cigarette*) Stacia brun' thim.

Raphael Did tha have their breakfas'?

Portia A cuurse tha did, whah ya tache me for ah all.

Raphael Jus' axin' Portia.

Portia Well don't arrigh'! An' if yar thah worriet abouh thim why'd'n ya mine thim yarsilf!

Raphael An' you'll go ouh an earn tha mona?

Portia If ya never med another penny we'd still be rich . . . Tae.

Raphael Naw.

Portia Busy ah tha factory?

Raphael Aye.

Portia Ud's me birtha taday.

Raphael Thah a fac'?

Portia Imagine, ah'm thirty . . . Jay, half me life's over.

Raphael Me heart goes ouh ta ya.

Portia Have wan wud me an me birtha.

Raphael Ah this hour, ya mus' be ouha yar mine.

Portia pours one for herself.

Portia (*defiantly*) Slainte.

Raphael takes package from his pocket, throws it to her.

Raphael This be why ah cem bache this mornin'. Happa birtha Portia.

Portia Though' ya forgoh.

Raphael Did ya now.

She opens package. A vulgar diamond bracelet: she is dismayed at their flashiness, her taste is better.

Portia Diamonds.

Raphael Why noh.

Portia Thanks Raphael . . . ud's lovely. (*Stands there looking at it.*)

Raphael Portia.

Portia Whah?

Raphael Wha's wrong a' ya?

Portia Natin'.

Raphael Natin' . . . well ah'd behher geh bache. (*About to exit.*) Wha's thah yoche there?

Portia (*looks at old musty box*) On'y an aul box ah pullt ouha tha river las' nigh'. (*Looks at box transfixed.*)

Raphael Whin a' ya goin' ta stop?

Portia Stop whah?

Raphael (*waves an arm wearily, about to exit*) Puh thah someways safe, ater settin' me bache five gran'. (*Exits.*)

Portia throws bracelet in a drawer, goes to box. We hear Gabriel's voice, very faint. She listens, rummages for a CD, puts it on to drown out the sound. The sounds merge then CD, opera, dominates and Gabriel's voice disappears. Exit Portia.

SCENE TWO

Enter **Maggie May Doorley,** *an old prostitute, black mini skirt, black tights, sexy blouse, loads of costume jewellery,*

high heels, fag in her mouth, she carries a large parcel.
Followed by **Senchil Doorley**, *her husband, half the size of*
her, skinny, fussy, lovely.

Senchil (*following her, half dance, half run*) Leh me carry
thah peh.

Maggie M (*talking through fag*) S'arrigh' peh, ah have ud,
anaways didn' tha doctor say as ya've ta mine yar heart.
(*Calls.*) Portia!

Senchil Ah'll turn down tha music or ud'll brin' an yar
migraine.

Maggie M Lave ud, lave ud, ah liches ud Senchil.

Senchil Do ya, will ah turn ud up so peh?

Maggie M S'fine peh. Portia!

Senchil Ya sure now peh?

Maggie M Am peh.

Senchil (*indicating parcel*) Here puh thah down peh.

Maggie M S'arrigh' peh, Portia!

Senchil Don' strain yar vice peh.

Maggie M Arrigh' peh. PORTIA!

Senchil S'thah Italian he's singin' peh?

Maggie M Is peh, tache tha cigareh ouha me mouh,
stingin' tha sockets a' me eyes.

Senchil (*takes cigarette out of her mouth*) Ya want
another puff afore ah puh ud ouh peh?

Maggie M Aye. (*Has another puff, Senchil holds it.*) Ah
wonder is she gone.

Senchil Her char's ouside anaways, sih down peh, yar

varicoses, ya shouldn' be wearin' thim high hales peh, don' know ha mana times ah toult ya thah.

Maggie M Portia!

Portia (*off*) Whah?

Senchil She's here peh.

Maggie M On'y yar auld aunt.

Portia Sihdown ah'll be ouh in a minuhe.

Maggie M Ligh' us a cigareh there Senchil.

Senchil (*lighting one fussily*) Yar smochin' too much Maggie May an' ya didn' geh yar lungs chicked ouh this five year.

Maggie M Ah will, ah will peh.

Senchil Whin?

Maggie M Soon, soon.

Senchil Ah'm tiret machin' appintmints for ya now, Maggie May.

Maggie M Ah know y'are peh, an' sure why wouldn' ya be.

Senchil Sa long as ya know ah'm noh ta be tachen avantage of Maggie May, now.

Maggie M (*not listening to him, smoking away*) Ah know peh.

Senchil An' yar no use ta me dead Maggie May an' tha's tha truh of ud now.

Maggie M Noh a sign a' me dyin' Senchil, noh a sign.

Enter Portia, dressed in skirt, sandals, jumper. The same outfit for Acts One and Three.

Maggie M There y'are.

Portia (*kisses Maggie May*) How'ya Senchil?

Senchil Ah'm vera well thank ya Portia an' yarsilf, beauhiful day, beauhiful, beauhiful, a day ta seh tha bull among tha heifers, a day ta hop tha ram in an tha ewes.

Maggie M (*looking at him*) Aye if there war e'era bull or a ram around Portia for yar birtha. (*Hands her the parcel.*)

Portia Ah there was no nade Maggie May.

Maggie M A Godchile's a Godchile, thah righ' Senchil?

Senchil Is peh.

Portia Whah is ud?

Senchil Open an' see now for yarsilf.

> *Portia takes a three-foot white delft horse on its hind legs, from wrapping.*

Portia God Ammighy, ah may jump up an him an' ride off an him wan a' these days.

Maggie M Sem as ah though' mesilf whin ah seen him.

Senchil Goh him ah tha garden cintre.

Portia Ah love ud Maggie May, yar fierce good ta me. (*Kisses her.*)

Maggie M Oh Senchil puh in for ud too.

Senchil Will ah mache a chup a tae peh?

Maggie M Mache wan for yarsilf Senchil, ah'll have a brandy if Portia offers me wan.

Portia A cuurse ya will.

Senchil (*takes a packet of biscuits from his pocket, offers them around*) Y'all have wan Portia?

Portia Ah won't Senchil.

Maggie M No thanks peh.

Senchil Ya don' mine me brinin' me own biscuits do ya now Portia?

Maggie M An' why would she peh, sure don't Portia know yar heart be banjaxt.

Senchil Ya see, sem as ah war t'ahe a chocolah biscuih an' sem as tha crumb a' tha chocolah turnt inta a cloh an' sem as thah vera cloh wint up ta me heart. (*Pregnant pause.*) A goner.

Maggie M Stiche ta yar digestives Senchil, tha's all ah'll say an tha mahher.

Senchil Ah will peh, ah will. (*Exits.*)

Maggie M Yar fierce down in yarsilf Portia.

Portia (*drinking*) Am ah?

Maggie M For a birtha ghirl an' all.

Portia Ah.

Maggie M Raphael tratin' y'arrigh'?

Portia Aye.

Maggie M Glad ta hare ud, an' tha kids?

Portia Sure they're nearla min, Jason be twelve chome Dicimber, Peher tin an' Quintin's i'school arready . . . Ah had thim too young Maggie May . . . marrit ah seventeen, Jay whah war ah ah?

Maggie M Ah know peh.

Portia An' ah mimber ya tellin' me an' all.

Maggie M Nowan ever tachen my advice yeh, barrin

Senchil, an' looche ah tha stahe a' him . . . mebbe ya war behher off, marriet ta wan a' tha richest min i'tha county, beauhiful house, beauhiful clothes, beauhiful everthin'.

Portia An ah was goin' ta college an' all, had me place, buh Daddy says naw, marry Raphael.

Maggie M Aul' Sly Scully, never liked him, God forgimme talchin' abouh yar father liche this.

Portia Don' chare for him naither.

Maggie M Turnt yar mother agin me this years now.

Portia Mother war allas fierce wache.

Maggie M She warn't allas Portia, me an' her had greah times together, we'd paint tha town regular. Atwane yar father an' his aul' mother tha beah everthin' worth batin' ouha her. Thah an' losin' her son.

Portia She warn't tha on'y wan as lost him. (*Pulls over musty old box.*)

Maggie M Though' thah wint inta tha river wud him.

Portia Did an' all, found ud las' nigh', ah'm sittin' an tha banche an' ah hear tha waher sloshin' over somethin', ah looches down an' there's tha box . . . Maggie May ah though' ah seen a hand.

Maggie M Chome off ud Portia.

Portia Ah geh inta tha river ta drag ouh tha box an' ah feel somethin' clutchin' me leg.

Maggie M Mos' prob'ly ragworh nor sedge, tha roots a waher lilies, mebbe an eel, big conger fella.

Portia (*examining contents of the box*) This war no eel, he's chome bache ta geh me, an' ah was strugglin' wud him, los' me balance, wint under for a few seconds, he

tryin' ta tache tha box offa me, buh ah fough' wud him,
cem up wud tha box burstin' for air.

Maggie M Ya war dramin' ud childt.

Portia No, ah felt him, ud was him Maggie May, looche,
hes music. (*Holds up sheets of music from box.*) A
phohograph of him an' me, an' looche, our jar a money,
old money, we war savin' for whin we'd be grown . . .
clothes pegs (*Laughs.*) Gabriel said we'd nade thim,
robbed thim from all tha neighbours' lines, a couple a time
. . . crayons . . . we though' wherever we war goin' we'd
nade crayons . . . crayons . . . in this box we puh everthin'
for whin we'd be free an' big . . . we war goin' ta travel tha
whole worldt me an' him . . . Maggie May ah'm vera
afraid.

Maggie M Natin' ta be afraid a' Portia, on'y a box, rivers
is forever throwin' up stuff ya think is gone.

Portia Ah know ud war him, ah know.

Maggie M He's dead Portia an' ah have no truck wud
ghosts an' naither should you for yar pace a mine, forgeh
abouh ud an' peg thah box bache ta wheerever ud chem
from.

Enter Senchil with his tea.

Maggie M Ya med yar tae peh.

Senchil Ah did, ya want me ta do tha washin' up Portia.

Portia (*mind elsewhere*) Whah?

Senchil Tha washin' up.

Portia Jay no Senchil, ud's gran', lave ud.

Maggie M Senchil's mighy ah tha washin' up.

Senchil Ah do love ud, loochin' ouh tha winda ah Maggie

May's Arfrican marigolds an' washin' tha ware, don't ah peh?

Maggie M Ya do.

Portia (*packing up box*) This lamb of a day an' me stuche here for all eternihy. Ah have ta geh ouh Maggie May.

Maggie M Chome inta town wud us.

Senchil Aye do.

Portia Ah thinche ah'll go walchin', pull tha duur ater ye.

Senchil Bye peh.

Maggie M Quare mood.

Senchil Lonely in hersilf isn't she now Maggie May peh?

Maggie M She is.

Senchil Ah hope now if you was ever ta geh lonely an' fierce basement down in yarsilf, ah hope ya'd have tha dacency ta tell me.

Maggie M Cuurse ah would Senchil.

Senchil An' ah'd have ya righ' as rain e'er long.

Maggie M Ya would peh. Will we go or will ah have another wan?

Senchil Too erla peh.

Maggie M Don' start wan a yar lectures an drinkin' peh, chan't abide thim.

Senchil Ah won't peh, ah won't on'y ud's noh good for ya, brandy for breakfas' an' me ater choochin' tha full fri for ya. D'ya thinche would y'ahe ud, noh a bih a' ya, had ta peg ud ta tha chah.

Maggie M (*exiting*) Peh! Peh! Shu'p! Shu'p!

Senchil (*following her*) Manners Maggie May! Manners!

They exit.

SCENE THREE

Enter **Damus Halion**, *swarthy, handsome. By the bank of the Belmont river, he picks a clump of violets, arranges them into a bunch.*
Enter Portia.

Damus (*kisses her, puts a violet in her hair*) For tha birtha ghirl. (*Stands back, admires her.*) Ya'll soon be an aul hag Portia Coughlan.

Portia Mebbe ah will, don't seem ta deter you none anaways.

Damus Ah liches me women an tha mouldy side, liche cheese yees taste behher whin yees are goin' off . . . natin' a' more interest ta th'eye than a beauhiful woman beginnin' ta rust.

Portia Complimintra as ever. (*Sits on the bank.*)

Damus Whah tooche ya sa long?

Portia Maggie May an' Senchil arrived wud a big lug of a horse.

Damus Ah says ta meself aither she's gone offa me agin or aul Hop-along's finally found ouh.

Portia Ah toult ya noh ta call him Hop-along! Chan't abide ud! S'noh hes fault half hes fooh was cuh off.

Damus Well there's mana as says he done ud be purpose for tha chompensation.

Portia Well ud's lies an' ya know ud, who in their righ' mine'd cuh off their fooh for a few quid?

Damus Ah know plinty as may for half a million, buh ah find yar difince a' yar husband touchin' an' a wee bih sintimintal. Coughlan if ya war mine an' ya talcht abouh me tha way ya talche abouh thah excuse of a man a' yourn ah'd chop yar head off an' ahe ud for me tae.

Portia Well ah'm noh yours nor anawan ilses Damus Halion.

Damus A'ya noh now.

Portia Gis a cigareh. (*He lights one for her, she lies back and smokes.*) Lovela here.

Damus (*kisses her, a long lusty kiss*) C'man up ta tha boah house.

Portia In a minuh.

Damus Ah've ta be bache in an hour.

Portia Thin go if yar worriet.

Damus Wan a yar bitchy moods agin.

Portia Ah mane, for Jaysus sache Damus, chan't we jus' sih an' talche or d'ya noh want ta talche ta me. Why does ud allas have ta be thrashin' an' sweatin' i'tha boah house?

Damus Missus, ud was you gev me tha chome an an' now ya wanta talche.

Portia Ta my reckonin', bin a long time since ah gev you anathin' approachin' a chome an.

Damus Thah a fac' . . . (*Lies back, sucking grass.*) Whah kapes ya chomin' here so?

Portia Ah chome here because ah've allas chome here an' ah reckon ah'll be chomin' here long ater ah'm gone. Ah'll lie here whin ah'm a ghos' an' smoche ghos' cigarehs an' observe ye earthlin's goin' abouh yeer pintless days.

Mebbe ah'll see me father pickin' stones from hees forty
fields an' be able ta watch him athout shiverin', tha way ah
never could whin ah war livin'. Mebbe ah'll see you, older,
doin' some nigh' fishin' here an' mebbe, jus' mebbe, ya'll
looche up from yar fishin' for a second, jus' a second, an'
ya'll have seen me or felt a breath through yar hair thah
warn't tha wind, or heerd a rustle from tha copse thah
warn't some nigh' animal. Thah'll be me. Mebbe. Mebbe
me sons'll be min an' ah'll walche amon' thim an' mebbe
ah'll be longin' ta be livin' agin, though ah don' thinche
tha's a possibilihy.

Damus An' mebbe yar an eegit, cracked as yar twin.

Portia An mebbe yar as thick as tha rest a' thim. Though'
ah'd tache y'ouha tha slime buh ud's still drippin' offa ya.

Damus Wasn' far from slime ya was reared yarself Portia
Coughlan. Yar aunt tha village bike! Yar father gettin' aul
Tim Lahane drunk an' stalin' hees land offa him.

Portia Me father bough' thah land fair an' square.

Damus Aye an' Tim Lahane scuttered under tha table an'
he signin' ud over, never a soult ud an' him sober.

Portia Ya don' know whah yar talchin' abouh so kape yar
big thick mouh shuh 'till ya do.

Damus Yar more trouble nor anathin' else Portia
Coughlan, allas war, led me a dance this years. Wance ud
was me ya war goin' ta marry buh ah warn't good enouh
war ah, wance ya clapt yar greedy eyes an Raphael
Coughlan an' hees big char an hees big factora an' pound
signs lewin' in hees eyes.

Portia Tha's righ', geh ud offa yar chest, ya'll feel behher.
Jaysus yar so fuchin' bihher!

Damus Yar noh exactla a picture a bliss yarself, looche ah ya.

Portia Yar righ' ah'm noh continted an' have noh bin this long while bache. (*Stamps out cigarette.*) Ah have ta go.

Damus Tomorra.

Portia If ah fale liche ud. (*Throws flowers into river, and begins to exit.*)

Damus Ah don' know whah ud is ya want from me.

Portia An' ya never will.

Damus Fuche ya! (*Exits.*)

SCENE FOUR

Enter Portia and **Stacia** (*the Cyclops*). *They sit at the bar of the High Chaparral.*

Stacia An' Quintin was ballin' hees eyes ouh, had ta drag him from tha char inta tha classroom.

Portia (*barely listening*) Fierce difficult, Quintin.

Stacia He's on'y a childt Portia, ya may go softer an him.

Enter **Fintan***, the barman of the High Chaparral.*

Fintan Ladies yees are loochin' extremla beauhiful this sultra summer's day.

Stacia Ud's Portia's birtha.

Portia Now's yar excuse ta gimme a khiss. (*Proffers cheek.*)

Fintan G'way ouha thah wud yar cheeche. Cheeche's is for grannys an' aul' spinster aunts. Ah on'y ever khisses women an tha lips nor tha legs.

Stacia D'ya hare him, tha cheeche a'ya!

Portia (*offers leg*) Be tha leg so, me lips is Raphael's, God help him.

Fintan kisses her leg.

G'way now an' lave me leg alone afore ya swally ud'.

Fintan Ah've swallyed worser.

Stacia A bottle a cider Fintan, an' Portia whah're ya havin'?

Portia Sem as ever.

Fintan Branda an' ginger chomin up.

Stacia He's fierce forrard isn' he now? Whah d'ya think a' me new eye-patch Portia?

Portia Suits ya.

Stacia Pigskin. Goh four a thim, wan's blue, wan's grane, wan's yella an' wan's blache for mass an' funerals. Sint away t'Englan' for thim.

Portia Ah don' know Stacia, sometimes ah thinks if ah had me eye gouged ouh ah'd wear nera patch ah all.

Stacia Ah no Portia, ud'd frighten tha childern, as ud is they're a bih ashamed a' me.

Portia Pihy abouh thim.

Enter Fintan with drinks.

Fintan An tha house ladies, a sourta birtha present, whah age a'ya anaways?

Stacia Ya know well whah age she is, ya'd know less an' you a class ahind her in Miss Sullivan's school. Yar on'y machin' small talche so as ya chan ogle her over.

Fintan D'ya know whah ud is Stacia Diyle, you're gettin' more observant since ya lost th'eye.

Stacia All tha behher ta see through you wud Fintan
Goolan. Have ya no worche ta be doin' instead a sniffin'
'roun' tha skirts a' two marriet women.

Fintan Don't overestimate yarself Stacia Diyla whin ud
chomes ta my intintions an' for yar information, ah never
sniffs wheer there an't a scint. (*Looks at Portia and exits.*)

Stacia Kape away from him Portia, bad news, bad news.

Portia Ah he war on'y jossin' us, yar too serious Stacia.

Stacia Ah'm tellin' ya now Portia, thah fella'd have ya
pillowed an' thin broadcast ud an tha mornin' news, goh a
cousin a' mine up tha pole las' year, denied ud ta tha hilt.
Ah don' liches him wan bih.

Portia Well cheers anaway. (*Drinks and smokes.*)

Stacia Raphael tachin' y'ouh ta celebrahe tanigh'?

Portia Celebrahe . . . Me an' Raphael . . . (*Laughs.*)
Chan't imagine ud.

Stacia He noh tachin' y'ouh for dinner or somethin'?

Portia Nah, we're pas' thah kinda larche, lasteways ah
am.

Stacia God, Justin an' me goes ouh regular, ya nade time
be yeer selves Portia.

Portia An' whah d'yees talche abouh, yarself an' Justin,
whin ye'er be yeerselves.

Stacia Whah d'ya mane, whah do we talche abouh?

Portia Ah mane, be there ana differ sittin' opposit him
wud a chandle stuck atwane yees thah there would be if
yees war ah home facin' wan another in armchairs.

Stacia A cuurse there be.

Portia Asplaine ud ta me thin, whah tha differ be.

Stacia Well, Jaysus, dunno if ah chould righly say whah ud is.

Portia These days ah looches ah Raphael sittin' opposite me i'tha armchair. He's allas tired, hees bad leg up an a stool, addin' up tha books from tha factora, lost in heself, an' ah thinks tha pair of us migh' as well be dead for all tha jiy we knock ouha wan another. Tha kids is aslape, tha house creachin' liche a choffin, all thim wooden duurs an' fluurs, sometimes ah chan't brathe anamore.

Stacia Ya nade ta do more things Portia, geh ouha tha house, geh away from thah river, why'd'n ya geh him ta tache y'an a holida. Whin's tha las' time ya had a holida?

Portia An't never bin an wan Stacia.

Stacia Jay tha's righ, y'ant never had a holida. Tha's shochin' Portia! Shochin'!

Portia Ah don' want wan, don' think ah'd survive a nigh' away from tha Belmont valla.

Stacia Don' be daft, a cuurse ya would, migh' aven enjiy ud.

Portia Oh ah'm sure ah'd live through whah other folks calls holida's buh me mind'd be turnin' an tha Belmont river. Ah'd be wonderin' war ud flowin rough or smooth, was ud's banks mucky nor dry, was tha salmon beginnin' their awful rowin' ta tha sae, was tha frogs spawnin' tha waher lilies, had tha heron returned, be wonderin' all a these an' a thousan' other wonderin's thah river washes over me. In a former life ah'm sure ah war a river.

Stacia (*looks at her*) A river??

Portia Aye . . . (*Drinks.*) Another?

Stacia School's nearla over, kids'll be waitin', jus' go ta tha loo.

Exit Stacia. Enter Fintan.

Fintan Ya chould kape behher compana nor tha cyclops a Coolinarney.

Portia Don' call her thah i'front a' me an' if ya want ta screw me Fintan Goolan, have tha dacency t'ax me liche a man 'stead a' fussin' 'roun' me liche an aul cluchin' hin!

Fintan Fierce sure a' yarself, an't ya.

Portia Ah seen ya loochin', nigh an ever' time ah chome in here, asides there's noh a man i'this counta ah couldn' have if ah wanted.

Fintan Thah a fac'?

Portia An' ya know ud.

Fintan Well ah'm free this avenin'.

Portia Ah bet y'are. Seven, tha Belmont river.

Fintan Ah'll tache ya for dinner.

Portia Chan have dinner ah home, on'y want ta fuche ya, fine ouh if yar ana good, see if there's anathin' ahind a' thah cowbiy swagger an' too-honeyed tongue.

Stacia returns, both exit.

Fintan (*looking after her*) Jaysus H! (*Exits.*)

SCENE FIVE

Enter Gabriel Scully, wandering by the Belmont river, singing. Effect must be ghostly.
   Portia is in her living room, eyes closed. Leaning against

the door, listening. Hold a while. Doorbell rings. No move
from Portia. Again. Still no move. And yet again,
impatiently, aggressively, still no move.
   Marianne Scully, *Portia's mother, appears, watches*
Portia leaning against other door. Eyes closed.

Marianne So ya don' aven bother answerin' tha duur
anamore.

Portia (*eyes still closed as song gets fainter and Gabriel*
drifts off) Knew be tha witchy ring ud be yarself an' ya'd
be bargin' in afore long because ya never learnt, Mother,
t'allow people space an' quieh.

Marianne Wan a yar bad timpered moods agin. (*Begins*
tidying up the living room.) Tha stahe a' tha place, looche
ah ud.

Portia Lave ud.

Marianne (*ignoring her*) Ya'd sweer ya war never taugh'
how ta hoover a room or dust a mantel. A bledy disgrace
tha's whah y'are. (*Shouts off.*) Sly chome an in she's here.

   She puts a cushion from the floor onto the couch, Portia
   throws it on the floor again.

Marianne (*picking it up again*) An' wheer's yar childern?
Playin' 'roun' tha Belmont river ah suppose. You be luchy
tha don' fall in an drown thimsilves wan a these days.

Portia Ya'd liche thah wouldn' ya, weepin' ah tha grave a'
wan a' yar darlin' gran' sons. Be histora rapatin' udself,
wouldn't ud now, be liche buryin' Gabriel all over agin. Ah
knows how your bihher mine works, ya think thah if wan
a' my sons was drownt thah mebbe ya could asplaine away
how me twin was lost. Well mother, natin'll ever asplaine
thah, natin'.

Marianne Ah would ya stop such nonsinse, don' know

whah yar talchin' abouh, yar so darche Portia, allas war.

Portia Ah rades subtext mother, words dropt be accident, phrases covered over, sintinces unfinished, an' ah knows tha topography a' your mine as well as ah knows ever' inch an' ditch an' drain a' Belmont Farm. So don't you bluster in here an' puh a death wish an my sons jus' acause ya couldn' save yar own. My sons'll be fine for if ah does natin' else ah laves thim alone an' no marche be behher than a blache wan.

Marianne Y'ave nera righ' remindin' me a' Gabriel in such a bleache an' blameful way.

Portia He woulda bin thirty taday aswell . . . sometimes ah thinche on'y half a' me is left, tha worst half . . . D'ya know tha on'y rason ah married Raphael? Noh because you an' Daddy says ah should, noh because he war rich, ah chares natin' for mona, naw, tha on'y rason ah married Raphael was because of hees name, a angel's name, sem as Gabriel, an' ah though' be osmosis or jus' pure wishin' thah wan'd tache an' tha qualihies a th'other. Buh Raphael is noh Gabriel an' never will be . . . An' ah dreamt abouh him agin las' nigh'. Was wan a' thim drames as is so rale ya think ud's actualla happenin'. Gabriel had chome ta dinner here an' ater he goh up ta lave an' ah says, 'Gabriel stay for tha weechind', an' Gabriel demurs ouha poliheness ta me an' Raphael. An' ah says, 'Gabriel, ud's me Portia, yar twin, don' be polihe, there's no nade wud me' . . . an' thin he turns an' smiles an' ah know he's goin' ta stay an' me heart blows open an' stars falls ouha me chest as happens in drames an thin ah wache an' he's gone . . . We war so aliche, warn't we ever . . . Mother?

Marianne Tha spih, couldn' tell yees apart i'tha cradle.

Portia Cem ouha tha womb howldin' hands . . . whin God war handin' ouh souls, he musta goh mine an'

Gabriel's mixed up, aither thah or he gev us jus' tha wan
atwane us an' ud wint inta tha Belmont river wud him . . .
Oh Gabriel ya had no righ' ta discard me so, ta floah me an
tha worldt as if ah war a ball a' flotsam, ya had no righ'
. . . (*Portia begins to cry hysterically.*)

Marianne Stop ud! Stop ud! Stop ud righ' now! (*Shakes
her.*) Tha's enough a' thah! If yar father hares ya! Control
yarself! If ya passed yar day liche ana normal woman there'd
be none a' this! Stop ud! Stop ud! Ah'm tellin' ya now!

Enter **Sly Scully** *pushing* **Blaize Scully** *in a wheelchair.*

Blaize Would ya lave me chair alone! (*Whirrs forward.*)
Ya'll destriy me braches. (*Does a whirr in a circle to check
brakes.*)

Sly Marianne do somethin' wud her, she have me diminted.

Marianne Y'arrigh' there Mrs Scully?

Blaize Am, Mrs Scully, thank ya vera much!

Sly Happa birtha Portia.

Silence from Portia who stands with her back to them.

Blaize (*manoeuvring her chair into position*) Birtha's,
load a bollix.

Sly Ah toult ya Mammy, noh ta be cursin'.

Blaize (*irascible*) An' ah toult you ah spint tha first eigh'y
years a' me life howldin' me tongue, fuchin' an' blindin'
inta tha pilla. An' Jaysus, if God sees fih ta gimme another
eigh'y, tha'll be spint spachin' me mine foul nor fair.

Sly Yar mother an' me Portia, seh a thinkin' whah'd
Portia liche for her birtha an' we rached our brains, didn'
we Marianne?

Marianne Aye.

Sly There be natin' tha ghirl nades nor wants was th'ony conclusion we could chome ta.

Blaize Sly havin' trouble partin' wud mona agin Portia, ah sweer ta Jaysus Sly if hell war free ya'd go there sooner than pay a small intry fee ta Heaven.

Sly Natin' tha ghirl nades nor wants, thah righ' Marianne.

Portia So yees jus' brun' yeerselves.

Blaize An' me wud thim, won't lave me be me own anamore Portia, afeard ah'll fall inta tha fire, jus' wanted ta lie up agin tha range radin' me books an' listenin' ta Count John McCormack, d'ya think would tha leh me! (*takes a swipe at Sly's leg.*)

Sly Ow Jaysus Mammy stop!

Blaize Fuche ya! If ah had tha power a' me legs agin!

Marianne (*to Portia, who is pouring herself a drink*) Ah this hour!

Portia Ya know where tha duur is if ya can't stan' tha sigh' a' me.

Sly Ana sign of a sup a' tae or is thah too much t'ax.

Portia Mache yarself ah home Daddy. Granny Blaize, here's tha radia for ya.

Blaize Don' want nera radia, p'an tha Count, Portia.

Marianne Ah'll mache ya wan Sly, seen as yar daugher haven't tha manners ta.

> *Portia goes to look for CD of the Count. Sly comes over to her.*

Sly Ah seen ya wud young Halion agin taday down be tha Belmont river.

Portia Spyin' an me agin.

Sly Goin' abouh me business mendin finces an tha shalla side. Portia whah're ya doin wud him? He's no good thah fella, nor ana he cem from.

Blaize Tha Count, puh him an, puh him an.

Sly Ah'm talchin' ta ya ghirl.

Portia (*looks at him*) He knew Gabriel.

Sly Gabriel, forgeh Gabriel, thah unnatural childt thah shamed me an' yar mother so.

Portia Forgeh Gabriel . . . how can ya forgeh somewan who's everwhere. There's noh a stone, a fince, a corner of ana a' your forty fields thah don't resemble Gabriel. Hees name is in tha mouths a' tha starlin's thah swoops over Belmont hill, tha cows bellows for him from tha barn an frosty winter nights. Tha vera river tells me thah wance he war here an' now is gone. An' you ax me ta forgeh him. Whin ah lie down ah th'end of another awful day, ah pray for tha time ah'll be in tha ground aside a' him. Daddy ya don' understan' natin'.

Sly Don' talche down ta me ghirl. Ah've workt an' built Belmont Farm up from twinty acre a' scrub an' bog ta wan a' tha fines' farms i'tha county, wud thim there hands. Ah saved an' bough' fairla, mine you, ever piece a' land as could be bough' 'roun these parts. Thah don' happen jus' liche thah! An' for you ta be hangin' 'roun tha liches a Damus Halion. Sur' thim Halions wouldn' geh ouha bed i'tha mornin' ta milche tha cows, an' wha's Raphael think a' all a' this, hah?

Portia Daddy ah war on'y talchin' t'him.

Sly More nor talchin' ah seen, looches bad Portia, fierce bad. Don'n ya know everwan be's watchin', hopin' ya'll turn ouh liche yar aunt Maggie May.

Portia An if an did, ah migh' be behher off.

Sly Ah done me best ever ta diluhe thah wild Jiyce strake an yar mother's side, strange ud passed her over, buh you, you an' Gabriel, yees war ever unperdictable, never knew whah ye be thinkin'.

Portia Daddy ah'm a grown woman an' whah ah do is none a' your concirn. (*Goes to exit.*)

Sly Don' you walche away from me whin ah'm talchin' ta ya, ya rip ya!

Portia Don' you talche ta me liche thah in me own house! Now aither ye lave or ah'm lavin'.

Sly You watch yar tongue ghirl.

Blaize Tha Count, wheer be tha Count?

Marianne (*coming in with Sly's tea*) An' where're you off ta an' visihors i'tha house.

Portia Visihors! Jaysus, permanent fixtures be more liche! (*Exits.*)

Sly Sometimes, Marianne, ah do wonder be thah ghirl stable ah all?

Blaize Ah warnt ya an' ah toult ya Sly ta kape away from tha Jiyces a' Blache Lion, tinkers tha loh a' thim.

Marianne We war never tinkers an' well you know ud.

Blaize Oh yes yees war! Cem inta this area three giniration ago wud natin' goin' for yees barrin' flamin' red hair an' fah arses. An' tha counta council buildin' ye houses from our hard ernt monies. We don' know wheer ye cem from, tha histories a' yeer blood. Ah warnt ya Sly! D'ya thinche ya'd fuchin' listen! There's a divil in thah

Jiyce blood, was in Gabriel, an' ud's in Portia too. God protec' us from thah blache-eyed gypsa tribe wud their blache blood an' their blache souls!

Marianne Ya goin' ta stan' there an' jus' leh her talche ta me liche thah!

Sly Ah now Marianne she don't mane ud.

Marianne She mane's ever bih of ud! (*Goes over to Blaize in wheelchair.*) An' whah war you afore ya war marriet? Wan a' tha inbred, ingrown scurvied McGoverns! Tha say yar father war yar brother!

Blaize Ya fuchin' tramp ya!

Sly Ah Jaysus women! Jaysus!

Blaize All a' tha McGoverns was bred fair an' square which be more nor ya chan say for tha Jiyces!

Marianne Thin why is there nera father an yar birth cert. Ah'll tell ya why, acause ya had none, y'igorant aul hag, talchin' down ta me an' loochin' down an mine this thirty year nor more!

Sly Marianne! Y'arrigh' Mammy? She don' mane ud.

Blaize Shu'p ta be fuched you!

Sly Arrigh' ah'm sayin' natin'! Khill wan another for all ah keer!

Blaize (*getting out of wheelchair*) You Missus!

Sly Jaysus Mammy, yar hip!

Blaize Fuche me hip! YOU MISSUS! Ah know wha's atin' you an' ah've watched ud ate tha vera heart ouha ya this fifteen year!

Marianne Ya know natin'!

Blaize Ya kilt yar son! Yar beauhiful son who had a vice liche God hesself.

Marianne Ya don' know whah yar talchin' abouh!

Blaize Ya kilt him an' ya know ya did!

Marianne Yar lyin', an' ya know y'are jus' tryin' t'upseh me, ya vicious evil minded yoche ya!

Sly Lave ud now tha pair a' ye.

Marianne Ah never led a finger an him an well you know ud!

Blaize Ah fingers! Who's talchin' abouh fingers! Whin tha whole worldt knows ya can kill a body jus' be loochin' ah thim if ya looche long enough an' ya looche wrong enough! Ah know yar darche aul fuchin' Jiyce strake an' whah ud does to a person! Looche ah Sly! Y'ave turnt him inta a lump a' jelly afore me eyes. Tha's tha Jiyce power Sly, gets hoult a somethin' beauhiful an' pure, liche Gabriel, an' crushes ud till there be natin' left buh tha shell.

Sly Mammy tha's enough.

Marianne Ah don' want her nex' nor nare me agin. Ya may tind her from here an in. Ah'll sih i'me bedroom if ah have ta, tha way she med me do whin first ah war a bride. Amimber thah y'aul witch, sindin' me up ta me room whin all tha work was done, an Portia an' Gabriel wud me. Six a' clache an' summer evenin's, sint ta tha room, tha sun shinin' as if ud was midday, acause ya couldn't bear ta share yar kitchen wud a Jiyce. An' you leh her an' kep yar head down, doin' yar farm booches, dramin' a' acres, an' whah good are tha ta ya now, ya've nowan ta lave thim ta, an' tha twins an' me above i'tha room, too hot ta slape, wonderin' whah ud was we'd done ta be banished from our own kitchen. (*Begins to exit.*)

Sly Marianne.

Marianne Don't chall me in thah self-pihyin' vice, sickens me Sly, sickens me this long time gone. Tache yar mother home an' mine her, tha way ya shoulda minded me an yar childern, for we nade yar harsh chare namore. (*Exits.*)

Sly Well ah hope yar happa now.

Blaize Tache me home ta John McCormack an' don' worra abouh thah wan, tough as an aul booh, she be in tha duurway, po-faced, feelin' sorry for sheself afore dusk.

Sly and Blaize exit.

SCENE SIX

Enter Raphael Coughlan. He begins tidying up the place. Puts on some music. Sets the table for two, lights candles. Opens bottle of wine. Let this go on simultaneously with what's happening by the Belmont river.

Dusk. Enter Portia by the river. Smokes. Throws leaves into river. An owl hoots. She sits on her hunkers looking into the river. Enter Fintan. Stands there. Watches her a while.

Fintan Yar two hours lahe.

Portia (*up from a dream*) Whah?

Fintan Chem ah seven liche ya says.

Portia Oh righ'.

Fintan Couldn' geh away, ah says ta meself. Luchy ah chem bache. (*Takes out a naggin of whiskey.*) Whiskey?

Portia Why noh.

Fintan (*pours whiskey into two plastic cups*) Cheers.

Portia Yeah. (*Drinks.*)

Fintan Fierce close ta home . . . don't yar father's land go by this place?

Portia Aye . . . an' sur ah live on'y up tha lane.

Fintan Ya liche flyin' i'tha face a' everwan, do ya.

Portia If'n ya want tha hones' ta Jaysus truh Fintan ah forgoh all abouh ya. Ah chem down here acause ah allas chome down here.

Fintan Forgoh all abouh me! Ya mache ud vera hard for a man Portia Coughlan.

Portia (*barely listening*) Do ah.

Fintan Aye, ya do.

Puts a hand on her arm, she looks at the hand, he removes the hand.

Fierce quieh here.

Portia Ya chan hear tha salmon goin' up river if ya listen well enough, strugglin' for tha Shannon, an' up inta tha mouh a' tha sae an' from there home ta tha spawnin' grounds a' th'Indian Ocean.

Fintan Thah so.

Portia Aye. (*Steps into the river.*) They've never med thah journa afore, jus' born knowin' tha rouhe tha'll travel.

Fintan Chome ouha tha river, ya'll fraaze, ud's dape in there.

Portia stands there in the river, utterly still.

Chome an ouh Portia, ud's dangerous in there.

Portia goes in further.

Jaysus chome bache!

Portia Ever hare tell a' how tha Belmont river chem ta be callt tha Belmont river.

Fintan Heerd tell arrigh' . . . forgotten ud now . . . somethin' abouh a river god . . . Miss Sullivan used ta tell us in school. Chome on ouha tha river.

Portia Aye, buh afore thah there war a woman; more a ghirl tha say, an' she war tha stranges' loochin' creature ever seen in these parts, dark an' thin an broody she war an' all was afraid a' her acause she had tha power a' tellin' tha future. If ya lookt her in th'eye ya didn't see her eye buh ya seen how an' whin ya war goin' ta die. Ah wouldn't a bin afraid for ah know how an' whin ah will go down. Knowed ud this long while now. Anaways tha people 'roun' these parts grew aspicious of her acause everthin' she perdicted happened. Tha began ta belave thah noh on'y war she perdictin', buh causin', all a' thim terrible things ta chome abouh. So wan nigh' tha impaled her an a stache wheer tha river now is, mayhap righ' here, an' tha left her ta die. Ud's a slow deah, cruel an' mos' painful an' for nights an' nights ya could hare her tormintid groanin'. Bel, tha valla god heerd her, an' her cries near druv him mad. He could noh unnerstan' how her people could treah her so for she war wan a' thim, on'y a little different. He chem down tha valla in a flood a' rage, coverin' houses an' livestoche an' churches over, an' tooche tha ghirl in hees arms, down, down, all tha way down ta tha mouh a' th'Atlantich. Tha say Bel tooche more nor tha ghirl whin he chem down tha Belmont valla, ah don't know enough abouh thah buh ah thinche tha do say righ' for this place mus' surela be tha dungeon a' tha fallen worldt. An' ud's alsa said thah whin tha river be low 'roun' high summer, ya chan hare tha cries a' tha ghirl beggin' for release. Gabriel used ta hare her; sayed ud was liche an aria from a

chave; sayed there war no soun' i'this worldt ta match ud;
sayed if God tooche ta singin', be tha soun' he'd mache . . .
Ah never heerd thah soun' . . . yeh.

Fintan Load a' bollix if'n y'ax me.

Portia Ah'm noh axin' ya! Λh'm tellin' ya! An' your
apinion an' these mahhers or an ana mahher for thah
mahher don't interest me Fintan Goolan acause yar a
fuchin' clodhopper liche yar people afore ya an' liche those
ya'll spawn ater ya in a weh ditch an a weh nigh' in a
drunken stupour.

Fintan Y'ave a lug an ya an' a way abouh ya Portia
Coughlan thah'd turn bache a funeral! An' y'ave a toungue
an ya thah if ya war mine ah'd bate tha big shoh, stuche up
bejaysus ouha!

Portia Ah'm noh afeard a' you. Sa don't waste yar time
threatenin' me . . . thinche ah'll wade home be tha river.
(*Starts wading upstream.*) Nigh'.

*Fintan watches her disappear around the bend. He flings
the cup on the ground.*

Fintan Fuchin' mickey ketcher! (*And storms off.*)

SCENE SEVEN

*Focus back on Raphael finishing bottle of wine. Candles
have burnt down. He walks around impatiently. Portia
appears in doorway, barefoot, carries her sandals, stands
there.*

Raphael An' wheer war ya 'till this hour?

Portia (*looks at table*) Tha chandles an' tha wine. (*Leans
against doorway wearily.*)

Raphael Aye . . . chooked dinner for ya an' all, spiilt now.

Portia Dinner . . . Tccch. (*Sighs.*)

Raphael Nigh an midnigh' Portia.

Portia Is ud.

Raphael Bin home sense seven, tha kids atin' rubbich an' watchin' videos, no homework done, naither lunch nor dinner in thim. Wheer war ya?

Portia Ah Raphael, lave mc alone.

Raphael Quintin cryin' hes eyes ouh all avenin' for ya.

Portia He'll grow ouha me ivintualla. (*Sits, dries her legs with a cushion.*)

Raphael Ah for Jaysus sache Portia he's on'y four!

Portia Ah knows whah age he is an' ah want as little as possible ta do wud him arrigh'! (*Pours the end of the wine for herself, sits and smokes.*)

Raphael Yar own sons.

Portia Ah ncver wanted sons nor daughers an' ah never pertended otherwise ta ya, toult ya fron tha start. Buh ya though' ya chould woo me inta motherhood. Well ud hasn't worched ouh has ud. Y'ave yar three sons now so ya behher mine thim acause ah chan't love thim Raphael, ah'm jus' noh able.

Raphael Portia ah know thah taday of all days yar down an' ah know why. Now ah don' mache ouh t'unnerstan' tha breadth an' dipth a' you an' Gabriel. Ah have heerd thah tha bond atwane twins be ever strange an' inexplicable, buh surela now ud's time ta lave ud go an' try ta mache yar life athouh' him.

Portia (*erupting, like a madwoman*) Gabriel! Gabriel! Ha

dare you mention hees name! Tha problem's noh Gabriel,
ah'm over him this years! Tha problem's you! Ah fuchin'
hate ya! Moochin' up ta me wud yar sliche theories an
wha's wrong a' me! Ya haven't a fuchin' clue y'igorant aul'
fuchin' cripple ya! A chan't bear tha sigh' a' ya hobblin'
'roun' me wud yar bad fooh an' yar custom med cowbiy
boots!

Raphael Stop! Stop! Portia! Stop!

Portia An' whin you touch me at nigh', sometimes ah've
jus' goh ta slape, often tha first slape a' waches an' ah'm
slidin' inta a drame thah'll tache me away from this livin'
hell an' you touch me an' lurch me bache ta Belmont valla,
an' times yar lucky ah don't rip ya ta pieces or plunge a
breadknife through yar lily heart!

Raphael Portia ya don' mane ana a' this, yar upseh, ya
chan't mane ana a' this.

Portia (*shaking with rage*) Ya thinche ah don't! Thin hare
this an' le's be free of all illusions for evermore. Ah despise
you Raphael Coughlan, wud yar limp an' yar chape suits
an' yar slow ways! A chompletla an uhherla despise you
for whah y'are in yarself, buh more for who ya will never
be! Now lave me alone! An ligh' namore chandles for me
for fear ah blinds ya wud thim! (*Snuffs out candles
violently.*)

Raphael Portia please, don' spache ta me liche this, please
thinche whah ya're sayin', this isn' you . . .

Portia Tha fool chomes bache for more! Well there's
more! Y'axed me wheer ah war tanigh', well now ah'll tell
ya. Ah was screwin' tha barman from tha High Chaparral!
Gettin' angry now a'ya? Good, beginnin' ta hate me,
behher still. Ah wants none a' yar wahery love Raphael
Coughlan an' while we're an tha subjec' he war useless,
jus' as ah knew he would be, useless, as useless as you!

G'wan cry away, breache yar heart Raphael Coughlan,
ud'll hale, don't worra, ud'll hale, an' ah'll go guarantor
for you thah wance ud's haled there'll be natin' under sun
or moon thah'll ever lance ud's tough hide agin.

Lights down.

Act Two

SCENE ONE

*By the Belmont river. Evening. A search light swoops
around the river. Raphael, Marianne, Sly, Stacia, Damus,
Fintan, Senchil and Maggie May complete the group. They
stand in silence as a pulley raises Portia Coughlan out of
the river. She is raised into the air and suspended there,
dripping water, moss, algae, frog spawn, water lilies, from
the river. Gabriel Scully stands aloof on the other bank, in
profile, singing.*

    Ensemble choreography, all movements in unison.
All take a step back as Portia is raised.
All stop when pulley reaches its height.
All take another step back.
All look up at the dead Portia.
*Portia sways there, pulley creaking, Gabriel singing, water
dripping.*

Marianne Oh no.

Maggie M Swate sufferin' Jaysus.

Senchil Will somewan for Chris' sache cover her.

    *Portia wears only a slip. No one moves, transfixed by the
elevated image of the dead Portia. Senchil takes off his
jacket, tries to cover her, she's too high, jacket falls,
suspends on her foot, hangs there.*
    *Hold a minute. Then lower pulley. Raphael moves
forward to take her in his arms. Fintan moves to help.*

Raphael (*a measured growl*) Kape yar paws offa my wife.

    *Fintan moves back. Sly Scully takes rope off pulley.
Portia is now free of pulley and in Raphael's arms.*

Marianne Ud's happent agin! (*Begins banging Sly on the chest.*) Ud's happent agin an' ya toult me ud would never!

Sly puts arms around Marianne, allows her to beat him.

Oh Maggie May, whah have she gone an' done.

Raphael Portia! Portia.

Maggie M Ah don' know peh, ah don' know.

Raphael Ah suppose ah may tache her up ta tha house. (*Looks around hopelessly.*) Whah?

Sly Ah.

Raphael begins moving off with Portia, stumbles, intake of breath from Raphael, intake of breath from all, all stumble, and follow him off. Fintan and Damus left looking after them. Fintan offers cigarette to Damus, they light them, stand smoking in silence.
   After a while.

Damus Strange bird allas . . . Portia Coughlan.

Fintan Aye.

Damus Tha twin too.

Fintan Aye.

Damus Aye.

Fintan Gabriel.

Damus Tha's righ'.

Fintan On'y fifteen.

Damus Exac' sem spoh he war pulled ouha too.

Fintan Thah a fac'.

Damus Lookt liche a ghirl.

Fintan Sang liche wan too.

Damus Aye . . . wan thin' ah allas found strange abouh thim Scully twins.

Fintan Whah?

Damus Ya'd ax thim a question an' tha'd boh answer tha sem answer ah tha sem time, exac' inflexion, exac' pause, exac' everthin'.

Fintan Ah'd forgotton thah.

Damus Ya'd put thim in different rooms, still tha sem answer.

Fintan Aye . . . mimber now.

Damus Amimber tha school tour.

Fintan Which wan?

Damus Tha wan ta Behhy's Town.

Fintan Naw.

Damus Portia an' Gabriel sah up i'tha front a' tha bus in red shorts an' whihe tay shirts.

Fintan Aye.

Damus Whisperin' ta wan another as was their wont. We goh ta Behhy's Town, still have tha phoha a' tha whole class, still chan't tell wan a' thim from th'other. Anaways whin tha time chem ta geh bache an' tha bus, Portia an' Gabriel war missin'. A mad search wint an, nera sign a' thim, tha coastghuards callt in, helacopters, lifeboats, tha worches. Tha pair a thim found five mile ouh ta sae in a row boah. Tha jus' goh in an' started rowin'. Poor aul' Miss Sullivan in an awful stahe. 'Whah war yees ah childern, whah war yees ah, ah all?' 'We war jus' goin' away says wan a' thim.' 'Away! Away wheer i' tha name a'

God' says Miss Sullivan. 'Anawheer' says th'other a thim, 'jus anawheers thah's noh here.'

Fintan Anawheers tha's noh here, Jaysus.

Damus Aye.

Fintan Sur aul' Hop-along chould never manage her.

Damus Luchy ta geh her, though ah wouldn't chare for hees shoes now.

Fintan Whah'd she ever see in him?

Damus Chould a' had anawan, Portia Coughlan.

Fintan Ah, she chould.

Damus Anawan . . . anawan.

Both exit.

SCENE TWO

Lights up on Blaize and Stacia manoeuvring Blaize's wheelchair into Portia's living room. Stacia gets her into position.

Stacia A'ya arrigh' now?

Blaize Am Mrs Diyle thank ya.

Stacia Ah'll lave ya here so, an' gch th'aheables ready afore tha chome bache from the funeral.

Blaize P'an tha Count first.

Stacia Don' know if ah should seein' as tha day as is in ud.

Blaize G'wan ghirl. Portia loved tha singin'! P'an Count John McCormack. G'wan ud's there loochin' ah ya.

Stacia If anawan axes ud was you med me arrigh!

Blaize Puh ud an ghirl, ah'll dale wud thim, don' you worra.

Stacia puts on the Count. Blaize listens a minute.

An't he magnificent . . . an't he now? (*Crooning along with the Count.*) There war a gramaphone an' wan rechord in our house whin ah war a ghirl. Was tha Boston McGovern, a uncle who brun' ud home, war a rechord a' tha Count an' ah listened ta thah rechord 'till there war natin' left of ud . . . so ah did.

Stacia Did ya?

Blaize Aye . . . ah did. (*Listens some more.*) An' d'ya know whah war an tha radia this mornin'?

Stacia Whah?

Blaize Ater findin' Afghanastani cines 'roun' these parts.

Stacia Afghanastani whah?

Blaize Afghanastani cines ghirl.

Stacia An' wha's thah goh ta do wud anathin'?

Blaize Ah'll tell ya whah ud's goh ta do wud anathin. Wance there war Afghanastanish i'tha Belmont valla. Thah's whah ud's goh ta do wud anathin'. Manes wance mebbe ah war an Afghanastanish or ah tha vera laste me ancestry talked wud Afghanastaners. See ghirl these cines tha foun' be vera old, man an tha radia says, older nor tha Vikings. Mebbe wance this war Afghanastan afore ud war Ireland.

Stacia Afghanastan?

Blaize Beauhiful word, afghanastan, afghanastan. A word ya could say all nigh' inta tha pilla an' chome bache ta i'tha mornin'. Afghanastan, Jaysus. An't been righ' Stacia sense ah heerd th'afghanastaners war here. Man an tha radia

says biggest slave markeh i'tha Europe, time a' tha tinth
centura be in Dublin. Jay, ta be a slave ghirl in tinth
centura Dublin.

Stacia Ya be raped an' beh up an' soult for small change
Mrs Scully, soult for a chattel.

Blaize Dipind an who ya war chatteled ta Stacia Diyle.
Chould be a khing, nor tha saltrap a' Babylon, nor mebbe
Alexander tha Greah. Imagine bein' hes chattel now. Ever
mornin' ya wache up, a new continent. Imagine thah
Stacia Diyle if y'ave e'er a magination. No yees paple
'roun' here chan't imagine anathin' beyant nex' Frida i'tha
pub an' a bag a' chips an tha way home. Portia now, she'd
imagine ud. In a sourta way Portia war an Afghanastanish.

Stacia Thah she war.

Blaize (*listening to the Count again, conducting his
signing, miming along with him*) God bless ya
McCormack, a midlander liche me, born on'y up tha road
Stacia, on'y he goh away, say a prayer Count wheerever
y'are for us all who stayed . . . Turn him off now Stacia for
fear tha be accusin' us of disrespec' for tha dead. Tha'll be
here afore long, tomb eyed, stinkin' a' tha new dug grave.
Ah hahe tha smell a' choffins don't you Stacia?

Stacia (*turning off the Count*) An't smelt enough a thim ta
know Mrs Scully.

Blaize Vera partichular smell, cross atwane honeysuchle
an' new mown putrefaction.

Stacia Ah wishes if ya'd talche gintler abouh tha dead Mrs
Scully.

Blaize Ah my age Stacia, an't natin' left ta talche gintle
abouh. From here an in ud's jus' bihherness an' gums.

Stacia Portia was me friend Mrs Scully, me onla friend an' ah realize now ah didn' know her ah all. Sure ah knew she war unhappa buh who isn' these days, mus' be terrible lonesome ta do whah she done Mrs Scully. An' Maggie May toult me abouh Sly an' Marianne . . .

Blaize (*defensive*) Whah'd she tell ya abouh Sly an' Marianne?

Stacia Well she toult me all abouh how tha war . . .

Blaize Don' mine thah wan! Liar! Maggie May Doorley! A rusty tandem tha's all she be! Fit you behher Stacia Diyle ta mine yar own business an' noh be listenin' ta tha fabrications of a hoor.

Stacia Ah'm sorra Mrs Scully, ah didn' mane t'upseh ya.

Blaize (*calming down*) Noh upseh childt, noh upseh ah all, jus' don' pay ana attintion ta thah wan.

Enter Raphael followed by Senchil, Sly, Marianne, Maggie May. All wear black.

Stacia Sih down Raphael an' lave tha hostesseries ta me.

Raphael There's drink an' food an' all thah sourt a' stuff i'tha kitchen.

Enter Maggie May from kitchen with tray of drinks. Senchil runs to help her, nearly knocks her down.

Senchil Leh me carra thah peh?

Maggie M Jay Senchil, watch wheer yar goin', near knoched me flah.

Blaize (*to no one in particular*) Buriet is she?

Maggie M Aye, God rest her Mrs Scully.

Blaize (*to Raphael*) Bereft be ya? Fuchin' cheeche a'ya marryin' her i'tha first place! Who d'ya thinche y'are hah!

Raphael (*calls off*) Sly ya may chome in here an' tache charge a yar mother.

Blaize None a' ours ever had truche wud new money afore you chem skulkin' down the valla wud natin' goin' for ya ceptin' yar chompensation cheque in yar arse pocket!

Raphael (*half to himself*) Ah don' nade this taday of all days.

Sly Mother behavin' yarself. Ah'm sorra Raphael she's a bih upseh!

Blaize (*to Marianne*) Dry yar eyes ghirl, bin chomin' this fifteen year. (*to Sly*) Warnt ya an' ah toult ya! Would ya listen! (*to Maggie May*) Whisky! Black Bush, Black label!

Maggie M Ya knows yar whiskies Granny.

Blaize Mrs Scully ta you.

Silence. They all drink awkwardly, some sit, stand, lost in grief, exhaustion, whatever.

Senchil Lovela Sermon.

Looks around, glare from Blaize. Silence from the others.

Maggie M Was peh, was.

Blaize An' whah'd aither a' ye know abouh sermons, lovela nor otherwise. (*to Maggie May*) Tha sigh' a' you in a church ud blush tha host an' pale tha wine. Fuchin' tinkers tha Jiyces, allas an' ever wud thar waxy blood an' wanin' souls. Dirta igorant blood tha liches a' which Belmont has never seen afore. Slainte! Ta tha Jiyces! (*Drinks.*) Ta Portia i'tha murchy clay a' Belmont graveyard wheer she war headin' from tha day she war born, cause whin ya brade animals wud humans ya chan on'y brin' forth poor haunted monsters who've no sinse a' God or man. Portia

279

an' Gabriel. Changelin's. Slainte. (*Finishes her drink, smashes glass against fireplace.*) Tache me home, tha nex' funeral'll be me own!

Whirrs chair into reverse and then forward. Sly gets up to follow her.

Sly (*to Marianne*) Be bache in a while.

Marianne If ya chare ta.

Sly (*erupting*) You blem me for everthin'! For Gabriel an' now Portia. Ah war never hard an tha lad! Never! Leh him do whahever he wanted whin ah should a' bin whippin' him inta shape for tha farm.

Maggie M Ah now tache ud aisy Sly.

Sly No! Lave me be! Ah druv thah childt twice a wache, ever wache ta Dublin for hees singin' lessons in tha hay sason, whin tha chows was chalvin, whin there war more than enough worche ta be done ah home. Ah druv him, (*Points to Marianne.*) acause you says ah should, liche a fuchen slave, seventa mile each way an' he'd sih i'tha bache a' tha char, radin' hes music booches, hummin' to heself, wouldn' gimme tha time a' day noh if hes life dipinded an ud. Ah war hes father an' he leh me know he wanted no part a' me. God forgimme, buh times ah'd looche ah him through tha mirror an' tha though'd go through me mine thah this be no human childt buh some little outchaste from hell. An then he'd sing tha long drive home an' ah knew ah war listenin' ta somethin' beauhiful an' rare, though ah'm no judge a' these things, an' me aul' rough heart'd milt though he did noh sing for me. An' ah'd be proud, so proud thah this odd creature war mine. Chome, Mother, home, boh me children is gone, me grey-eyed ghirl, me son, me cold, hard twins.

Marianne Yar greah ah feelin' long ater tha nade ta feel be ghone. Why couldn't ya a' lookt ater thim whin tha war alive!

Sly Why! Ah'll tell ya why Missus! Ah war never leh!

Marianne An' ah suppose ud was me as stoppt ya! If in doubt blem me, ah chan do natin' righ!

Sly Ah'm fuchin' siche an' tiret a' yar martyr dance! You interfered ever time wud me an' tha twins! You pushed me ouh 'till ah war na more nor tha shada of a shade! Well now they're gone an' ah'll noh abide yar sorra Marianne. Ya done ud all be yar own.

Blaize Jaysus, y'ave a bachebone ater all Sly! Don' stop now ya started! Puh thah upstart in she's place wance an' for all!

Raphael Will somewan geh thah woman ouha me house.

Maggie M Ah will. (*Begins wheeling Blaize backwards.*) Wan a' these days ah'm goin' ta climb i'tha winda an' burn ya in yar bed . . . (*Whispers.*) an' another thing, did ah ever tell abouh tha time ah gev yar husband a quiche wan down Mohia Lane.

Blaize (*a hiss*) Liar, ah don't belave ya!

Maggie M Oh yes ya do, acause you know an' ah know wha's realla goin' an here, you know an' ah know whin tha roh began an' how tha roh began.

Blaize Don' know whah yar talchin' abouh! Hoor ya.

Maggie M Ah did aye, gev him a job down Mohia Lane, tha dirta aul' dog. Ped me wud yar egg mona, fifta quid, an' d'ya know whah he said abouh you.

Blaize He said natin'! Yar machin' ud up.

Maggie M He says ya war a bihher aul' hag an' he'd rather hump a bag a' rats an a bed a' nittles.

Blaize Oh listen ta tha filth a' tha hoor wud tha brochen bottle! We war vera happa ah'll have you know.

Maggie M Happa, war yas, happa! Thin ha chome he bet tha lard a' ya evertime he lookt ah ya . . . ha chome waches an' waches'd go by an' nowan'd have seen Blaize Scully ouh an' abouh acause her face war in a pulp agin . . . ha chome . . .

Blaize Sly tache me home! Sly!

Sly begins wheeling her off and both exit.

Senchil Whah war ya sayin' ta her peh? (*Eating a biscuit out of his pocket.*)

Maggie M (*to Stacia, coming in with sandwiches*) Dechlare ta God Stacia, forgoh all abouh ya.

Stacia Raphael ate somethin, y'ave noh touched natin' this three days.

Raphael Tha kids Stacia?

Stacia They're gran', over in my house, me sister's loochin' ater thim.

Raphael Quintin?

Stacia He's gran' . . . gran'.

Marianne Ah jus' chan't believe ud, ah jus' chan't.

Maggie M Ya wanta chome an' stay wud us a while Marianne?

Senchil Y'ad be vera welcome.

Marianne Stay wud yees? No, ah'll go home, tha'll be nadin' me there.

Gabriel Scully sings a lament from the banks of the Belmont river. All drift off.

Act Three

SCENE ONE

Lights up on Portia Coughlan's living room. It is set as it was at the end of Act One. Portia dozes on couch, wearing the clothes she wore at the end of Act One. It is the morning after her thirtieth birthday. We hear the sound of Gabriel Scully's voice. Portia wakes to this. It grows fainter, she strains to hear it. It stops. Portia, half sits, half lies there. Lights a cigarette.

Enter Raphael Coughlan, fresh suit. He limps across the room to collect his account books, looks at Portia, she looks at him. He turns away. Goes to open curtains.

Portia Lave thim.

He does.

Raphael Ya goin' ta get tha kids ready for school or will ah?

Portia You do . . . plase.

Raphael looks at his watch. Stands there.

Raphael Portia.

Portia Whah?

Raphael Ah'd be willin' ta forgeh whah ya said las' nigh' if y'ad on'y tache ud bache.

Portia Oh thah . . . D'ya want dinner this avenin'?

Raphael Whah?

Portia Dinner?

Raphael Yeah . . . be nice.

Portia Whah d'ya want?

Raphael For dinner?

Portia Yeah.

Raphael Well anathin' ah suppose.

Portia Arrigh'.

Raphael Righ' so. (*Goes to exit, stops at the door.*) Ya wanta come inta tha factory for a few hours?

Portia Naw.

Raphael Be good, get ya ouha tha house.

Portia Can't abide tha place Raphael, ya know.

Raphael Ah . . . (*Stands there lookin' at her.*) Well is there anathin' ah can do Portia? . . . Anathin'?

Portia Ah'm gran' hones'.

Raphael comes over, goes to kiss her on the cheek, instinctively she jerks her head away from him.

Don't . . . jus' don't touch me.

Raphael Quintin wants ya ta dress him for school.

Portia Will ya jus' stop! Lave me alone! Toult ya! Ah chan't! Arrigh'! Ah'm afraid a' thim Raphael! Afraid whah ah may do ta thim! Don' ya understan'! Jaysus! Ya think ah don't wish ah could be a natural mother mindin' me children, playin' wud thim, doin' all tha things a mother be asposed ta do. When ah looks at my sons Raphael ah sees knives an' accidents an' terrible mutilations. Their toys becomes weapons for me ta hurt thim wud, givin' thim a bath is a place wheer ah chould drown thim. An' ah have ta run from thim, lock thim ouha tha room, for fear ah cause these awful things ta happen. Quintin is safest when ah am nowheres near him, so teach him ta stop whingin' for me for fear ah dash his head agin a wall or fling him through a winda.

Raphael Portia yar noh well, yar noh.

Portia Ah'm arrigh' an' stop lookin' ah me as if ah'm goin' ta murder ye all in yeer beds, for ah won't as long as ye lave me in peace.

Raphael Portia ud's noh normal, tha way you're talchin' an' tha way ya be thinkin', noh normal ah all.

Portia Look, if ah was goin' ta do somethin' dreadful do ya think ah'd be tellin ya abouh ud. Naw, ah'd jus' go ahead an' do ud. Tha fac' ah'm even talchin' abouh ud manes ah wont.

Raphael An' whah sourta logic is thah?

Portia Me own, th'on'y logic ah knows.

Raphael Ya stayin' home all day?

Portia Ah may.

Raphael Will ah ring Stacia ta collec' tha kids from school?

Portia Whahever.

Raphael Portia?

Portia Whah?

Raphael Ya got me scared now, ya wouldn't do anathin' ta thim, would ya?

Portia Toult ya ah wouldn't, an' ah haven't, noh a mark an thim an' ah never will. Ah jus' wants thim noh ta want anathin' from me, tha's all.

Raphael Arrigh' so . . . see ya this avenin'.

Portia Yeah.

Goes over to him, looks at him, puts her arms around him, kisses him, loses interest immediately, goes to mantelpiece and looks away. A sigh from Raphael. Looks at her, can't make head nor tail of her shifting moods. Leaves the room. Portia stands there a minute. Sounds of Gabriel singing comes over, he appears at the river.

Portia Gabriel.

She runs from the room.

SCENE TWO

Gabriel Scully begins departing as Portia reaches the bank of the Belmont river. He disappears around the bend as she appears, out of breath. She stops, pants, looks around, senses him. Silence, except for the flowing river and birdsong. Damus Halion stands there watching her, unobserved.

Portia (*shouts at the air*) Chan't ya lave me alone or prisint yarself afore me! Is heaven noh sa lovela ater all? Are ud's streets noh paved in gold? Do th'angels noh sih drinkin' coffee an' prunin' their wings along th'eternal boulevards a' paradise? D'ya miss me ater all? . . . Whah's ud liche? . . . Gabriel.

Damus Talchin' ta tha dead now Coughlan?

Portia (*turns sharply*) An' whah if ah am.

Damus Some do say he still walches.

Portia Tha do say righ' . . . who toult ya anaway?

Damus Still nights he chan be heared singin' in hees high ghirly vice. Aul Mahon sweers he heared him, an' he chomin' home ater a night's poachin' up an O'Connor Morriss' bilt a' tha river.

Portia Ah aul Mahon, he sweers everwan who's dead walches.

Damus (*puts an arm around her*) Well ah'm alive an' dyin' for ya me prehhy little ghos' fancier, an' though ah chan noh haunt ya as ghosts chan, ah chan lave me marche an ya well enough.

> *Kisses her. Portia neither resists nor complies.*

If'n ya spint less time thinkin' abouh thah silla little brother a' yourn an' more thinkin' abouh how ah chould plase ya, ya'd be a happa woman Portia Coughlan.

Portia Ah'm past all pleasures a' tha body Damus. Long past. An' if ya realla chare ta know, ah've allas found sex ta be a greah leh down, all thah suchin' an sweatin' an stickin' things inta wan another maches sinse ta me na more. Gimme a jigsaw or a good opera ana day or tha Belmont river. Ah'd liefer sih be tha Belmont river for five sechonds than have you or ana other man aside a' me in bed.

Damus Strong sintimints from a little cock taser who used ta geh her jiys an' thrills from watchin' men drool as she churved by, an' who, aven as she professes ta have found sex ta be a greah leh down, is lanin' up agin me an' a flame crapin' up her throah all tha way from tha bachestairs of her hoh little arse.

> *Portia moves away from him. Looks into the river, pulls tufts of grass, flings them into the water, watches their journey.*

Sulchin' now are we.

Portia Ah didn't chome here ta see you Damus Halion. Ah chem here acause this here's me father's land. This be our part a' Belmont river. So g'wan off wud yarself an' yar crude radin' a' tha worldt an' ud's inhabitants.

Damus (*goes over to her*) Ah Portia c'man don't be gettin' thiche o'er natin'.

Portia (*shrugs him off*) Tha discos an' hotels is full a' youn' wans who'd be on'y too glad ta have ya maulin' thim. Lave me be. Ah won't see y'agin, so there's no pint in chomin' here anamore.

Damus Portia ah bin chomin' her an an' off this sixteen year.

Portia Ah know ha long ya bin chomin'.

Damus Don't thah chount for anathin? Wance ud war me ya wanted an' no wan ilse, or have ya forgotten thah, have ya?

Portia Ya war never more nor a distraction Damus Halion.

Damus Ah don't belave ya.

Portia Belave whah ya liche, ud's tha truh.

Damus An' who knows buh wan a' your youn' lads isn' mine.

Portia Thim's all Raphael's, God help thim, ah med sure a' thah.

Damus Yar lyin'. We war ah ud hoh an' heavy afore, durin' an' ater all a' your pregnancies. Ah've a mind ta go an' see thah cuckold a' yourn, an' tell him hees sons is noh hees sons buh mayhap mine.

Portia Tell him whah ya liche, don't give a tinker's curse anamore if tha whole worldt knew.

Damus Looche Portia, tha las' thin' ah want ta do is mache your life more difficult nor ud is. All ah want an' all ah've ever wanted is ta be wud you. Why'd'n ya lave him liche ya used ta say ya'd do.

Portia Used ah say ah'd lave him?

Damus Ya used.

Portia (*laughs a little madly*) Whah did ah belave in then, wheer did ah think ah war goin', for there's nowheer ah chould go Damus for if ah left tha Belmont valla ah would surela die. Anaway ud maches no differ ta me whether ah'm wud you or Raphael.

Enter Maggie May, unobserved by Portia and Damus.

Damus Yar a heartless fuchin' bitch an' ah wish ta God ah'd never led eyes an ya! Ah have never done things be halves, an' ah have loved you ta tha hilt a' me heart, puh up wud yar messin', an' yar runnin' bacheards an' forrards atwane ma an' Raphael an' yar twin, all tha time belavin' thah wan day ya'd be mine an' on'y mine an' you turn roun' ater all thah an' tell me ud maches no differ ta ya whether yar wud me nor Raphael. Whah sourt of a mongerel lamb d'ya tache me for, slavin' ater ya. Well ud's over now for wance an' for all, an' don't you chome loochin' for me whin yar mood changes agin because ah'll noh be there for ya, yar empta as a sached grave Portia Coughlan. Go ta yar twin, ah hope he won't be there so you migh' learn thah heaven war here, noh there, for tha tachin'.

Exit Damus, Portia sits there, rigid.

Maggie M Portia.

Portia Over here.

Maggie M (*sees Damus departing*) Halion righ'.

Portia Righ'. (*Lights a cigarette.*)

Maggie M Ah'm noh wan ta chaste aspersions an extra-marital dalliances buh ya chould do behher nor him. Raphael know abouh this?

Portia Raphael. On'y thing Raphael knows be how ta mache mona an' thin how ta save ud, sem as Daddy. Raphael! . . . an' aven if he did fin' ouh he jus' be doin' a bih of a cuckold jig an thin ud'd be bache to hees bank balance, hees factora, hees darlin' sons. Ah'm jus' hees chattel, hees decoration for tha Christmas party wud tha biys, ah'm tha cook whin tha Germans an' tha Finns an' tha Bulgarians chome loochin' for dales. He puts thim talchin' ta me, ah entertain thim, tha dale be done. Ah'm through wud all a' thah Maggie May, he chan do hees own fuchin' dales, find somewan ilse ta tache to hees parties; ah wish ta Jaysus he'd run off wud somewan an' tache tha brats wud him. Noh a hope, noh a hope in hell. Men; ah jus' want ta castrate thim.

Maggie M Jay Portia, thah's noh righ'.

Portia An't natin' righ' abouh me Maggie May, natin', an' me mother, d'ya know whah ah want ta do wud her?

Maggie M Whah?

Portia Ah want ta rape her, thah's noh righ is ud.

Maggie M Jaysus, tha mind boggles Portia, as how you'd go abouh ud.

Portia Ah've imagined ways, don't worra, don't tell anawan ah said thah, so ya won't, Maggie May.

Maggie M A cuurse ah won't.

Portia She's a darche fuchin' witch an' ah chan't abide tha sigh' a' her. Never chould, may God forgive me.

Maggie M She's jus' fierce damaged Portia. She'd an awful time growin' up herself an our mother war particulara hard on her. Senchil's above i'tha house machin' heself tae, s'arrigh.

Portia Aah.

Maggie M Lovela here.

Portia Aah.

Maggie M Me an' me father used ta chome nigh' fishin' here.

Portia Used yees.

Maggie M Caugh' a piche here wance, bigger than a yennin' ewe.

Portia Mimber tha time . . .

Maggie M Whah?

Portia Natin'.

Maggie M G'wan tell me.

Portia Jus' thinkin' abouh tha time tha cemetara gates fell an Gabriel.

Maggie M Aye, had ta be rushed ta hospital, everwan though' he war a goner.

Portia Mimber tha pair of us was unconscious for a wache, ah thinche ud was a sign.

Maggie M Sure ud was.

Portia He was never righ' ater thah . . . whah'd ya thinche ud meant Maggie May? Is there signs i'tha worldt? Is our lives followin' a minuhe an careful plan designed an high or are we jus' flittin' from chance ta chance?

Maggie M Well there be some as says ud's impossible for a body ta be other than th'are, buh then there's others as would claim thah ya choose yar own life an' yar own machin' of ud. Personalla ah prefers ta belave thah everthin' ah've done be planned be somewan else down ta tha las' detail. Ah'm a fah aul' hoor wud bad legs Portia an' ah'd hahe ta have ta blem ud all an meself.

Portia When ah war a childt Mother an' Daddy used ta brandish you as a threah. For years ah though' tha worst as could ever happen me was t'end up liche you. Now ah wishes ah chould.

Maggie M Liche me peh, sure ah've natin' goin' for me ceptin' Senchil. Did ah ever tell you how ah chem ta meeh Senchil?

Portia Naw, ya didn'.

Maggie M People's allas laughed ah him, thinches he's an eegit, mebbe he is, buh ah seen another Senchil thah no wan chares ta looche for. Ah war in London worchin' King's Cross, big angra fuchers wud too much mona an' no respec'. Had this rough chustomer wan nigh', showed me hees fists, done hees job, tooche me mona an' ran off wud me shoes so's ah couldn' folly him. Ah'm lyin' there i'tha duurway of an aul' warehouse, feelin' a little sorra for meself, an' along chomes Senchil. He's a nigh' watchman. He taches me inta hees huh, maches me tae, turns ouh he war brough' up noh twinty mile from Belmont valla. We talche all nigh' abouh Belmont an' other things an' i'tha mornin' he buys me a pair a' shoon. T'war tha shoon thah did ud.

Portia Allas liche Senchil, though he's fierce fernichity, liche an' aul cluchin' hin.

Maggie M Senchil warn't born, he war knihhed an a weh Sunda aternoon, na mahher, ah feel safe whin he's around acause he's so fuchin' borin' natin's e'er bound ta happen.

Portia bursts into tears, Maggie May looks at her in consternation, gets up.

Wha's wrong peh?

Portia (*roars, just standing there*) Oh Maggie May.

Maggie M Ah peh, wha's wrong a' ya? G'wan ya chan tell me.

Portia Ah don' know, ah don' know.

Maggie M Is ud Raphael?

Portia Ah'm afraid he won't be there whin ah go.

Maggie M Go wheer, who? Whah're ya talchin' abouh peh?

Portia Afore ah was allas sure, was tha wan thing as kep' me goin'. Now ah don' know anamore, an' yeh ah know thah somewhere he lives an' tha's tha place ah want ta be on'y ah don' know how ta geh there.

Maggie M Jay peh don't be talchin' liche thah, frightens me.

Portia Ah chan't help ud, years now, this years ah cuh tha worldt in two, ther's wud Gabriel an' there's withouh Gabriel an' everthin' else ceases be thah division. An' y'ax me abouh Raphael, Raphael don't figure i'my plans, never has, never will. Maggie May ah don' know if anawan realizes whah ud is ta be a twin, everthin's synchronized, tha way ya thinche, tha way ya move, tha way ya speache, tha blinkin' a' yar eyes, tha blood in yar veins moves be unison. Thah time tha cemetary gates fell an Gabriel, tha migh as well've fallen an me too, amimber ah war found unconscious aside of him, wud noh a marche an me, five feeh from wheer tha gahe fell. Tha's on'y a small example of how we ware. Ah'm dead Maggie May, dead an' whah ya seen this long time gone be a ghost who chan't fin' her restin' place, is all.

Maggie M Ah know ya miss him peh buh . . .

Portia An' ah knew he war goin' ta do ud. We'd planned ta do ud together an' ah tha las' minuhe ah goh afraid. Stupid! Stupid! An' he jus' wint an in athouh me an' ah challed him bache an' he didn' hare me an account a' tha swell an' jus' kep' an wadin' in an' ah'm standin' an tha banche shoutin' ah him ta chome bache an' ah tha las second he turns thinkin' ah'm ahind him an' he sees me standin'. Hees face Maggie May, tha looche an hees face an' ah'm roarin' buh no soun' is chomin' ouh an' he tries ta mache tha banche buh th'undertow do have him an' a wave washes over him an' he's gone wud our box a' things . . . jus' liche thah . . . Don't tell Mother thah so ya wont Maggie May, nor Daddy, for tha hahe me enough as ud is.

Maggie M Buh ud warn't your fault peh.

Portia (*hunted animal*) Don't tell thim okhay! Shouldn't a' toult you aither!

Maggie M Peh, ah won't say a word.

Portia Tha's arrigh' so. (*Cold.*)

Begins walking off.

Maggie M Wheer ya goin'?

Portia Home a cuurse.

Maggie M Ah'll chome wud ya.

Portia C'man so.

They exit.

SCENE THREE

The High Chaparral. Fintan Goolan cleans a table. Enter Stacia followed by Portia with a bag of groceries. Fairly dishevelled by now.

Fintan Ladies. (*Cool.*)

Portia just looks at him.

Stacia Bottle a' cider, Portia?

Portia Natin'.

Stacia goes over to jukebox, begins putting on music.

Fintan (*cautiously attempting to flirt*) Overdone ud an tha whiskey las' nigh'.

Portia Ah never drinche whiskey, Fintan Goolan.

Fintan Thah a fac' now. (*Sneers.*)

Portia Aye. Drinchin' wud you don' count . . . (*Examines him.*) More liche a non drinche . . . you're tha sourta man as cancels yarself ouh as soon as y'appear, more nor thah, th'eye fails ta register ya, you're tha kinda cowbiy as gets shoh i'tha first scene of a bad western . . . (*Wearily.*) jus' geh Stacia her drinche.

Fintan D'ya know whah you nade, Portia Coughlan?

Portia Whah do ah nade?

Fintan Ya nade tha tongue ripped ouh, an' tha arse flayed offa ya.

Portia An' d'ya know whah you nade?

Fintan Whah do ah nade?

Portia Chompassion.

Fintan Chompassion . . . wha's thah whin ud's English?

Portia Aye. Athouh ud an't noboda human. An' d'ya know whah we boh nade Fintan Goolan?

Fintan Wha's thah?

Portia Ta be pounded inta dust an' med all over agin . . . geh Stacia her drinche!

Fintan Ya chan buy everthin' ceptin' good manners, thim ya has to be born wud.

Stacia A loh he'd know abouh good manners.

Portia begins jiving expertly, Stacia joins her. Fintan arrives with drink for Stacia, stands there, thick as a bull.

Fintan Wan nintey.

Portia Brandy an' ginger.

Fintan Changed yar mind.

Portia Aye.

Enter Maggie May and Senchil.

Maggie M Portia peh, glad to see y'enjiyin' yarself aven if ud is on'y two a' clache i'tha day.

Portia Chome an' dance wud us.

Stacia You too Senchil.

Senchil puts his hand on his heart for reply. Maggie May takes off her shoes and begins jiving, expertly.

Senchil (*to Fintan*) A poh a tae, tae bag . . .

Fintan Ah know, ah know. Poh a tae, tae bag an tha side, kittle jus' off tha bile an' a brandy an' ginger for himself. (*Points to Maggie May. Goes off in fury.*)

Senchil Yes, thank you.

Portia comes over to table to drink, her mood has changed again. She stands there looking off into space holding drink, cigarette, looks upstage to river. Gabriel is there, in profile, singing, we see him but don't hear him.

Arrigh' peh?

Looks at Senchil, knocks back drink, devilish glee, throws glass at Fintan who has been watching her.

Portia Sem agin! C'man Senchil. (*Takes him by the hand, they waltz.*)

Senchil Jus' for you peh.

Maggie May and Stacia sit down, drink, watch Portia and Senchil a while.

Maggie M Yar vera good ta her Stacia.

Stacia Portia allas bin good ta me, whin ah los' th'eye, (*Touches eye-patch.*) No wan behher . . . she's noh well, Maggie May.

Maggie M Ah know.

Stacia An' her kids is troublesome. Ah'm noh sayin' ud as a complaint buh they're noh minded ceptin' whah Raphael does an' they're vera violent an' destructive an' ah don' know how ta tell Portia. Buh she may tache charge a' thim soon . . . mebbe ah'm worryin' too much. Portia herself war a demon of a childt buh she grew up arrigh' . . . didn' she Maggie May . . . Aven if she be a bih odd.

They watch Portia and Senchil waltz a minute.

Maggie M Did ya know thah Marianne, Portia's mother, war a twin too.

Stacia No, never knew thah.

Maggie M There's few as does, ah'm noh aven sure Marianne knows. Marianne an' Sly is brother an sister. Sem father, different mothers, born ithin a montha wan another.

Stacia Jay, ha chome.

Maggie M Me mother toult me an her deathbed thah Marianne was aul' Scully's childt. 'Roun' tha sem time Blaize Scully was expectin' Sly. She knows, th'oul bitch! Allas knew! Thah ah'm convinced a'.

Stacia An' she let thim marry.

Maggie M Done her bes' ta thwart ud, buh'd never own up ta tha why a' thwartin' thim. Too proud ya see; an' me mother, too ashamed, asides me father'd have kilt her if he foun' ouh, an' ah mane kilt her. Youn' Gabriel Scully war insane from too much inbreedin' an' ah'd near sweer he walched inta tha Belmont river be accident. Aither thah or hes antennae war too high, couldn' tache th'asphyxiation a' thah house.

Stacia Portia know all a' this.

Maggie M Naw, buh her blood do. Crossin' me mind these days ta tell her if ah though' ud'd do ana good, buh ah thinches ahm abouh thirta year too lahe . . . Ah don' have ta tell ya Stacia ta kape ud ta yarself.

Stacia Wont aven tell Justin an' ah tell him everthin'.

Maggie M Good ghirl.

Focus on Portia and Senchil dancing. Switch from Patsy Kline on the jukebox to Gabriel taking up the song. No one notices this. Portia rests, Senchil has closed his eyes, Fintan sways from side to side watching them, Maggie May and Stacia sway, drink, smoke, lost in themselves. Senchil takes a biscuit out of his pocket, nibbles on it, with his other hand he pats Portia's head lovingly. Portia looks at him.

Portia An judgement day Senchil ya'll be atin' yar biscuits sittin' opposite a' God.

Senchil May aven offer Him wan.

Portia How'd ya geh ta stay so unsiled Senchil?

Senchil Unsiled, thah how ya'd ascribe me.

Portia Aye, yar clane as snow fallin' an snow.

Senchil Ah'm on'y an aul eegit Portia, whah tha worldt'd chall a failure an' liche tha snow fallin' ah'll milt athouh a trace.

Portia Be thah sa terrible?

Senchil Be . . . never meh a body yeh as didn' wanta lave a marche, some sign, however small thah they was an th'earth ah a pint in time. Be some as laves a good marche; some as laves a bad wan; we shada people lave none ah all, an' still we be necessara, a necessara bachedrop for tha giants who walches this world an' mayhap tha nex'. (*Takes a bite of his biscuit.*)

Stacia Portia, behher geh a move an. Tha kids is well ouha school.

Portia and Stacia are about to exit.

Fintan (*thick*) Sa high an' mighy now yees don' fale ud necessara ta pay for yeer drinches.

Portia Here! (*Fifty-pound note.*)

Fintan Ah don' have change for fifty pound.

Portia Thin kape tha change. Buy yarself a new medallion.

Exit Portia and Stacia.

Maggie M Whoa. (*Grabbing fifty-pound note off him.*) Ah have change. Senchil! A fiver!

Senchil produces a fiver in a flash. Fintan grabs it, storms off.
Exit Maggie May and Senchil.

SCENE FOUR

Back in Portia's living room. Curtains still closed. She sits perched on the table, ear cocked, like some demented bird,

listening to something, inaudible to all but herself. Beside
her are the dishes and wine glasses from last night's
aborted dinner attempt by Raphael.
  Enter Marianne Scully, looks at her.

Marianne Portia.

  No answer from Portia except an involuntary shudder.

Ah said Portia.

Portia (*eyes closed*) Ssh.

Marianne Whah i'tha name a God's wrong a' ya. Portia!

Portia Listen.

Marianne Whah?

Portia D'ya hare ud.

  Portia, enraptured, listens to Gabriel's voice.

Marianne Maggie May rang me up, says ya warn't
yarself, whin is she, says ah. Geh down offa thah table this
minuhe youn' lady!

Portia (*looks at Marianne a while*) Ah've allas wanted ta
liche ya Mammy buh ah never chould.

Marianne Ah would ya stop such nonsense talche! Now
geh down! (*gently*) Will ah help ya Portia?

  Offers a hand, Portia looks away.

Is ud Gabriel?

Portia Jus' don't! Ah don' wanta hare you talchin' abouh
him, ya sully him an' me, allas.

Marianne Gabriel war fierce difficult, over-sinsitive,
obsessed wud hees self an' you.

Portia Ah said not ta talche abouh him!

Marianne Well ah am an' he war obsessed wud ya! Chem ouha tha womb clutchin' yar leg an' he's still clutchin' ud from wherever he is. Portia yar goin' ta have ta cop an ta yarself. Yar home is a mess, jus' looche ah tha cuh of ud! (*Waves an arm.*) Yar childern is motherless. Raphael has ta do ud all.

> *Portia looks at Marianne, a look of complete and utter hatred.*

Stop loochin' ah me liche thah! If ah didn' know ya for me daugher ah'd sweer ya war some avil goblin perched up ther glowerin' ah me.

> *Portia leaps, a wildcat leap from the table onto her mother, knocks her down and falls on top of her.*

Portia! Me bache! Have ya lost tha run a' yarself . . . thinche ya brochen me leg!

Portia (*flailing at Marianne who is pinned under her*) Y'ave me suffochahed! (*Shakes her viciously.*) So ah chan't brathe anamore!

Marianne Lemme up! Lemme up! Portia plase, yar mother!

Portia Why chouldn' ya a' jus lavin' us in pace! Me an Gabriel! We warn't doin' natin'! Why'd ya have ta sever us!

Marianne Yar noh righ' i'tha head! Leh me up!

Portia (*wallops Marianne across the face*) Allas spyin an us!

> *Roars from Marianne.*

Interferin' wud our games! Ouh challin' us in yar disgustin' hysterical vice! Why chouldn' ya a' jus' lavin' us alone! Why!

Marianne Lave yees alone, ta yeer unnatural ways an' stupid games an' privahe med up langage thah none chould understan' barrin' yeerselves! Savages! Thah's whah yees war! Savages!

Portia We warn't hurtin' anaboda! (*Belts mother again.*)

Marianne (*wallops Portia back*) Don' you hih me ghirl! Thah's enough!

   Portia sits there, takes the blows.

Portia We jus' wanted our own worldt wheer nowan buh us existed an' we damn near had ud until you chem alon' an tore us asunder. D'ya know thah me an Gabriel hahed you. We used ta drame up ways a' gettin' rid a' ya. We used ta khill ya daila down be tha Belmont river! An' whin Gabriel an' me grew up, we war goin' away an' we war goin' ta live tagether alone, away from everwan. An' you an' Daddy would never see nor hare from us agin.

Marianne (*brushing herself off, nursing her wounds*) Yar own mother! Th'abuse of ud.

Portia You meant natin' ta him! natin'!

Marianne Fuchin' bitch!

Portia Ah'm jus' tellin' ya how ud war! Me an' Gabriel locked i'thah room listenin' ta you sobbin' inta tha pilla, thah soun', ah thinche hell be a corridoor fulla rooms like thah wan wud thah soun' chomin' from ever'wan a' thim. An' thin ya'd turn an us acause we war wacher an' smaller than you, buh thah war natin' chompared wud yar fable attimps ta love us. We'd sooner have yar rage anaday, yar hysterical picnics, wud yar bottle a' orange an' yar crisps. 'An't we havin' a greah time' ya used ta say an tha three of us miserable, an' ah'd see Gabriel loochin' ah a sharp stone or a pinted stiche. Mother ya don' know how nare an' how offen ya chem ta . . . Know whah we used ta chall ya? Tha stuche pig! A chan't abide a bone in your wache body, so lave my house an' don't ever chome bache.

Marianne Ah don't know wheer ah goh you an Gabriel buh ah'll tell ya this ah wish if ye'd never bin born.

Portia We wished ud too an' more. We wished never ta have been, which be a different thing. Ta never have bin born, manes yar alreada here. Never ta have been, manes ya chompletla an' utterla never war.

Marianne Ah don't have tha langage ta dale wud your devilry na more. An' ah'd say yar nex' stop'll be th'asylum, ah'd have ya comihhed on'y ah don't want ana more blood an me hands. Yar crazier than yar twin an' he war a demon.

Portia Geh ouh afore ah smear ya an tha walls.

Sly comes in unnoticed.

Marianne Ah'm goin', an' jus' you amimber this, tha close a' yar days an' th'an't far off tha way ya be goin' an. Jus' you amimber this, Gabriel war tha wan ah loved, never you, you war on'y hees shada. He had all tha gifts an' you had none. He war tha fire, you, jus' tha charred remains.

Sly Ah've heared ya Marianne an' ah've heared enough an' ud all be lies. Portia, you war tha firs' ghirl ta chome inta tha Scully household in over wan hunderd year. Ah'm an on'y son, me father, wan a' three min, his father an on'y biy, an' hees father afore him, wan a' five sons. You war tha first ghirl in our house in over a centura, tha first ghirl an' therefore precious, precious for chomin' inta tha worldt a ghirl, an' precious beyant valua for bein' born ta me. (*to Marianne*) Ha dare you tell my child she war noh naded for ud isn' true, she war wanted more, achres mor nor ana mirachle. Go home woman ah'm sichened be yar abidin' cruelty.

Marianne You don' know whah she's bin sayin' ta me.

303

Sly Ah don' chare Marianne, ah don' chare!

Marianne (*final bullet to Portia*) Well ya know wheer ah am if'n ya want ta apologize.

Portia Ah do Mother, an' tha'll be transportin' Dodo's ta Jupiher afore ah chome knochin' an your duur.

Marianne (*to Sly*) D'ya hare her?

Both look at her.

Arrigh' ah'm goin', know wheer ah'm noh wanted, on'y thing ah've ever known . . . trula. (*Exit.*)

Silence.

Sly Portia.

Portia Whah.

Sly Gabriel.

Portia Ah.

Sly Ah try an' try ta thinche whah ud war ah done or whah ah failed ta do . . . tha marra be stript from tha privates a' me bones wud hees passin' as if ah war no more nor an ear a' chorn ah tha threshin'.

Portia We all of us thinches thah eache of us war hees individual minion . . . Gabriel didn' give a damn about ana of us.

Sly Yar righ' childt, buh oh tha substance of him do folly me everwheer.

Portia Ah knew he war goin' ta die . . . noh in ana tangible way buh amimber tha way he used ta sing ah mass up i'tha balcona . . .

Sly On'y rason ah wint ta mass. Did ya know Portia, atwane tha milchin' an' tha sewin' or tha lambin' or tha chalvin' or tha savin' tha hay or whahever ah had ta do, atwane all a' thah ah'd wander in ta listen to hees practisin'. Ah'd stan' there i'tha vestra stinchin' a' animals or new thinned swades an' jus' listen . . . Ah sweer ah knew tha words a' all hees songs be heart.

Portia Wan Sunda he war singin' or mebbe ud war a weddin' he war doin', chan't amimber, anaway he war up an tha balcona, hees head jus' above tha parapeh, ya know tha high side a' Belmont chapel . . .

Sly Aye ah do, built an an incline, church divin' for tha river. D'ya thinche he ever knew ah war there Portia? Whah's ud mahher now anaway. Times ah nigh' ah wache an' ah'm i'tha vestra a' Belmont chapel, an' tha smell a silage be everwheer an' above ud be Gabriel an' those high notes a' God he loved to sing . . . (*turns to Portia*) What war ya goin' to say childt?

Portia Natin'.

Sly (*looks at her*) Ah may geh back ta the farm so.

Portia Aye.

Sly Righ'.

Exit Sly.

SCENE FIVE

Evening. Portia lays the table for dinner. Lights candles. Opens wine. She looks at the table without pleasure. Pours herself a drink. Leans against door, drinks.
Enter Raphael. Portable phone, car keys, factory account books. He looks around. Apparent pleasure at the sight. Not a usual occurrence we take it.

Raphael Greah smell from tha kitchen.

305

Portia Is there.

Raphael Kids in bed?

Portia Aye.

Raphael Goh held up ah the factora.

Portia Did ya. (*Pours him a drink.*)

Raphael Thanks . . . falin' behher?

Portia Fale jus' fine.

Raphael Glad ta hare ud.

Portia Ah'll brin' i'tha dinner if yar reada.

Raphael Aye.

Portia serves up the dinner. They eat a while in silence.

Ah wint ta see tha barman a' tha High Chaparral . . .
Sweers he never led a finger an ya.

Portia Did he.

Raphael Is ud true. Ud is isna? Portia why'd ya lie abouh
somethin' liche thah.

Portia Mayhap ta hide a bigger wan.

Raphael Whah ya mane?

Portia Chan't ya lave ud Raphael! Looche! Ah chooked
yar dinner, ah seh tha table. Ah poured yar wine, ah bahed
Quintin, read him a story an' all.

Raphael Ah'm glad ya spint time wud tha childt Portia an'
ah hope ud do signal behher things ta chome. Ah've long
realized thah ya want vera little ta do wud me an' ah'm
prepared ta live wud thah buh ya mus' tache chare a' tha
childern.

Portia Ah may have wanted more ta do wud ya if ya

warn't allas sa chalm an' unnady Raphael, ah jus' never
learnt how ta dale wud thah.

Pushes away her food, lights a cigarette.

Me an' Gabriel med love all tha time, down be tha
Belmont river among tha swale . . . from th'age a' five . . .
well thah's as far bache as ah chan amimber anaways, buh
ah'm sure we war lovers afore we war born. Times ah close
me eyes an' ah fale a rush a' waher 'roun' me, an' above we
hare tha thumpin' a' me mother's heart, in front of us tha
soft blubber of her belly, an' we're atwined, hees fooh an
me head, mine an hees foetal arm, an' we don' know
which of us be th'other an' we don't want ta, an' tha waher
swells 'roun' our ears an' all tha world be Portia an'
Gabriel packed for ever in a tigh' hoh womb, where there's
no brathin', no thinkin', no seein', on'y darcheness an'
heart drums an' touch . . . An' whin ah war fifteen ah slep'
wud Damus Halion an' ah liched hees distance an'
igorance a' me an' ah began ta slape wud him regular
down i'tha swale be tha Belmont river . . . Shoulda
knowed behher, he meant natin' ta me . . . never did an'
Gabriel seen, Gabriel seen an' never spoche ta me ater.

Raphael Damus Halion?

Portia Yeah.

Raphael Thah eegit. Though' ya'd have higher standards
nor him.

Portia Thah all yar worriet abouh. Ah'm tryin' ta tell ya
abouh me an Gabriel.

Raphael Ah've long suspected whah ya toult me abouh
you an' Gabriel. An' ah don' know whah ta say anamore
Portia. Ah don' know ya ah all. Chan't we jus' forgeh tha
whole thing. Damus Halion, Jaysus. Ah'm weary of ud all
Portia, ah'm goin' ta bed.

Portia Please Raphael don't lave me here an me own, here have more wine. (*Pours for him.*)

He sits back down, doesn't drink, looks at her.

Raphael Ah don't know whah ah'm asposed ta say or do Portia.

Silence. Hold as long as possible.

Portia (*eventually*) Wance ah war listenin' to him i'tha Belmont chapel. High mass or a weddin'; chan't amimber, me an unsifted ghirl, him a green sandalled biy, small for hees age, ah'd long outgrown him. An' ah turned ta watch him above i'tha balcona an' we caugh' wan another's eyes as we used often do whin he'd be singin'. Then ouha nowhere a rip a' pain wint up me side an' ah'm writhin' i'tha pew tryin' noh ta scrame an' ah see Gabriel i'tha balcona clutchin' hees side as if we war bein' sliced from wan another liche a scab from a livid sore, an' don't ax me how buh we boh knew he'd be dead chome spring. An' Gabriel sang through ud all, sang for me an' in hees song we seen him walchin' inta tha Belmont river; seen me wud you an our weddin' day; seen me sons, this barn of a house; seen tha lane ta tha river an a darche nigh'; grake darche aspite tha pile up a' stars; an' me walchin' along tha lane carryin' an aul box, older an' wiser than ah've ever bin; we seen ud all Raphael down ta tha las' detail.

Raphael Whah? Seen whah? A'ya drunche or whah Portia?

Portia (*laughs a little strangely*) Aye ah am.

Gets up, goes over to Raphael. Kisses him full on the lips.

Raphael (*pushes her away*) Y'ave me all a twaddle woman; don't know whah way ah'm asposed ta behave wud ya anamore. Ya thinche ya chan do whah ya liche wud me; wance ya could, noh anamore. Ah'm noh ta be

played wud tha way you play wud me an' ah won't turn
into an eegit whin ya turn thim soft eyes an, so lave off an'
lave me be. Y'ave savaged me ta tha scuh an now ya want
love talche. Go 'way woman; ah don't want you nare me.
(*Pause.*) Ah'm goin' ta bed an' don't bother follyin' me up.

Exit Raphael.

*Portia stands there. She goes to follow him. Stops.
Returns to living room. Gets box. Lets herself out of the
door. Gone. Gabriel's voice comes over. We see her
standing by bank of the Belmont river.*

Afterword

The origins of *Portia Coughlan* are eclectic. I am a
Midlander: I grew up in a place called Gortnamona which
means 'field of the bog', seven miles outside Tullamore in a
place famous for having hanged the last woman to be
hanged in Ireland. Nearby is Banagher, where Charlotte
Brontë spent her honeymoon. For years I castigated her on
her choice; who on earth would spend their honeymoon in
Banagher? Now I think it must be like her beloved moors,
though I've never been there, the open spaces, the
quicksand, the biting wind, the bog rosemary, the gothic
ruins of old castles and big houses, the rough exoticism of
the English spoken, for we speak differently there.
'Newspeak' has left little evidence of itself in the Midland
mouth. We talk long and slow and flat, we make a meal
out of giving someone directions. If someone asks us the
time we want to know who his grandfather was, we
hunger for stories, details, any morsel that will take our
eyes off the bogholes. Our place names are mythical: Pallas
Lake, Rhodes, Belmont, Rue de Rât, Pullagh (this last
Hiberno English, coming from the Irish 'pull' [hole]). And
the list goes on.

Another contributory factor to the genesis of *Portia
Coughlan* is my nightly forays back to that landscape. I
have not lived there for fourteen years, in the flesh that is,
but I find myself constantly there at night: lights off, head
on the pillow and once again I'm in the Midlands. I'm
wrestling, talking, laughing, reeling at the nocturnal traffic
that place throws up. Now I think it's no accident it's
called the Midlands. For me at least it has become a

metaphor for the crossroads between the worlds.
   Finally, at twelve I learnt my first passage of
Shakespeare by heart. I have never forgotten it.

   In Belmont is a lady richly left
   And she is fair, and fairer than that word,
   Of wondrous virtues: sometimes from her eyes
   I did receive fair speechless messages:
   Her name is Portia, nothing undervalued
   To Cato's daughter, Brutus' Portia:
   Nor is the wide world ignorant of her worth
   For the four winds blow in from every coast
   Renowned suitors . . .

               The Merchant of Venice, William Shakespeare

                              Marina Carr
                              November 1995
                              Dublin